Praise for *The Gathering Tide*

'*The Gathering Tide* creates its c ___.. of song-line along the edge of one of England's last and richest wilderness areas – Morecambe Bay… Full of earthy realism, authentic observation and quiet lyricism. It is a hugely impressive debut.' MARK COCKER, AUTHOR AND NATURALIST

'Beautifully written, weaving fact and personal reflections fluidly and with real skill.' ERIC ROBSON

'Lloyd's exquisite descriptions take us through the seasons of this 'infinite blue space reflected in the skin of the water'…with a forensic attention to detail that sparkles with lyrical imagery, mapping the history of the shores and sands of this endlessly fascinating bay.' MIRIAM DARLINGTON, *BBC WILDLIFE*

'Undeniably beautiful writing … Lloyd's lyrical prose is smooth, like a pebble softened by the tide… A tribute by a gifted writer to the place she calls home.' KATE FELD, *CAUGHT BY THE RIVER*

'This poetic book is a map, a layered account of Morecambe Bay, its birds, rivers, names, bones, weathers, ghosts, tides and lives, its dangerous beauty, its tragedies … In mapping a place and sharing its beauty … she arrives at her own sense of belonging.' GILLIAN CLARKE, POET

'A vivid book with a landscape at its heart, redolent with the tang of original imagery. The hallmarks of good nature writing are in place – a seeing eye, that willingness to watch alone that deepens the bond between nature and writer, and the capacity for celebrating what Hazlitt called "the involuntary impression of things upon the mind."' JIM CRUMLEY, NATURE WRITER

'⸻ ⸻ ⸻ ⸻ history, to stories
⸻ ⸻ ucceeds magnif-
⸻ *SUNLIT SUMMIT*

The
BLACKBIRD
DIARIES

A Year with Wildlife

KAREN LLOYD

Published by Saraband
Digital World Centre
1 Lowry Plaza, The Quays
Salford M50 3UB
www.saraband.net

ISBN: 9781910192962
ebook: 9781912235100

Printed in the EU on sustainably sourced paper.

10 9 8 7 6 5 4 3 2 1

CONTENTS

For Andy
and the lovely girls, Freya and Eva.

Climb then, carrying your thoughts
to the steep hill's summit
where the eagle builds her nest
and the waterfall is born.
And here, in remote obscurity,
reflect, think, learn.

GIOVANNI PASCOLI

INTRODUCTION

One memorable spring, as we traipsed in and out of the house hefting bags and cases and outdoor gear and boots, a pair of blackbirds was busy building a nest. In between each of our trips to the car, the blackbirds swooped into the garden bringing twigs and moss and plant material. Each time, they waited until the coast was clear, then darted inside the clematis that rambles in disorderly fashion above a wooden archway. Newly emergent leaves would soon grow and fill the spaces in between the clematis stems, and the nest would become invisible, hidden inside. Although our annual Easter pilgrimage to Scotland was an enticing prospect, part of me wanted to stay home and watch the blackbirds. A week later as we returned, carrying everything back in to the house, it felt as if we were invading the blackbirds' personal space. But soon I settled in, and waited for the arrival of the young.

◉ ◉ ◉

Our garden is no grand affair – just an ordinary plot at the back of a terrace of five Edwardian houses on the outskirts of Kendal. There's a lawn (or near enough), herbaceous borders, and a stately silver birch we had planted as a stripling not long after we moved in. The clematis runs rampant over the wooden trellis and down the three steps from the paving outside the back of the house to the lawn and flower beds. From the kitchen window, I keep a constant lookout – for the goldfinches and blue tits, the jackdaws and swallows and swifts, the chaffinches and robins, but most of all, for the blackbirds. I like to consider them our neighbours, but even more than that, they share our living space. The blackbird is a species, above many others, with which humans often feel a deep sense of connection, forged entirely because of this close habitual proximity. They are highly visible birds, and more than other garden species will tolerate our presence in a way that might suggest that the relationship is two-way. How many gardeners, busy weeding a border on their hands and knees, have not looked up to find a blackbird close by, head cocked to one side, waiting for a turn of worms?

This book charts my encounters with birds and wildlife over the calendar year of 2015, both in my garden and in the wider South Lakeland landscape. It begins with the blackbird's subsong, the limited out-of-season call, pulsed into the new year's early morning from a neighbour's Scots pine, and culminates at the year's end, as the landscape has found some kind of equilibrium after the devastating floods of Storm Desmond.

Along with observations of our garden and the wider landscape of South Lakeland, I chronicle journeys north to Scotland, to the Solway in search of geese, finding thousands of barnacles overwintering there from their summer breeding territories in Arctic Svalbard – and with them comes the memory of something that happened on the morning of my father's funeral, something I have never been able to explain, or to forget. On the island of Mull, I encounter whales and whale-watchers and spend a mid-summer evening with puffins on the nearby island of Staffa – a jewel in the Hebridean crown. I stake out a sea eagle eyrie where, in the setting sun, I watch through my binoculars as the last rays glint in their eyes like crystals. In the rural shires of Shropshire and Wales, and working as part of a team of artists, I help to raise awareness of the serious decline of one of our most iconic birds, the curlew. I visit curlew nests with the project's ornithologist, and write curlew poems with scattered rural communities. Late in the year, a story breaks about the skeleton of a wolf found in a cave on Kendal Fell, a site which lies a mere ten minutes' walk from my back door. What does the wolf represent amidst all the current talk of rewilding, and how does it link with the demise of England's last golden eagle?

◎ ◎ ◎

It is the proximity of the wild, of the fell across the road, that brings with it the gift of birds all year long. The birds that inhabit the fell travel down into the gardens and back up to the fell in constant two-way traffic. Yet it is to the blackbirds that my attention is drawn continually throughout the year. The common blackbird, a species whose presence is stitched throughout our urban and rural landscapes, beavers away in the background of our lives, providing a soundscape that is so familiar yet deeply affecting. Indeed, it was this music that played into my subconscious in the suburban avenues of my childhood home: a cock blackbird, singing after rain, somewhere in the old walled garden of a cottage. The garden is long gone, but the blackbirds themselves remain, ubiquitous, and enriching. The male blackbird's song is variously spirited, aggrieved, cautious, wistful, melancholic. Amongst the first birds to sing in the morning, they offer the last of nature's generous solicitousness at the closing of the light.

Every day I quietly revel in their proximity, watching for the cock bird's sun-ringed eye, and for the quiet, soft, umbered grace of the hen as she turns to look over her shoulder, watching me. I think they know I am beguiled.

KAREN LLOYD
August 2017

One

INTO THE LIGHT

January 1

The first song of the new year was a blackbird's. It was tentatively sung, as if testing the idea of singing into the grey early morning. It was only a matter of days past winter solstice, and already here was an emissary from the lighter seasons of the turning year.

The song was made up of short phrases, optimistic and nostalgic, delivered in staccato rhythm. The full, surging version of the song comes later, in the spring. The sound called me from my bed, and I went to the window. There he was, the blackbird whose territory is *our* territory, on the topmost branch of a neighbour's Scots pine. As the caroller sang, I watched his beak opening and closing, his body pulsating as he pushed the phrases out, then the short pause in between. His head moved from side to side as if to catch any onlookers – like me – watching him, enthralled.

A scuffle in the lower part of the tree, and there was the female, hopping up the network of branches, moving closer and closer to the male, coiling a pathway towards him. Or perhaps it was as if he was winding her up towards *him* with an invisible thread.

I thought that she, too, was enthralled, that she couldn't believe that both he and this opening song of the year were hers for the keeping.

◎ ◎ ◎

Our house sits on the road heading north of Kendal towards Windermere, and before we bought it, the first thing that drew our eyes was the back garden. Our first son, Callum, was two years old then. Here, unlike the treacherously steep gardens of houses for sale elsewhere in the town, a mere couple of steps lead down from the paving outside the kitchen door to the small lawn and flower beds. Once we'd seen the view from the back windows of the house, we were sold. The views from our previous house in Gateshead were restricted to urban terraces, chimneys and rooftops. Any pretensions to wilder landscapes were limited to a distant glimpse, visible only from the attic skylight, of the hills above the Tyne valley. On summer evenings, once Cal was asleep in his small room, I'd go up there and stand on the bed to gaze out at the hills, and take in the fading light.

From the back-bedroom windows, the land drops away towards the valley of the River Kent before rising again in the east. It's a bird's eye take on the world – looking over the rooftops and chimneys to follow the narrow lane at the side of the house down to the crown of the small mixed woodland on Kendal Green. Over the tops of the trees, further beyond the river valley, the rolling summits of the Whinfell Ridge range along the eastern horizon. In winter, without the density of leaves to block the view, the deftly drawn lines of dry stone walls are visible, striding up the flanks of Castle Howe, Shooter Fell and Whinfell Beacon. Further north, where the ridge runs close above the A6, blocks of forestry dominate Ashtead Fell. On Mabbin Crag, a dark conifer plantation rests like a toupee over the summit, and slightly to one side. North again, little Whiteless Pike is sometimes difficult to find unless picked out by late afternoon sunlight. It lies in the shadow of the larger Bannisdale fells from whose uplands springs the River Mint – one of two tributaries that merge with the Kent upstream from Kendal. North-west lie the brackeny slopes of Potter Fell, upon whose summit two tarns nestle, eponymous Potter Tarn and the other, named perhaps in some lost dialect, Gurnal Dubs. Both are small gems of water and are hidden from view until one is almost upon them.

One airless summer's day a few years ago, we had packed a picnic and trodden the steep path following the rushing beck up towards Potter Fell. We arrived at the place where Potter Tarn should have been, but became confounded. Had we walked past it already? We attempted reorientation. Scouting the hillside, it was only the simple forward propulsion of a mallard, lazily cruising the far edge of the tarn, that allowed us to recognise the sheet of water for what it was; the surface had become perfectly still, with the undisturbed reflection of the surrounding hills creating the perfect simulacrum of land.

Both tarns are favourite summer swimming haunts – a perfect reward after the hour-long pull up the steeply climbing path, following the splashy delights of the cascades and pools that course, mostly hidden, in the stream-cleft beyond a screen of oaks and wizened hawthorns.

Below Potter Fell, England's fastest rising river – the aptly named Sprint – begins its westward swing, emerging from the quiet alluvial floodplains of the Longsleddale valley. The Sprint is born high in the headwall of Harter Fell. Its journey commences as two dirty, leaking runnels in peat hags a quarter of a mile apart, only metres below the summit ridges of Harter and Little Harter. Once the two streams merge, the river quickly gains momentum, turning out of the blind valley and rapidly becoming a clear-running stream bustling over the grey, white, jet-coloured and rusty-red cobbles of the stream bed. It plunges over small cascades and crashes at breakneck speed into and out of the deserted slate workings of Wrengill Quarry before turning south-east to fall in spectacular fashion alongside the ancient packhorse route of Gatescarth Pass. Here, mountain shadows fall early: Kentmere Pike, Steel Rigg, Raven Crag, Goat Scar and Shipman Knotts. The Sprint falls further, washing over gravel beds before singing itself underneath the packhorse bridge at Sadgill and ploughing onwards through the fields of the valley proper before its eventual confluence with the River Kent, close to the village of Burneside.

Now to the area's star attractions, the Kentmere hills: the illustrious summits of Froswick, Ill Bell, Yoke, Thornthwaite Crag and the summit of High Street, along with paler, more distant Red Pike. That first summer, I must have spent hours looking out from the windows once Callum was asleep. I'd look up to the hills and, transfixed, watch the night sky shift from turquoise to midnight blue, the light evolving, becoming that particular luminous citrine sheen that lingers close to the rim of the hills. Oh, how the glow of that *simmer dim* remains long after night has fallen – memories of being drawn back to the windows for just one more look, staying as the darkness grew around me and feeling the unfamiliar shadows of the new house beginning to turn familiar. Memories of how, over weeks and months, the teetering piles of boxes were emptied and sorted and the place began to grow into a home.

◎ ◎ ◎

Each of the five terraced houses has a small square front garden facing the road and long gardens to the rear. Built in 1910, they are made of limestone hewn from a small quarry up on the fell across the road. After the stone was blasted from the quarry, it was transported on wagons down a tramway built especially for the purpose. Much of Kendal is built of the same stuff, giving rise to its familiar pseudonym 'the auld grey town.'

In our first years, as we began to put our own stamp on the garden, every spadeful of earth turned up shard after shard of broken glass: greenhouse remnants. But making a garden of our own was revelatory after the small brick yard and handful of potted plants we'd had at our previous home in Gateshead; this was heaven.

The neighbouring gardens continue to evolve, of course. New residents tear up someone else's patio and install their own concept of what a garden should be. Sheds have come and gone. Neighbours, too. In 2014, we lost our favourite neighbour, Joan. Ever the planner, wanting to be as little bother to anyone as humanly possible in her later years, Joan sold up, swapping the house that had been her family home for fifty years for a bungalow on the other side of town with a minimal garden. I can't imagine how hard that must have been.

On the hot July day we first arrived in Kendal, we pulled up on the rough parking space at the bottom of the garden – the place where my study now stands – and saw our new neighbours, Joan and her husband Colin, walking up their garden path to greet us. Hands were shaken over the garden gate, two-year-old Callum was admired and welcomed, a symbolic cup of sugar and a pint of milk were handed over the garden wall. Just before Christmas that same year, Colin died suddenly, at home. Joan dealt with her grief privately, and by the time spring came – the time for gardening, for chatting over the wall – she was composed, already planning which shrubs needed 'showing who's boss.'

After Joan moved to her bungalow, we missed her enormously. Her new garden, designed to make life easier, was a patch of clean, multi-coloured gravel on which stood the few tubs and plants she had taken with her. That winter, I bought and planted for her a trough of spring bulbs as a house-warming gift. Joan lived long enough to see the daffodils and tulips coming up. Six

months later, she was gone, having caught, and ultimately succumbed to a virulent infection.

That summer and autumn I took a series of photographs of
'Joan's garden' – as it would ever be to me, even after delightful
new neighbours had arrived – of the snowball viburnum bursting with creamy-white pom-pom flowers, the spears of white
lilac graced with butterflies, the bright yellow firework clusters of
mahonia and the sweeping grace of the burgundy-bronze weeping beech. I took pictures of the garden path leading up to the
back door and the wall over which we talked, over which Joan
talked to our children. I can see them now, the boys showing
Joan tadpoles or Lego, or wonky iced cakes. After the funeral, I
sent the photographs to her sons. David got in touch. He and
his brothers were all, he said, moved to tears. This, the power of
a garden.

Today, the five neighbouring gardens are dominated by two
major trees: our own silver birch, planted as a sapling by 'Trevor
the tree man' which now stands as tall as the garden is long, and
two gardens away, close to the back wall of the middle house,
a Scots pine. These two trees create shelter, food and stopovers
for innumerable birds throughout the year. There is a scattering
of Japanese maples, ruby-red, lime-green or golden-leafed, and
two weeping birches. There are climbing roses, rambling roses,
holly, ivy, clematis in every colour – one with leaves of a rich
rose-red that flings itself over the white corrugated sheeting of
a neighbouring carport roof every summer, softening the focus.
There are a couple of ponds, too, and herbaceous borders. Over
the dividing picket fence, sits Joan's raised bed, preparation for
the days when she might have difficulty bending as low as she
once could, packed with plants and shrubs – mahonia and mock
orange, a perfect habitat for young birds to shelter in.

Our avian garden neighbours are goldfinches, blue tits, great
tits, blackbirds, chaffinches, greenfinches, sparrows, dunnocks,

coal tits and more. The skies above the gardens are frequented by jackdaws, starlings, feral and racing pigeons, swallows and martins, and higher again, the swifts. Sometimes a frisson of excitement erupts as the occasional sparrowhawk scrutinises the area for food, or a buzzard comes soaring over from the fell, gliding in stately fashion above the rooftops. In the mornings, gulls pass over on their way to spend their days scavenging on and around the inland lakes and tarns. As evening falls they pass again on the journey back to roost on Morecambe Bay.

In twenty-two years of living here, new neighbours have come and gone, but the one constant is that a handful of people have created, largely unintentionally, an environment that is a rich habitat for wildlife. Here, across the five gardens, literally on our doorstep, is bird-land – bird and bird-watcher heaven.

◉ ◉ ◉

Not long after moving in, we discovered a path directly across the road. It led to an exuberantly ramshackle collection of allotments – home to hens, goats, ducks, geese and pigeon lofts. We'd walk up onto the fell, my young sons and I, and, holding one of them in my arms, shading our eyes from the sun, we'd watch pigeons flying in whirling circles above us, one or two sometimes dropping out of the flock to fall headlong towards the earth – the deception of the tumbler pigeon. As the pigeons flew close overhead, we could feel the draught of their wings on our faces, the boys enthralled by this proximity to these airborne dervishes.

We found another path too, leading first past the allotments and then passing through a tiny gated stile at the intersection of the allotments' wall and the adjacent fell wall. Progressing upwards through a steeply sloping field, another stile must be clambered through, and here it emerges onto Kendal Fell beside a copse of Scots pine and holly. From here, more paths lead by various routes up to the summit of the fell, then beyond to the distinctive limestone escarpments of Cunswick Scar and Scout Scar – and further still towards the outlying fells of the Lake District. We didn't know when we bought the house that all this was on our doorstep, and that from our back door, we could walk as far as our sense of curiosity, or legs, would carry us.

◎ ◎ ◎

In the early afternoon, I walked north from Helsington along the edge of Scout Scar, so that the mountain panorama lay ahead of me. The drear cloud that had hung around for weeks had finally begun to lift, and whilst an ambivalent edge of cloud still threatened, ragged and ancient, beyond it lay the promise of blue. Close by, a raven materialised from the cliffs under the edge of the Scar. Then, at the zenith of its momentary arc, the wings folded, emptied of air, and it fell back to the rough bounds below. In the mere seconds of its presence I noted the sweep of its eye charting the plateau. For a while nothing else moved.

Being on the Scar is to stand on the edge of space and immeasurable distances of air. There is volume, space to think. It's a bird's eye perspective on the landscape.

Down in Brigsteer Woods, the high-pitched shriek of a rusted gate rang out, followed by the clang of metal on metal. A pheasant cronked. A dog barked. Milly, our dog, ran to the edge and looked down but was soon recalled by the stronger force of scent trails. The mountains were snowbound, their gullies and edges the colour of dark steel. There was light at last though, and it moved over the mountain backdrop like stage lighting. A single beam traced the silhouettes of the Old Man of Coniston and Brim Fell against more grey sky. Further north, the Langdale Pikes appeared like twin characters in a play, waiting in the wings for their moment to shine. Finally, the light slid over them, turning them the softest pink, veined like marble with cliffs and crags, the great defile of Stickle Ghyll in between.

Behind me, towards the south, long rolling layers of cloud over Morecambe Bay were lit like surf waves on an Atlantic shore. In the far west, at the edge of Cumbria, the outlying hills of Black Combe began to fade behind showers moving in from the Irish Sea. If the forecast was to be believed, more snow was on the way.

The Scar is an almost three-mile length of broken stony bluffs that ascend steeply from the farmland threshold, rising through rich woodlands, tree scrub and tumbles of shattered limestone that sparkle in sunlight, to a height of almost a thousand feet. The summit plateau is a mix of undulating grassland, heather and juniper scrub through which it is possible to follow a mazy network of pathways offering endless variety and ways to encounter new perspectives on the landscape. Across the plateau, ash trees grow, but not in their usual form; here they are short in stature and limb with branchlets bunched into knotted fists, clothed in the whitest of white skin.

The familiar herd of black, curly-coated Galloway cattle sheltered underneath a stand of ash, watching, impassive as always and chewing the cud as we weaved our way between them. Ubiquitous Cumbrian hawthorn populated the plateau, from younger, smaller bushes to full-blown, tightly compacted tree-forms: manna to small birds.

In the middle distance, a man strode out with an old-fashioned coat flapping open and six collies moving like miniature black-and-white clouds around him, flowing in and out, forming, breaking, reforming. Even from that distance I heard him talking to them continually. As they came closer, I noticed that five had the usual black and white collie markings, but the sixth was red-brown, bleached almost, as if he'd been left out in the sun too long. Underneath his gabardine, the man wore a battered suit, a striped pink shirt and a kipper tie. His hair was collar-length, Brylcreemed.

We drew nearer. I called out, 'Do you have enough dogs?'

'Aye, I do, but they cost me a fortune!' he said, and suddenly, a dog was sitting on each of my feet, four eyes looking up at me and two cold noses pushed into my hands.

'Are they from the same family?' I asked, nodding at the dogs.

'Oh yes, I bred them all. That's the father,' he said, using his carved walking stick to point at the one with the curious coat.

'I like that one,' I said. 'He's an unusual colour.'

'It's not supposed to be that colour.'

'Oh?'

'He was wearing the coat off another dog, a red coat, given to me after the dog died, and the colour ran in the rain, and since then he's been that funny colour.'

'Well, he looks good to me,' I said, and gave the doe-eyed collies a final pat. 'Enjoy the rest of your walk.'

'Oh aye, I will. You have to, don't you? Get out, I mean? We may not get the light again for another month!'

I knew what he meant. Seize the moment, get out into the light. As we moved further and further apart, the collies blurred back into small clouds again.

January 7

The treecreeper appeared suddenly. It was close enough that if I'd reached out, I could have touched the red bark of the Scots pine where it had foraged, briefly, before hop-skipping away to the far side of the trunk. The detail of the bird's cream chest and throat, the grip of its upwardly grasping claws, its short, curving bill probing the crevices, the camouflage of its upper body and raggedy stripe of white above the dark eye – I noticed all of this in the merest snatch of time, before the treecreeper spirited itself away.

This particular pine is one amongst a group of a dozen that stand high on Helsington Barrows, overlooking the Lyth Valley.

Close by are the bleached remains of other long-fallen pines, lying together in all their architectural ruin. South-east of the great limestone prow of Scout Scar, Helsington Barrows has a sense of the primordial landscape about it – it feels like an ancient, untrammelled place. There are acres of deep, dark green yew trees, and larches that in January are cinnamon and nutmeg-coloured with thin, golden tendril-like branches, sweeping down to the straw-coloured winter grass.

Close to Helsington Barrows are Barrowfield Woods, Barrowfield Farm, Barrowfield Lot and the village of Underbarrow. The views to the west are dominated by Whitbarrow, on the summit of which is Wakebarrow. Any archaeological hunches, though, need to be firmly reined in. Though the word 'barrow' is a common signifier of burial places, in this part of Cumbria, the word's origins infer a woodland place.

The sky was brilliant. Sunlight illuminated the edge of cloud-galleons that were pushed along by a fresh northerly wind. To the south, Morecambe Bay glimmered like glass reflecting the sun; the tide was in. To the north, new snow had fallen on the mountains, and there was more on the way.

Further in, another Scots pine was spotlit by low sunlight, the pine needles brightened to an intense green and the bark was sun-painted a deep red, as if it glowed from within. Then – *rrraaaa, rrraaaa* – a pair of crows dived together through the air overhead, working in tandem, following tight in the wake of a buzzard. The raptor swivelled and dodged above the larches, revealing pale under-wing bars. The crows were ruthless and determined, not resting until the buzzard had dropped out of sight over farmland. My feelings – as usual – were with the underdog.

The shallow cleft of a narrow valley dissects the common. At its centre stands a grove of oaks, and suspended on generously long ropes from an elongated branch hangs a swing. It has a wooden seat, cut and shaped for the job, and three names carved into the surface. I find its lure irresistible, so I sat and swung, idling the minutes away, looking up through the network of branches to the sky. With each pass of the swing, the buds at the tips of the branch brushed the earth momentarily, and I listened in to the soft creak.

January 13

Dawn broke like the end of an affair. Ruby light towards the east soon became subsumed by banks of deep grey cloud. Walking the rising ground from the car park up the path to Scout Scar, a wren, deep in the hawthorn scrub, ticked the morning awake.

In the west, the sky cleared and before long the morning was awash with new blue, though the Coniston hills remained cloud-wrapped. Further east, new snow brightened the mountains. Above the Langdale valley, Bowfell and Esk Hause resembled the upturned hull of a boat. With its splayed wingtips finger-ing the wind, a crow broke out from the edge of the Scar and glimmered darkly over the long band of wintering woodlands, hundreds of feet below. Following the trajectory of a perfect cir-cle, the crow flew back in towards the Scar again, landing in the topmost branch of a hawthorn, facing into the wind and over the valley below, like a ship's figurehead. A second crow followed suit, closely followed by a third, as if this were some early morning ritual – the getting of air under one's wings to begin the day. I knew how that felt.

To the south, on the edge of the bay at Arnside, street lights flickered orange and were extinguished. Dog walkers out earlier than me were already returning along the edge of the Scar, and as we passed each other, we exchanged notes on the emerging day:

'Better weather?'

'About time!'

'I think we deserve it.'

And yes; we did.

I stood at the edge, watching Mistle thrushes and blackbirds surfing through the trees on the undercliff, then continued on, my goal the great white cairn of limestone rocks. Arriving there, I added another small piece to the jumble, as usual, and turned for home.

I became conscious of a familiar whistling in the hawthorns ahead of me. A pair of small birds flitted across the path: bullfinches. Another pair joined them, and yet more. I counted them quickly, though the birds seemed in no hurry to move on. Seven pairs, no, eight; twelve. Against the snowy attire of the Langdale Pikes, Sergeant Man and High Raise, in amongst the spiky web of branches: the bright red breasts and black hoods of the male bullfinches, each accompanied by the softer, browner females, all contact calling as they foraged.

January 14

We woke to a smattering of snow, the kind that will inevitably melt as the morning continues. I put food out for the birds on the wall and cast breadcrumbs and the remains of fruit bread beside the bird bath, pouring hot water to melt the skin of surface ice. Then, like Hansel, I made a trail of crumbs, with the added temptation of raisins, leading from the birdbath and ending close by the back door.

Soon enough, the female blackbird arrived, her feathers puffed out against the cold. I set the camera ready and sat down on the kitchen step behind the glass door. I watched as she followed the crumb trail, pausing between each delicate peck. As she arrived at the door our eyes momentarily met. I wondered what, if anything, she made of me.

On she came, closer still, eventually settling on the snow-covered doorstep. I pressed the shutter to catch the moment: freeze frame.

I have that photograph on my study wall. If my gaze wanders and I see it, I'm reminded of the birds I think of almost as family. In the picture the female is poised, her toes making only the slightest intrusion on the surface of the snow. Her tail is down and her head is turned to the side, a note of ochre yellow on the tip of her beak. She seems self-assured, her brown eye calmly observant and her feathers puffed out to reveal that rich, autumnal brindling and stippling of golden tones beneath the more mundane browns.

Later that morning, another trail of prints appeared in the snow. The hen, or perhaps her mate, had carefully negotiated the food by the bird bath, working from the outer edge of the crumbs inwards. The result was an almost perfect spiral of blackbird prints, each set of them representing a new stance, a scan of the garden and the sky for potential threats before taking another crumb. Another click of the shutter: the printed spiral preserved.

January 16

Drawing the sitting room curtains in the early morning, a black silhouette shifted onto the cotoneaster beside the front door: a cock blackbird, foraging for berries. Behind him, beyond the confusion of dense, spiny branches, dawn broke rosy.

January 17

As the snow began to fall, I took my black gloves into the back garden to catch snowflakes. Some fell in little crystal tangles, or aggregates, and others singly. I studied them closely, revelling in their intricate structure. Whenever I do this – which is almost every time it snows – I recall how late in life it was, in my forties, that I discovered the crystalline structure of snowflakes can be seen with the naked eye. Of course, we learned about the structure of snow crystals at primary school, as most children do, and made our replica paper snowflakes to hang at the classroom windows in the weeks leading up to Christmas. But our teacher hadn't said (perhaps she hadn't known) that if you look closely, you'll see the complex crystal structure – the thing that scientists refer to as sixfold radial symmetry – with your own eyes. No need even for a microscope. For a more intimate view I peered through my hand lens to unlock the secrets of each unique crystal.

This year I made another discovery – the existence of a path on the far side and lower reaches of the Helm, the crested ridge which frames the eastern view from the town. Walking there the morning after the snow had fallen, it was joyful to see the landscape transformed. After weeks – no, months – of gloom and rain, all was bright again. There was a sense of a collective sigh of relief; the land had been remade by the simple, unifying beauty of fresh snow.

On the untrodden path through the woodland, another first: a woodcock. Disturbed by my approach, it launched itself suddenly from under my feet; I don't know which of us was more surprised. Spooked, the woodcock jinked away, passing between the trees and disappearing into the sloping fields of the Stainton valley. I followed the wavering line of its flight and saw sheep grazing, a frozen tarn, buzzards circling and mewing overhead. The thin *tsee tsee* of tiny goldcrests filtered down from the tree tops above.

The path led on to the open fell. I climbed upwards between islands of gorse, crossing the semi-frozen trail of a small beck. In the distance, the herd of Fell ponies that lives on the Helm all year round were grazing, their black forms easy to identify against the white snow. I always relish seeing them, a native breed that is doing well, fetching record prices at pony sales, though on the uplands there are uncertainties as older farmers and other keepers retire or die. Finding newcomers to take on the herds does not prove easy. But the breed's intrinsic hardiness is maintained by the upland grazing herds, and if their long-term viability is compromised, this fundamental characteristic may eventually become lost.

Why, I wondered, import Polish Konik ponies, as some wildlife reserves have, for use as conservation grazers, when we have many perfectly-suited breeds here in the UK, including Fell ponies?

Fell ponies look comfortably at home in our wild Cumbrian landscape. Unfazed by the snow, they grazed as if it were just any other day. I walked towards them, then hunkered down in their midst to take close-up photographs of their shaggy black faces. One of the ponies had highlights of a very becoming sienna tone amongst the dark-umber of her mane and a forelock that swept almost to her nose. She was very beautiful in a rugged, northern kind of a way. I lingered, taking photographs and telling the ponies how lovely they were. One of them came close and began to nudge my back pocket.

January 20

Gunshots. Never a good way to begin a walk, particularly with a dog whose natural inclination is to run immediately in the opposite direction. Nevertheless, we walked forward along the flood banking at the edge of the bay, dog held firmly on the lead. On the rim of the saltmarsh, a line of geese had settled, though you had to look hard to find them; the white and black of a shelduck in their midst drawing the eye in. More shots, but the birds seemed unperturbed. They fed on grass, preened, occasionally stood tall and ruffled their feathers. Further along, four swans floated like sculpted ice on a semi-frozen pool of water. In the distance, inland, the mountains lay under snow, the air entirely still.

Something was running towards me across the marsh. The creature appeared out of nowhere. A large animal, white, head erect and for all the world resembling a llama, its gait unfamiliar. It ran in a strange lolloping motion, turning its head from side to side, periscope-like. It was a fallow deer, startled by the guns and running away from the direction of the shots. It must have become badly spooked and disorientated to be so out of kilter, in such unfamiliar open territory, and alone.

As the deer moved closer to me it slowed to a walk, stood stock still and held its head erect: it was like a creature from a fairy tale. From the top of its head, a band of pale colour ran down the back of its neck, broadening over the body and stippled with white. It was the exact colour of last summer's sedge, through which the deer then began to run again. The creature had about it an air of not quite believing where it had found itself, and soon enough it set off again, quickly gaining speed and travelling towards the sanctuary of Dallam Park.

I felt a tug of panic; to gain the safety of the park and join the herd of fallow deer that live within its boundary, this deer would have to cross the coast road, along which traffic was speeding. The deer careered over the edge of the marsh, bounding a fence into the field, then covering the distance in seconds, leapt the wall onto the metalled surface of the road as two cars approached from opposite directions. Dodging them both by mere yards, it hurtled to the far side and skittered through the wide gateway leading into Dallam Park at such a speed, its hind legs seemed almost to crumple beneath it in the sharp turn of its curve. And then, as if by sleight of hand, it vanished.

◉ ◉ ◉

In a soft explosion, a flock of foraging fieldfares surfaced from the marsh and passed chattering ahead of me into the cover of hawthorn hedges bordering the marsh road. The fieldfares had not, it seemed, been startled by the intrusion of a deer into their midst – it had clearly passed straight through the feeding flock; it was me, me and the dog, highly visible on the bank top, who were the provocation for their flight.

January 23

Snowdrops. Looking out from the kitchen window, the year's first flowers helped to banish the gloom of recent weeks. I relished them, their nodding, fresh, soft green-fringed heads signifying that spring was coming. I went out to cut a small bunch, and wrapped them round with a narrow ribbon made of tiny embroidered stars, then placed them in a small blue jug on the windowsill.

Two

LARKS, ASCENDING

February 5

It wasn't difficult to work out that the buzzard I had seen on an early morning walk up the fell was a youngster. It sat on the dry stone wall which divides the long sloping field – the sledging field – from the footpath and the beginnings of common land. The raptor remained immobile as I walked closer and called the dog to heel. Seen in profile, the buzzard surveyed the land and the sheep below – lambs due any day now – then turned its handsome profile to look straight at me. There, that inscrutable eye, the hooked beak and pale throat, the cream and hazel chest, wing feathers rimmed with pale colouring underneath its tail. Another moment and the buzzard turned and lifted itself into the breath-cold air, moving lethargically towards the summit of the fell.

Later, coming back round the front of the fell, the buzzard was there again, flying reconnaissance. I wanted to divert from the path to follow, but the fields it soared over were behind gates that had been zealously wound with barbed wire.

February 6

My usual morning round of the fell, straight up to the top, over the smooth intervention of the golf course, and down the fields where my favourite cows, the Banded Galloways, tore at wintry grass. We skirted the northern edge of the fell and passed the restored field barn from where a group of rooks began their sorties, emerging one by one from the high barred windows and dissolving away over the fields.

The footpath dived through a small wood below the ridge line of the fell. Something moved overhead – the buzzard again, gliding without any shifting of wing position. It floated over the fields in widening circles, then with a small dip down and final upward swoop came to land on a fence post. Immediately, two rooks took off from the field and began to systematically harangue the raptor. Like prison wardens, they alighted on fence posts to either side of the buzzard, the buzzard moving not a feather. One of the rooks took off again and began to make small circles of flight, moving forwards, upwards and back again. At the end of each rotation it touched down upon the post for the briefest of moments before rising and resuming the strange dance.

The buzzard, meanwhile, appeared unruffled, shoulders hunched, occasionally turning its head, although not, it would appear, to keep the would-be gaolers in sight. The flying rook, however, became apoplectic with rage, dive-bombing the interloper from above, the buzzard shifting only slightly with each pass, ducking its head with an air of vague annoyance. As I observed the fracas, a pair of mature buzzards travelled in from the north. One of them dropped through the air towards the juvenile, just once. The youngster acquiesced immediately and flapped away.

I didn't see the lone buzzard on the fell again for a long time. I wondered where it had come from, and if the pair of buzzards that had driven it away might have been its parents, teaching their offspring a lesson from the school of hard knocks: *Son, it's really time you moved on.*

February 7

Every now and then something stirs, calling me back to the west. I feel the pull of the quieter valleys I spent copious amounts of time in during my twenties. Having acquired my first car (for the vast sum of £700, a bronze Datsun Sunny with 120,000 miles on the clock), there was no longer any need to wait for the offer of a day out from friends; in that part of the world, buses were infrequent at best, and rarely went where I wanted to be. The Duddon Valley was a favoured wild place, crossed and re-crossed by more footpaths and green lanes than many of Lakeland's other valleys. I'd head up there during the short, atmospheric, daylight hours of winter and return home, leg-weary, my face tingling from exposure to the cold. But once the long, lingering days of summer arrived, I would stay late into the evening, waiting to see the sun set over the sea in the west, from the top of one fell or another, then drive home in the not-quite dark. There were, too, the delights of tea and scones in the Square Café on the way back home, and once a swimming party at Duddon Bridge after a summer day's walk with friends, followed by a long evening at the Newfield Inn. Then, stopping on the way home, we night-swam in the starless dark through the deep pools under Ulpha Bridge, and with the swimming came the realisation that, far from warming the body, the alcohol in my system made the shock of the cold water worse. And then there were the midges. Flying, or hanging about, waiting for unsuspecting food – like us – to arrive, the midge hordes travelled just above the surface of the river. Invisible, they ended up in our mouths, reducing the romance and tranquillity of our night-swim to the spluttering noise of a bunch of oafs destroying the peace of the valley.

◎ ◎ ◎

A clear day, and with my eldest for company, we set out. Road-works and long delays on the A590 conspired against us. We turned off into the Lyth Valley, onto the fell road towards Newby Bridge. We followed curves and hills and hollows past village pubs with names that Dickens would have approved of: the Punch Bowl at Bowland Bridge, or the Mason's Arms at Strawberry Bank that was built into the hillside below the steep bend in the road where only first gear will ever do.

Cresting the next hill, a line of 4x4s straddled the soft verge, short-wave radio aerials protruding from their roofs. Men and women glanced over their shoulders at us as we passed, others scanned the fell and the fields below through binoculars. A fox hunt – illegal of course, but nevertheless, in full swing.

The law on blood-sports remains unambiguous, but still the fox hunts continue. Since the ban came into force more than ten years ago, I've seen – or more often heard – a number of hunts in progress. I've heard hounds in Kentmere tracking rapidly across the open ground of the higher fells, their baying echoing around the valley. Or down by the river, men with terriers, turning to see who was driving past. Up here in the Lakes, the hunt has always been on foot, but for all the lack of pomp and red coats, long leather boots and money, I still loathe it.

As we passed the last of the vehicles, Cal recognised a lad he'd known at school, someone he remembered talking about hunting, of following in his father's and grandfather's footsteps, of keeping the tradition alive. Regardless, I willed the fox they were after to get away.

◎   ◎   ◎

We set out to walk in the Woodland Valley, the sun already past its zenith. Beyond Ring House Farm the path turns into a green lane running between dry stone walls and eventually breaking out onto the open fellside. Sunlight filtered through the branches of a small plantation of young birches. In that low sunlight, each tree appeared super-lit, each interlacing branch holding a network of silvered spider webs. Deeper in, the complex, shimmering construction of webs within webs.

I took a photograph of Cal walking the green path ahead of me. Passing the plantation, he shades his eyes from the slantwise sunlight. Beams of light pass on either side of him through the grove of white. In the next photo – taken looking back along the way we'd travelled – the birches are all willowy, wrapped up in the purple mist of their buds, and not a single web to be seen.

◎ ◎ ◎

As a teenager, I was finally able to indulge my passion for all things equine. I saved money from summer and weekend jobs and with the help of a loan from a family friend, I bought a horse. He was stabled at a farm just a few hundred yards from our house on the new estate at the edge of Ulverston. Riding out from there was a joy. A network of quiet roads and a green lane led up to Birkrigg Common where views opened out over Morecambe Bay and up to the Lakeland fells.

During my A-level year, Mr Buttress, a fruit and veg stall holder on Ulverston's street market whom my mother had befriended, offered to look after my horse for me, to free up time for study. Well – that was at least the theory...

Three generations of the Buttress family lived in the valley, in a farmhouse and the cottage next door, tucked into the bottom of the fell. The Sunday morning ritual involved practising my driving skills on the journey from Ulverston to Woodland, then riding my pony up to the summit of the fell, over the Iron Age settlement with its views along the valley into the west and out to the Irish Sea, along the ridge and down to the eponymous hamlet and the valley again while Dad, Nev, Sheila and Mr Buttress Senior drank coffee and caught up. That golden year was soon over, though. By the age of seventeen I'd found the stronger intoxications of boys, cigarettes and alcohol.

I hadn't been back to Woodland for years – no, decades. I remembered that the Buttress family's farm was in the valley bottom, but I couldn't work out where. Navigating by our noses rather than the map, Cal and I walked through a large farmyard and passed a grand house – Woodland Hall. There were ponies in a paddock, calves in a barn, a monkey puzzle tree and ancient yews in the walled garden. We wandered down the farm lane to a small, dammed and semi-frozen tarn where we picked up stones to skim out across the icy surface, listening to the looping *ping-ping* and echo as they skeetered along and stopped, then aiming the next missile at a growing scatter of others. We came to the small metalled road that threaded through the valley. Here was the junction with the steep narrow road over the fell, the road that Dad and I drove every Sunday, me practising hill starts halfway up. Then I saw the gates where the farm lane curves and drops into the farmyard tucked below, and a memory surfaced, of the day my pony was sold on, once I'd finally admitted to myself that that particular part of my life was over.

He was sold to a farming family from the Whycham valley, near Millom. Twice afterwards, Dad and I drove over to visit and, pleasantries done with, I would walk alone to the field where the pony grazed. When I called his name – Solomon – he'd raise his head and, recognising my voice, charge up the field to meet me, pushing his soft black nose into my hands.

I heard later that they'd sold him to a riding school; he'd not made the grade at the local gymkhanas and the farmer's daughter was ambitious. I harboured the guilt of having owned and sold an animal that could not be kept for life and whose future care could not be guaranteed. Once in a while, I still dream about him. It is always the same dream: there is the utter joy of being reunited followed by the realisation that I'd forgotten him, left him abandoned in the stable on the outskirts of Ulverston, that he'd not been fed for months on end. And I wake always then, not just with an aftertaste of guilt, but with a profound sense of loss.

◎ ◎ ◎

On the journey home, Cal and I called in for tea and scones in Broughton village. A small gathering of goldfinches zipped above our heads as we walked down the hill towards the café. Close by, we could hear the sociable chattering of many more – dozens of them, high up in the branches of a mature beech tree in a walled garden. The tree was startlingly lit by the lowering sun, the effect intensified by the pale-yellow painted walls of the house catching and reflecting the light, and a backdrop of dense black clouds. Perhaps hundreds of goldfinches called and fidgeted, illuminated, gaudy and glowing. Then, like brightened leaves carried by the wind, they were off, flitting in their unmistakeable way, rising and falling and rising in bouncing yo-yo flight. Travelling in noisy, sociable little groups, they journeyed to another garden, some crossing back again to the beech trees. I wondered if this super-flock, and the birds' unceasing restlessness, foretold the end of winter.

We drove home in the last of the light. Beyond Newby Bridge, a fox morphed out of the roadside bushes and crossed the road not fifty yards ahead of us – in horribly busy traffic. I stamped on the brake and watched as the fox disappeared into the scrub beyond the tarmac. I fancied it was the same fox the hunt had been after that morning: having outwitted the hunters, it was on its way back to its own territory. Smart fox.

February 14
Goldfinches have been bringing their quirky performances into the garden. Like a private troop of jesters, they arrive and feed in pairs, one on each side of the sunflower feeders under the

clematis arch, deftly splitting the kernel of seed and immediately going back for more. Other goldfinches come in and are momentarily transformed into hummingbirds as they attempt to take their turn. As one pair feeds, another five or six take refuge in the intertwined, winter-bare clematis stems before bursting out from cover – and the show begins again.

In recent years, the explosion in goldfinch numbers has been an extraordinary phenomenon, bucking the more usual downward trend in species. Not so many years ago, I'd been delighted to witness flocks of them zapping out of hedgerows as our car passed along the coastal lanes in Dumfries and Galloway. 'Goldfinches!' I'd announced – though the young people in the back seat remained unimpressed. These gaudy finches might then have passed through our garden just once or twice a year, if you were lucky, to feed on the seed heads of teazle before flitting away like small colourful apparitions. In those years, the brightest addition to the garden were the greenfinches, the male with plumage almost as intensely coloured as budgerigars. These days, any visiting greenfinch is more of a rarity, and worthy of comment.

February 16
At the summit of the Shap road, I stopped the car. We were 1,350 feet above sea level, and it was 10.30 at night. Together with Fergus, our youngest, I pushed the door open and climbed out into the icy air. Slight, vaporous clouds evolved over the face of the moon and dissipated again on the other side; it was as if the moon was breathing. So many stars and so intensely cold; the glitter and spangle of crystals crackling in the darkest sky.

February 22

The thing that made washing the breakfast dishes less of a chore was eight goldfinches performing their morning acrobatics on the sunflower feeders. A smattering of greenfinches joined in, and for several moments the feeder was balanced by a goldfinch on one side and a greenfinch on the other.

Then a new sound came in – high-pitched and indistinct – a foraging party of long-tailed tits. They bustled into the shelter of the clematis and took up positions on both peanut feeders. It is rare that they come this close to the house, so the dishes had to wait. I fetched the binoculars and watched them feeding and flitting further into the garden, returning again and again to the feeders. When eventually they disappeared, I went outside and looked up into the tops of the silver birch, at the branches adorned by eight long-tails, four goldfinches, some half-dozen whistling starlings, a song thrush, a male blackbird, and four greenfinches.

The artery of the road passes between the house and the fell, but another, less visible pathway exists too, if one takes notice – one that is largely unobserved by people walking down into town and back, by kids on the way to school, by dog-walkers and postmen. It is the regular flightpaths of birds on their constant journeys up and down from the fell and the gardens. Various trees provide strategic refuges on the way: the ash trees near the bottom of the fell, the rounded frame of the copper beech in the garden across the road, our overgrown, contorted and blousy hazel in the front garden, our tall silver birch and the Buddleia in the back garden, to name but a few.

Last week a notice appeared on a lamppost in the lane: neighbours seeking permission to remove a cypress tree from their garden. I called the local council, wanting to arbitrate on behalf of the birds – the tree is a song post for blackbirds and thrushes. The planner told me that there is little, if any, regulation to the protection of unexceptional trees; the law exists chiefly to protect the *built* environment. Over the years, we've witnessed the felling of mature trees right in the middle of the nesting season. I asked the planner how many prosecutions there might have been here in South Lakes, for felling trees with active nests. A moment's pause. That, he said, was not his department.

◎ ◎ ◎

An email winged in. A friend was soon flying south to Israel to take part in a bird-spotting race, 'Champions of the Flyway,' organised by the Society for the Protection of Nature in Israel – part of the global alliance, BirdLife International.

The 'Flyway' raises awareness of the annual slaughter of twenty million birds (you read that right) on their migration routes across the Mediterranean. The cover image of BirdLife International's report entitled 'The Killing', taken in Cyprus, was of a lesser whitethroat trapped by a gluey lime substance that is routinely smeared onto sticks precisely for this purpose. Held fast and upside-down by the tip of its beak and its feet, the whitethroat is doomed to a slow, sticky death. That bird might have made it here, might have taken up residence and sung its wonderful affirmatory song in the woods near me, or near you.

The report cites Italy as the worst offender. Trappers catch birds in tension snares, where many die of thirst or exhaustion. Migrant birds are caught in nets and are sometimes used to trap other birds. They're kept in the dark and released into daylight in the autumn. Then, mistaking the light for spring, they sing and attract others to the trap. Birds are sold at high prices to restaurants and other private dealers as food. Vast numbers of Eurasian chaffinches, meadow pipits and song thrushes are killed in Italy alone. In France, the chaffinch, our much-celebrated robin (recently voted UK Bird of the Year) and the ortolan bunting are killed in large numbers. More chaffinches are killed illegally in France than almost anywhere else in Europe, and the ortolan bunting is served as a gourmet's 'rite of passage'. Despite the illegality, the killing is widely tolerated.

February 23

After a freezing two-hour blast of cold and bitter wind, feeling underdressed and thinking only of hot coffee, three buzzards materialised in that inaccessible, parallel space beyond the edge of Scout Scar. They began to display, soaring upwards and then folding their wings and falling. Each time they fell, they rose again on thermals that carried them far into the sky. Two of the birds interacted with each other, the third seemed more peripheral. They rose again, and in the stoop that followed one of them pivoted upside down, presenting its talons to the other. They clasped talons momentarily. Suddenly, I no longer felt cold.

February 24

Larks! Walking towards Cunswick Scar on a morning of clear blue sky and incipient warmth, I climbed the stile in the wall that divides the farmland from the wildness of the open fell and heard, caught on the slightest of breezes, larksong. I stood motionless, called the dog to heel and waited, but the sound did not recur. I've walked this route countless times before, but that day, for the first time, I noticed a path following a line underneath the fell and turned to walk into unknown territory. The path climbed gently, contouring around the northern end of the fell, and after a quarter mile the great, tumbled cairn of limestone rocks that marks the summit came into view. Along the northern horizon, the mountains at the head of Kentmere were rimmed with snow remnants.

Blackthorn bushes formed tight, impenetrable knots of spiked branches – not even enough room for a small bird, I thought.

Then lark song came again from below me on the far edge of the hill. There was a movement in the grass and, raising the binoculars, two larks appeared in my vision. They patrolled the ground, heads bobbing as they inspected the new season's breeding territory. They called to each other in a staccato version of their celebrated sky-borne song, and then a third lark voice joined in. I turned and caught its faltering, falling flight, sunlight filtering through its wings. It fell down the blue sky, alighting in the topmost branch of a blackthorn, and from there it seemed to survey me. If I'd not taken the unknown turn in the path, I'd not have been there, witness to the very beginning of the skylark's spring song, that potent symbol of the turning year.

The skylark, perhaps more than any other species, is an emblem of the British countryside. This much-celebrated songbird was a profound inspiration for Ralph Vaughan Williams' *The Lark Ascending*, amongst other musical works. Less well-known is the poem of the same name – the inspiration behind the Vaughan Williams composition written by English poet George Meredith. First published in 1881, it is a paean of 122 lines, a song of thanksgiving to a creature whose singing is one of the most affecting amongst all our native species of birds. Siegfried Sassoon described the poem as a lyric which sustains the recreation, or interpretation of lark-song – it 'soars up and up with the song it imitates, and unites inspired spontaneity with a demonstration of effortless technical ingenuity', continuing that a few readings of the poem will convince the reader of its precision.[1]

Both the poem and the music are given added poignancy when considered from our hundred-plus-years' vantage point. Both were written during the lead-up to the First World War. On the flyleaf of the musical score of *The Lark Ascending*, Vaughan Williams included a short section from the beginning of the poem, invoking the spirit that is present throughout the whole work:

He rises and begins to round,
He drops the silver chain of sound,
Of many links without a break,
In chirrup, whistle, slur and shake.
For singing till his heaven fills,
'Tis love of earth that he instils,
And ever winging up and up,
Our valley is his golden cup
And he the wine which overflows
to lift us with him as he goes.
Till lost on his aerial rings
In light, and then the fancy sings.[2]

But what of the structure of the skylark's song? David Hindley, a former head of music at Huddersfield New College and later of Homerton College Cambridge, made recordings of the skylark and slowed the results down. He concluded that the skylark's song is comparable to the work of composers of great music, noting the way it follows a classical sonata form: exposition, development, recapitulation. 'With invention, not repetition,' Mr Hindley stressed; 'If it was an automaton, it would repeat the music precisely.'

Each second of song delivers two hundred and thirty notes, all in ascending and descending cadences.

The lark's habitat ranges from the coast to the mountains, though it favours open grassland and meadow. But as with so many declining species, the skylark now appears on the Section 41 Species List, as well as the Birds of Conservation Concern 'red' list, having declined between 1970 and 2005 by as much as fifty-three per cent.[3] I was not surprised to read that, once again, this loss of species is directly related to changes in farming practices. The switch from spring to autumn sowing of cereals impacts on skylarks breeding later in the season. Increases in dog ownership, where dogs are at liberty to run free over heathland, also impacts on ground nesting birds. Fortunately for our larks, Milly runs to our heels.

◎ ◎ ◎

In the late afternoon, the light called me out again. In a few short hours, the snow on the mountain tops had all but disappeared. Dense shadows fell in an oblique line from Ill Bell across the high ground of the Kentmere valley-head. On the southern slopes of Thornthwaite Crag and Harter Fell, rocky ledges and crevices were scribbled marks of charcoal.

The low sun was cast in broad bands across the fields ahead of me, revealing the contours of medieval ridge and furrow. This ancient groundwork has marked the land for centuries, most noticeable under snow or slanting light.

Walking back down the fell towards home, a blackbird talked softly from somewhere deep inside the woven branches of the hedge: *cuck, cuck-cuck*. Catkins hung in bright green clusters, others the purple of early plums. A great tit sang optimistically from the top of a young oak. Everything was right with the world.

February 25

All the small birds dispersed; the neighbourhood thugs had arrived. The jackdaws dangled awkwardly from peanut feeders, stabbing into the contents with the table manners of a goat. Shattered peanuts fell to the ground. I went into the garden to place on the wall exactly one and three-quarter loaves of chopped-up wholemeal bread, laced with expensive pumpkin seeds, linseeds and more. My homemade bread had not, on this occasion, turned out to be edible – far from it. But I can say with confidence that the local jackdaws are given only the healthiest of foods. Whether or not they can fly weighed down by it all is another matter entirely. In twenty seconds, though, not a trace of bread – or jackdaws – remained.

The small birds returned. A robin lingered on the hanging seed feeder – unusual. As the tube rotated, his red breast flashed like a ruddy beacon.

◎ ◎ ◎

True darkness fell just after 6pm. Walking up the garden towards the house, from somewhere in the tangle of branches, a blackbird began belting out his full song of spring. Moments later, I saw him on the roof silhouetted the same inky black as the stovepipe next to him. Wood smoke rose and evaporated into the cooling evening. Above the fell, the sky was incandescent blue, like lapis. Clouds drifted. The first stars began to appear.

February 27

Walking home from Helsington, first along the three miles of Scout Scar, then on to lesser Cunswick Scar, in the company of robins. They sang from hawthorn and blackthorn bushes all along the way. This trickling song of theirs is an anthem to the close of winter, a reconnoitring of what has been left behind, and what is to come. It is the sound of a Lakeland beck singing over lichen-slow stones: a small waterfall of sound, a pouring of song that is as much the silence in between phrases as the song itself. It is a pause to let in the sound of the day breathing.

◎ ◎ ◎

In the dark soil below the dry stone garden wall, crocuses were beginning to open their slim, bright cylinders to the sun. As the day wore on, the petals fell flagrantly open, revealing the saffron-yellow stigmata, like satellites sending and receiving messages to the sun.

February 28

Hard, grey ice bloomed on the mountains and eastern fells. On Kendal Fell, something was astir.

The clatter of magpies on the wooded quarry path. Five of them flew in formation towards the lower ground, then as I came out of the wood they reappeared, but now only four. Together they moved across the sky in the magpies' characteristic 'dip, beat, soar and dip' flight, then came to land in the top of an ash tree higher up the fell. As the magpies travelled, they uttered their intermittent two-note high-pitched *chack-ack! chack-ack!* Almost instantaneously they took off again and dived over the fell, skimming the tops of the quarry wood trees before passing into the interior web of branches. I moved on again, and now the magpies lifted clear of the wood, crossing the field back towards the ash tree, though now there were seven of them.

This game, for I don't know what else it could have been, continued. The magpies repeated their journeys between the two woods, but always leaving one or two of the group behind, then subsequently collecting them, as if involved in some avian version of the playground game 'British Bulldogs'.

◉ ◉ ◉

The collective noun for a group of magpies, *conventicle*, is obscure enough for me to have to look it up. The Oxford English Dictionary defines this as 'a secret or unlawful religious meeting, typically of nonconformists,' and a British Trust for Ornithology report[4] on magpie behaviour, tells that younger magpies gather in larger groups in early spring to assist in the forging of pair bonds. The behaviour I witnessed did indeed appear to be a convened or intentional gathering, but the only secret thing about it was, had I not passed through their territory that morning, there would have been no witness to the ritual. Although such magpie gatherings are rarely witnessed, the old rhyme '*One for sorrow'*, etc, continues in common usage.

Historically, the word 'pie' originally referred to a mixture of colours, though in more recent times, the meaning has become reduced to the simpler definition of 'black and white'. The sixteenth-century Anglo-Latin name for the magpie is 'pica', and the Latin name *Pica pica*, has a direct link with the printing trade: a 'pica' is a unit of type size and length. Regional names for the magpie, as noted by Francesca Greenoak (see references), are 'piet', from the old county of Westmorland, 'piannot' from Cheshire, 'maggot-pie' from eastern England, 'Margaret's pie', and, resulting perhaps from the timbre of its 'football-rattle' call, 'chatternag', from Somerset.

Three

GEESE

March 1

I had a yen to go north, even for just a day. It had been a while since I'd been north of the border, a long time since I'd visited the Solway, and I wanted to see geese again. By 7am I was in the car, heading off into a brilliant morning.

As I pulled into the carpark at Caerlaverock, I watched small groups of geese winging inland over the buildings, low enough for me to hear the creak of their wings. I walked the wide path bordered by hawthorns that were garlanded by soft grey lichen, the intertwining branches forming an archway overhead, and walked out towards a bright band of distant water – the Solway Firth. At the end of the path was a wooden hide. I went inside. I had the place to myself. Looking out, the view spanned a wide margin of saltmarsh spangled with pools and channels towards the ebbing tide and the shining water. Across the Firth, England had almost disappeared. A church spire pierced a bank of low cloud and this, together with the silhouettes of Skiddaw and Blencathra, were the only intelligible features in that English landscape, the mountains holding shreds of strong yellow light.

Opening the narrow horizontal window, a cold, quiet wind pushed inside, blowing in over the marsh and accompanied by the unmistakeable sound of geese, though I couldn't see them.

I heard a skylark too – the Scot's 'laverock,' the bird for which both the reserve and the castle just further along the coast were named: Caerlaverock – 'Castle of the Lark.' I thought it a brave wee bird to be up in the air and singing with such gusto in the chill of that morning.

Three barnacle geese flew low to the earth; as they came to land I saw others, forty or fifty of them, foraging on the marsh, their contact calling an underscore to the wind. I like this, the constant social narrative of geese, their continual checking in with each other. And whilst it might not have been the hundreds of geese I'd hoped for, it was a beginning. Watching through the binoculars, every so often a small number peeled away from the group and began to fly in towards the fields, one goose on the perimeter of the flock remaining on sentry duty, its neck and head erect.

◎ ◎ ◎

Around the end of the twelfth century, Bishop Giraldus Cambrensis of Wales published in his book *Topographia Hibernice* that barnacle geese formed spontaneously from sodden driftwood, growing like goose barnacles. 'I have frequently seen, with my own eyes, more than a thousand of these small bird-like bodies, hanging down on the seashore from one piece of timber, enclosed in their shells, and already formed. They do not breed and lay eggs like other birds, nor do they ever hatch any eggs, nor do they seem to build nests in any corner of the earth.'[5]

On a previous memorable visit, I had seen something akin to Giraldus' description on a bitter cold December dawn. That morning I'd walked into the end of night along the lane from Caerlaverock farmhouse. The moon gone, owls were still at large, and the *keewick* of a tawny split the silence from a rumple-headed ash tree. At a farm, bright lights were already lit in the milking parlour, and radio pop music accompanied the beginning of the day. In the carrier bag at my side, two metallic flasks clanged against each other, and the din spooked a couple of sleeping horses behind the hedge into a sudden, snorting, chaotic gallop. I waited at a crossroads. The first hint of dawn's rosy inception glimmered, and somewhere out on the estuary I could hear the primordial conversations of geese. The minutes passed, though the friend who had offered to meet me for a dawn walk did not arrive. I began to wonder if I'd got the date or the place to meet wrong.

The distant thrum of a car travelling through the darkness toward the coast: I heard it slow down, then the shift of gears as it turned in at the junction half a mile away, the headlights breaching the early shifting of light. Grafted onto this, another sound, closer in, of something soft-trotting at speed towards me. A fox morphed out of the darkness, passing between me and the hedge, so close to the end of my boots that I saw its tenebrous outline perfectly, from the pointed nose to the paler tip of the balancing brush, and then, moving in fox-trot tempo, it was gone. A car pulled up, a door opened, and there was Dave.

A few minutes' journey, barely enough to warm up before we parked and began to walk the boardwalk out across the salt-marsh towards the Solway as night shifted to soft-focus grey dawn, woodland and mountain and sea-margins evolving with the light. We moved along between tall banks of sedge. Something was rattling and shaking as it sploshed a watery route away from the boardwalk. We followed the creature's progress by the shifting of the sedge-tops against the sky, looked at each other, mouthed, 'Otter!'

The hide was isolated out on the marshes, and stationed inside it, we saw dawn open more and yet more gaps in the cloud layer, behind which were luminous carmines and the blues of indigo and gentian. Through binoculars or the scope we looked out to the estuary, and there, on distant sandbars, surrounded by the incoming tide: barnacle geese. Settled in long roosting congregations, there were so many, so densely compacted together, it was as if a layer of black fabric covered the sands – or else sheets of darkened timbers cast out upon the sands.

Every few minutes, something began to move, and, as if lifted by an invisible finger and thumb, a corner of the cloth would lift and shift, becoming pixelated, breaking away from the mass. In small, inky constellations, the geese rose up and arrowed uproariously inland, shape-shifting, welcoming dawn in a squabble of voices. Over the hide they flew. We went outside, my hands not yet thawed, out into the bitter cold to watch them pass inland, 'V' after ragged 'V'. Holding their wings wide, they wiffled down into the fields to settle and lift, then settle and lift again in other fields.

Seen with our own eyes in the mid-winter darkness, Giraldus' barnacle geese had evolved from a place and in a way that, in the Middle Ages, could only have been imagined, and barely understood.

◎ ◎ ◎

As I came out of the hide at Caerlaverock that March morning, I looked up at the sky. Sheets of dense cloud were forming, swagged with wave after wave of bulging depressions, as if the sea and land had been inverted. Rain was imminent.

A large group of geese were busy feeding in one of the fields. I stopped momentarily to watch them, but it was their flight I wanted. I wanted the sky peopled by them, to watch them passing overhead in skein after skein of geese music. I thought of the long poem sequence, *The Fool's Errand,* by Irish poet Dermot Healy, in which he records and celebrates the sights and sounds of the barnacle geese overwintering on an island close to his home:

> *Since I began to*
> *look up*

at your psalm
all of the instruments

have turned into birds.[6]

◎　◎　◎

By the time I reached the Peter Scott hide, rain was falling stead-ily. Inside was a grander affair, with padded seats overlooking a pool through huge windows. At the back of the room, whoop-er-swan wallpaper decorated the long wall, the birds illustrated both in profile and face-on. It was, I thought, a touch of genius. As I sat down, a couple of older men said hello. Whoopers and mute swans paddled outside the windows in elegant white flo-tillas. Purple birches and the shambolic heads of sienna-coloured willows framed the pool.

I'd been here before, years ago. There had been hundreds of swans that day – the sky had been full of them, and I remembered the sensation of watching each great down-curved breadth of wing as they came in from the fields, manoeuvring themselves down from the sky onto the water. It had rained that day too – a deluge. Somehow a swan had been injured, and as I returned to the courtyard, a couple of wardens were trying to corner and catch it. One of the swan's wings trailed on the ground as it ran chaotically, evading capture. I joined in, waving my arms to help manoeuvre the large bird into a corner of the yard. After some time, the wardens finally got their bird.

Out on the water, the whoopers called continuously, the sound like a squeaky, rusty hinge or a child's scooter horn. More visitors came inside out of the rain, and more whoopers appeared on the outfield, standing with heads high like nosy neighbours. Then the warden came in and began to talk to us about the swans. He pointed out the differences between their bills: the mute swan's finer and more orange, the whooper's more a wedge-shaped, yellow mask with a black tip.

'Peter Scott,' he said, 'could identify three hundred individual swans simply from the slight differences in their facial characteristics.' Son of the famous Antarctic explorer, Scott was an influential leader in the early days of the modern conservation movement. He was instrumental in setting up Caerlaverock as a reserve, as well as the adjacent National Nature Reserve.

Someone said, 'Look – they're coming in,' and a group of whoopers, bright against the rain, their wingspan almost three metres from tip to tip, descended to the pool. Their feet glissaded momentarily along the surface of the water before, in close sequence, they folded their great wings back and upright into the distinctive position that lends swans such an unquestionably regal air.

The warden told us about the whoopers' coloured leg rings and how to read them, how you could look up an individual swan's story on a touch-screen console. I found the console, looked up 'Yellow 9AD'; it was a swan called Adiemum, a bird that had clocked up some forty-eight thousand miles migrating between the UK and its summer breeding grounds in Iceland.

'Many of the whoopers have already set out on the long journey back to Iceland – some eight hundred miles. Some of these birds have recorded journey times of a mere twelve and a half hours from Caerlaverock to Iceland.' From the front row seats by the windows came nods of acknowledgement.

'Our barnacle geese migrate from here to Spitsbergen in the Arctic, but pinkfoot breeding territories are in the highlands of Iceland.' I was beginning to feel the pull further north myself.

The warden left the hide, reappearing a few minutes later in front of the windows, wheeling a barrow-full of grain. The swans were the first to rise onto their feet, waddling out of the water and gathering on the gravel edge. The warden waited as a whooper swan put its head into the barrow, then picking up a scoop he began to fling showers of grain out over the water, over the geese and swans and ducks all gathered in anticipation.

'If I had my time again, I wouldn't do a desk job,' an older man said.

◎ ◎ ◎

I walked east between another avenue of trees towards the far observation tower. Rain fell and small birds scattered ahead of me, darting in and out of the branches – chaffinches, goldfinches and blue tits. I moved fast to get through the rain, dodging mud and sloshing through great puddles. Then, passing a slight gap between the sheltering trees and the protective banking, I momentarily spied a field brimful of geese. The split second of time as my figure shifted into their awareness, however, was enough. Instantly, an explosion of sound, like the roll of a thousand drums from the simultaneous beating of their wings as they lifted off from the ground. They separated, scattering and flying away from me, heading north. I was frustrated that the mere hint of my outline had driven them away. Through the gap, I watched as they formed into small jittery groups, waiting for that instinctual sense of direction to be transmitted through the flock's communal synapses.

'Come back!' I said aloud. The geese banked and began to turn. As they coalesced into semi-organised skeins, it seemed that they were intent on recreating order. I stood beneath the archway of tree branches, rain pouring onto my upturned face, and watched them begin to flow overhead. They flew towards the sea, and as they passed above me, the instruments began to play.

◎ ◎ ◎

In the last years of my father's life, his health and strength declined. Taking him for trips out was fraught with difficulty. He was tall, though stooped and heavy, and it became more than I could manage alone to manoeuvre him into and out of the wheelchair and the car. It was hard, telling him we could no longer go out.

The day of our last trip out into the world, it was cold. I'd wrapped him up with blankets and driven to Martin Mere Wild-fowl and Wetlands Centre, just a few miles from his home. I pushed him around the pathways, past enclosures with all kinds of exotic birds. At the edge of the reserve, I pushed him up a ramp into a hide overlooking the Mere, a vast wetland of pools and marsh upon which thousands of pink-footed geese were feeding. I opened up the window at wheelchair height.

'Can you see them, Dad?' I asked. He wasn't sure. 'Look out onto the pools – can you see the geese, Dad? There are thousands. Can you hear them?'

And Dad's rheumy eyes looked and he answered, like a child that hasn't yet seen the thing through the binoculars, 'I think I can.'

'It reminds me of home, Dad, back in Ulverston, when the geese used to come over in the winter – do you remember?'

'I'm not sure that I do.'

Pretty soon he needed to be back in the warmth, and I looked out at the geese and understood what it was that had gone, and how it would never come back.

◉ ◉ ◉

Early on the morning of my father's funeral, I went into the bed-room overlooking the back garden to draw back the curtains and let in the light. It was early June, and the summer was behaving itself. As my eyes adjusted to the intense brightness, I was met by something unexpected and surreal, though I later thought, something that *resonated*. I've never been able to account for what happened, nor to forget.

At the end of our garden, perhaps no more than twenty feet from the window, was a small group of geese. It seemed that they must have just at that very moment taken off, from right here

– in our garden, as if in the act of opening the curtains, I had provoked them into action and flight. I watched them, spellbound. They were a scene from an Arctic myth, or a fairy-tale. No geese had ever landed here before, and why would they? Small back gardens on the periphery of towns are not geese territory, and we rarely see them flying overhead.

The geese moved awkwardly, taking time to organise themselves, gaining altitude slowly, with difficulty. As they jostled and rose through the air, I saw that they were pinkfoots, the same geese I had watched from the hide at Martin Mere, and that dad may or may not have seen on his last ever trip out into the world. Before they passed out of view, flying towards the south and tracking behind the neighbouring chimney pots, something made me count them, and there were sixteen.

An hour or so later we were driving down the M6 towards Dad and the funeral service. I had with me the flowers I'd bought for his coffin – the bright yellow faces of sunflowers and the blue of irises as a way of recalling France, the place he most loved to be with his partner, Shirley. As we came close to the motorway turnoff my niece Eva said, 'Look – look at the geese!' Flying adjacent to us, along the perimeter of the motorway, orientated towards Martin Mere was a small skein of pink-footed geese. Something told me to count them again. I did; there were fifteen.

March 2
A confusion of weather. Snow squalls drifted in from the northeast, obliterating Potter Fell and the Whinfell Ridge. To the south and west, pale blue sky knitted with strands of cloud soon succumbed to this late manifestation of winter.

After the squalls had moved on, the gardens, houses and surrounding hills lay underneath fresh snow – almost too bright under the midday sun.

March 4

A new neighbour is proving to be a problem. Rather than the mellifluous tones we have come to love and expect, the singing of the thrush that has taken up residence in our birch tree is more Les Dawson than Beethoven, more apprentice hod carrier than diva. He had us awake from 5am or even earlier, bashing out his few phrases before the light arrived – far too early for discordant jazz. He sang all day and all evening until darkness mercifully fell, the repertoire confined to just three or four deafening phrases. The typical repertoire of the song thrush is a more multi-faceted affair. They usually develop a complex and extensive set of phrases that are picked out and delivered in linking chains of song. I wish someone had told this to our neighbourhood thrush…

He sang from the cypress tree across the lane or from the summit of our elegant birch, and sometimes sang unseen – which was when I knew he was on the roof of the house. Most mornings he visited the garden, perching sideways on the trellis to access the fat balls, feeding himself and simultaneously watching the blue tits, coal tits, chaffinches and goldfinches between bites. Yesterday brought a new arrival, a single siskin, staying only momentarily.

The snow thawed and dripped and the drips dissolved the remaining shreds of snow. A robin appeared, took umbrage at another robin and chased it out of the garden. The resident robin's tiny red engine glowed quietly from inside the tangle of clematis stems.

March 6

A feeding frenzy, late afternoon, on the feeder outside my study window: chaffinches, blue tits and the by now ubiquitous goldfinches. The window was open, and the timbre of irritable bickering and avian arguments filtered inside. I looked up, and there, complete with her black mask and buff-coloured chest: a female bullfinch. She took the sunflower seeds and peered all bright-eyed, through the window at me. Then the frap of small wings and her mate arrived, black headed and grey frock-coated, his chest as round and ruddy as a late September rosehip.

March 9

In the early morning quiet, before the rush for bathroom and breakfast began, I sat beside the fire, drinking the first mug of tea and listening to the spring love song of the collared dove that was, at that very moment, perched on the rim of our chimney pot. *Coo cooo cuk, coo cooo cuk.* He had been in residence these past few weeks. Every morning the song filtered down the flue, connecting me to the outside, to the shifting season.

March 11

On Scout Scar early. There'd been a film of morning mist covering the town, extending up to the Scar and blanketing the Lyth Valley, but as I began to walk, it started to unravel and dissolve. Sunlight broke through and the numerous ash trees on the Scar became brilliant, absorbing and reflecting white light. The dog ran on ahead following scent trails. Robins trilled phrases of song from blackthorn bushes.

I heard the unmistakeable call of geese, and looking up found a skein of pinkfoots travelling in two undulating, irregular lines with outriders close in. As they passed overhead, I watched them order themselves into the customary V-shape, altering their course as they did so, reconnoitring some internal navigational aid and heading north. Perhaps the Solway was their destination today – a refuelling stopover before the long haul into the *simmer dim* of summer in the far north and a nesting site beside glaciers or high on the summits of cliffs and crags. I watched them for a long time, and after picking up one final, distant, discordant note, they were gone.

Had anyone down in the valley heard that Arctic babble and looked up to see the geese, they would have seemed to be flying almost at cloud height. Up on the Scar, I was eight hundred feet closer to them, close enough to see their colouring, to see their beaks opening and closing, their wings using the air to push them onward. Into the silence that resumed after they'd disappeared came lark song – a single lark flying and falling, flying and falling over the blackthorn heath, over the shattered limestone terrain, over the ash trees reflecting the sun.

◉ ◉ ◉

Down the lane in our neighbour's kitchen, the talk was all about birds. Outside, a flurry of small avian visitors congregated at the seed feeders hung throughout the garden.

'Yesterday,' Brenda said, 'there was a blackbird with a beak full of worms flitting into the pyracantha by the front door.' A nest already on the way. Blue tits and coal tits came and went. Brenda said that a pair of bullfinches visits the garden every day, and for three years running a spotted flycatcher had taken up residence in the robin's nest box.

Cliff said, 'Two years ago, when the young fledged, they were caught by a neighbour's cat. We found the chicks' heads left on the grass – like gruesome trophies they were.'

Two years ago, the brood came good, but last year they'd found the female dead in the nest and one chick dead underneath. Their theory: a cat had done for the male bird, and the female, reliant on the male to bring supplies, simply remained on the nest, keeping the chick warm, sitting out the long, fruitless wait.

And so began a neighbourly game of bird one-upmanship.

Brenda and Cliff had bullfinches every day and long-tailed tits visiting regularly. We had goldfinches every day – so many I need to restock the feeders almost daily; they were eating us out of house and home. Cliff and Brenda had a dunnock nesting in their hedge. We had goldfinches on Christmas morning.

The conversation moved on to the tree surgeons we had all seen hacking at a mature ash near the allotments this morning. I'd walked across to ask what the plan was, the aggravating sound of the chainsaw preventing me from being able to work. The tree surgeon had been halfway up the tree, suspended by ropes.

'We're pollarding it, reducing it by about a half, then it'll be nice and healthy.'

Although I didn't say it, it looked as if the tree was perfectly healthy anyway. Cliff found the whole thing with tree removal difficult. 'They soak up water, don't they?' he said. 'And absorb carbon dioxide. Don't we need as many as we can get?'

Brenda talked about the way tree surgeons always arrive at the beginning of spring, just as birds are beginning to nest.

I told them of the nest I'd found earlier this week, tucked inside the hedge by the path onto the fell. It was a small, tight cup, intricately constructed around the joining stems of a young ash tree. The maker had wound, or rather embroidered, the construction with rounds of blue wool.

Before leaving, Brenda pointed out the squeezy bottle of water she kept on the doorstep – ready if a cat were to come anywhere near...

March 12

A male blackbird ferreted amongst the last of the snowdrops and the first of the small, bright *tête-à-tête* daffodils. This year, as last, the snowdrops arrived in January and lasted well into the spring, until the daffodils were in flower.

After a walk on the fell, passing the hedge, an absence: the handsomely woven nest had disappeared.

Whilst making the beds, I looked out to see a jackdaw peering down into the garden from his vantage point on the guttering of the kitchen. There were no crumbs on the wall, but ever the optimist, the jackdaw swooped down and strutted along, inspecting just in case.

Gripping the wooden rose trellis, the apprentice thrush fed enthusiastically from the fat balls suspended just above him. A robin studied the ground beneath the plant-pots, picking up crumbs. Missing nothing, the lone jackdaw noticed, crossed the garden and joined in. Blackbirds came and went, always in the undergrowth.

March 13

Bee-hum. Summer's sweet foragers had begun to wake, to work.

March 14

A bumblebee, ambling over the bright white, sun-warmed outside wall of my study, of such a size that it was visible from the far end of the garden. In close-up, its pulsing body imbibed the heat, warming up like an engine ready to begin production. A queen *Bombus terrestris*, the buff-tailed bumblebee, with that distinguishing, broad, dirty-orange stripe and buff-tipped abdomen: one of the earliest bumblebee species to emerge in the spring.

March 15

At the hamlet of Starnthwaite in the Lyth Valley, bees were working my friend's sunlit cottage garden, taking pollen from the nodding green or deep-pink headed hellebores. As we walked the narrow lane from the cottage we came across the carcass of a badger, dead these past two weeks, my friend said. It lay on the verge, as if it were merely asleep, like a dog with its hind legs extended behind, eyes closed and face resting on its two front paws. Nothing had touched it – not a crow, nor a fox, and there were, as yet, no signs of decay. The badger's thick hide is rarely penetrated by predators, who tend not to bother expending the energy required to break through, preferring to find easier carrion. So the badger's carcass awaits a long, slow disintegration.

March 20

Tree surgeons again. Two Land Rovers were parked in the lane, along with a machine for frazzling branches into tiny pellets. I knew there were blackbirds nesting somewhere in that garden, though I didn't know exactly where. I had seen the tell-tale signs of the male blackbird foraging in our garden, and carrying beakfuls of insects back across the lane in his usual swirling, banking flight. And on one occasion, he had winged past my ear as I pegged out the washing, before zooming away uttering his alarm call – letting me know unceremoniously that I was simply in the way.

I went to talk to the tree surgeons, to let them know about the nest, pointing to where it must have been. They were polite enough, but there seemed little intention to avoid disturbing the nesting blackbirds. The chipping machine stayed where it was, close to the nest area. The men began to lop branches off the cypress and feed them into the machine. The noise was deafening. Then the piercing alarm call of an adult blackbird sounded into the morning. Even for me, the stress was too much, and I headed off.

March 22

Spilled over on to the path, loose crumbs of earth. Mrs Blackbird had been gardening in her usual untidy manner. Watching from the kitchen window, I saw her work a patch of ground, flicking the soil from side to side with her beak, hunting for the juicy worm that was no doubt at that very moment pushing deeper into the earth. Later, she came close to the back door, and I enticed her closer still with raisins and dried cranberries; she was unable to resist. As she picked her way through the sweet dried fruit, she looked at me, then the sky, then at me again, as if she was working out exactly where this manna had come from.

The cock bird lifted from the lawn into a banking flight and flew over the lane in the direction of the nest. In the afternoon, a singular keening note pierced the air, penetrating even the closed window. The cock was high up in the silver birch. I watched his beak opening and closing as he gave the thin, keening whistle used to contact the young, either to entice them from the nest or call to them from the newfound territory of the garden once they've fledged. It was the sound of parental anxiety made manifest. I feared the worst.

March 25

For three days now, the pair of blackbirds have been feeding together. The nest was clearly lost.

March 26

Previously hidden behind the dense green foliage of the cypress, the view into our neighbour's garden now reveals the tracery of a Japanese maple, and in the topmost branch, the male blackbird sang as if nothing had happened, as if the nest had not been made in the closeness of the beech hedge, as if the early clutch of eggs had never been laid, as if the energy expended was of no consequence. He sang to the evening, for the simple, unequivocal impulse that is his life.

Our apprentice thrush has disappeared.

March 27

The cock blackbird bathed before breakfast. Overnight rain had refilled our birdbath – a large, shallow stone dish that rests on the paving amongst the flower pots. The blackbird pushed his bright yellow beak and jet-black head under the water surface, creating ripples and small waves, then scooped water up with his wings, sending it shivering in tiny sunlit beads that dripped and fell from his head and back.

◎ ◎ ◎

An early walk up to Cunswick Scar, dodging squally showers, bookended by larks.

The allotmenteers were preparing the ground for first plantings, and the pigeon men, Tommy, Peter and their pals, were calling to pigeons that whizzed in training flights over the haphazard collection of pigeon lofts, sheds and gardens. Wrens *chit-chitted* and scolded in the hedgerow, and robins sang their small waterfalls of song from the Scots pines up on the first wildnesses of the fell. Sunday morning walkers and runners were out in force. Owners exchanged greetings as their dogs approached one another, sniffed bottoms, and we called out to them: *come on!*

On the broad swathe of the summit, lark song came borne on soft gusts of wind. A fluster of larks passed overhead, singing and gliding. I stood still to take in the view – the valley of the Kent framed by the rolling backdrop of the Whinfell ridge and the Kentmere Horseshoe, the central fells and the Coniston hills in the west. I walked down the two big fields beyond the summit, crossed the dual carriageway by the footbridge, and entered another world. Cunswick Scar was visible ahead as a tawny landscape of winter grass adorned by dark stands of gorse and juniper. There was a sense of walking away from the mundane, towards a place where anything could happen. Gulls passed overhead, sunlit, silver-white on the front edge of dark and fast-forming rain squalls. Over the Lake District, rain fell.

The 'little-bit-of-bread-and-no-cheese' folk song of a yellowhammer floated over from the half yellow, half sea-green spiny branches of a gorse, the season not yet warm enough to release the heady coconut scent into the air.

I circumnavigated the great cairn of limestone rocks at the summit of Cunswick Scar, and, after looking longingly for a moment towards the mountains, turned for home again. Back on the fell, on the path below the little grassy crag, I heard larks again. One tiny songster moved through the air above me, its moth-like wings fluttering, the little out-breath when the body falls momentarily, then the resurrection into the high air as it rose up again, buoyed on stuttering wing-beats. Two goldfinches passed, their squeaky see-saw voices trailing in their wake as they zipped on towards the top of the fell.

Crossing the road into our lane, a clattering, rattling raiding party of jackdaws sailed over the gardens.

March 28

Like a portent, a wraith-like cloud of rooks drifted out from the edge of Cunswick Scar's northerly cliffs and over the woods below. Further on, three more were busy mobbing a pair of buzzards. One of the rooks stalled continuously, diving down and almost landing on one of the buzzard's backs before banking away. Behind them, a sunspot evolved out of the film of pale grey cloud. Towards the south, storms.

Four

CURLEW CALLING

Early Spring

'Have you written any poems about curlews?' my friend Mary
Keith asked in an email.

'Funny you should ask,' I wrote back. 'Just finished two. Why?'

This exchange marked the beginning of my time as part of a
team of people involved in raising awareness of curlew decline
and the urgent need for their restoration in the quietly wonderful landscape of the Shropshire-Welsh borders. Recruited by the
Stiperstones and Corndon Hill Landscape Partnership, we were
a small team: celebrated wildlife photographer Ben Osborne,
sculptor Bill Sample, Mary Keith as the project composer and
choir leader, and myself as writer and documenter. Together we
began to plan ways to celebrate the curlew and raise awareness of
its parlous state within local communities.

Why bring in a group of artists to do this? The Partnership's
project leader, Amanda Perkins, was clear: 'We can't go on bashing people over the head with the science and facts – it's too
depressing and a turn-off; people feel powerless. If the aim is to
celebrate, we'll have more success involving people.'

Last year the Partnership monitored twenty-one nests with
cameras. Every single nest was predated, predominantly by foxes,
though the cameras also recorded badgers and ravens. There was,

I saw, a strong sense of things being out of balance in the area. Not so many years ago, the local raven population was on the verge of extinction – now there are over seventy pairs. Raven? Or curlew? If it came down to it – and it seems in some places it clearly does – which species is more deserving of protection?

In early April, I met the project's ornithologists, Tony Cross and David Tompkins. We drove the winding, narrow lanes to look for curlew returning to their breeding grounds after over-wintering at the coast. We drove through settlements called Squilver, Snailbeach, the Bog, Gravels, Rattlinghope and Fish-pool. For me, this new landscape took some reconnoitring – it seemed all deep-set lanes mining through farmland, crossroads, and wild, overgrown hedgerows. I used the elongated ridges of the Long Mynd and the cragged Stiperstones for orientation, and Corndon Hill from where parascenders floated off beneath gaudy-coloured parachutes. Tony had already been staking out fields where he'd seen curlew. Our morning drive revealed many of them in the same fields; nesting would only be a matter of time.

◉ ◉ ◉

On my second day in Shropshire, Ben dropped me at Hemford Crossroads so that I could walk and learn by seeing that unfamiliar landscape alone. The path passed through mixed woodland where newly arrived chiffchaffs belted out their monotonous, optimistic songs from willow trees transformed by a new-grown fuzz of lime-green catkins. Higher up the hill, there was a gate to open, and fixed to it, a sign with the startling black and yellow graphic of an adder. A ladybird, woken and warmed by the sun, meandered over the image. I walked out onto Stapeley Hill. Somewhere below, on the rough ground to the east, rising like an off-pitch piccolo above the mixed woodwind of the woodland birds, I heard a single curlew.

Stapeley is not a big hill, but it punches above its weight for views. Across the valley, over farmland and woodlands was Stiperstones Ridge, where Cranberry Rock and Manstone Rock build themselves out of the shattered crags of the summit ridge and purple heather. The smooth rounded bulk of Corndon Hill and the Iron Age hill fort on Roundton Hill, which Ben and I climbed later that afternoon, were visible. From the top, we had watched the back of a red kite circumnavigate on thermals below us, and heard, but didn't see – despite scanning with binoculars for ages – a curlew in the steep, complicated clefts of the valley below. Blackthorn bloomed in hedgerows that radiated out across that subtle landscape, across western England and eastern Wales.

Someone told me that from Stapeley Hill you can see the weather coming through the Sarn Gap, a defile in the hills some twenty or more miles away, and sure enough, showers infiltrated the border into England then faded quickly into indifference. The border is a fluid, winding thing that divides England from what was once the Welsh Marches and Montgomeryshire and is now Powys – the county that chose for its symbol the red kite back when their presence here was remarkable, but they're ten a penny now.

From a thousand feet down the escarpment towards the Welsh border came an almost continual intrusion – the burr of what sounded like helicopters, taking off and landing, though whatever it was remained unseen. Several times I heard the distant distinctive rising warble of a curlew, carried on a wind that flowed in waves, messed about with my hair and made it difficult to see the map. Above me, skylarks belted out their complicated songs and moved like cursors against fast-moving white clouds. Gorse bloomed acid yellow. In the valley, a field of rape, though the yellow of rape does not sing. Clumsy bumblebees fizzed over the hill. Ravens roller-coasted on the wind. A pair of red kites passed through. Over towards Corndon Hill, a buzzard hung out. And over the summit of the ridge, a kestrel came close, engineering the headwind, hanging immutably in air.

I trod the ground over relics of field walls that were reduced to lines of occasional stones in the sheep-cropped grass. I scrambled down rocks at the far end of the hill, and into my sight came Mitchell's Fold Stone Circle. I had walked the old way through this new landscape, but I hadn't seen a single curlew.

The first cuckoo of the year kept me company as I walked past the standing stones. Blackbirds sang me along the path to the car park, and to Ben waiting for me beside his van.

◎ ◎ ◎

I met dairy farmers Jill and Bob at their farm with fields that straddle the border. As we walked away from the redbrick farmhouse and buildings, followed for a time by a ginger-and-cream cat, Jill said, 'We really don't want to lose the curlew. We love hearing them. When they come back, it's like seeing long lost friends.'

We walked to a meadow of buttercups and stopped at the field gate. Tony and Bob had sectioned off a generous third of the seven acres with an experimental electric fence. Hidden in the middle of that swathe of bright yellow and green, a pair of curlew and a nest. We talked in whispers, but even that low level of intrusion was too much: a curlew flew up, rising into the sky and casting out a two-note alarm – *courlie! courlie!*

Tony and I began moving towards the fence and, crossing it, a second curlew popped up from the grass: the female. We saw her head moving slowly, swivelling to keep us in sight. She walked right away from the nest, underneath the fence and then rose into the air, adding her own alarm to that of her mate.

'That's the female,' Tony said. 'She has a longer bill – more curved too. She walks away from the nest so its whereabouts are kept hidden.' Then he added, 'Take long strides – we need to disturb the grass as little as possible.' And so we loped in using seven-league strides. A black camera stood guard, orientating us to the nest amidst the sward.

The curlew patrolled the field above its ash tree borders, calling and calling against our intrusion. We looked down and there, the birds had fashioned a dinner-plate sized scrape of a nest by tramping the grass into a flattened circle. Inside lay four curiously pointed eggs, camouflaged in greens and browns. 'Pyriform', the experts call them, and to me they did indeed look like pears in a dish, each pointed end orientated to the centre of the nest.

'So they're not big on architecture then?' I said.

'Not at all,' said Tony. He began to weigh and measure each egg with callipers, numbering each with a waterproof pen, and placing them just so back in the nest. He took the memory card from the camera, replaced it with another, and we left.

Over mugs of tea and biscuits in the farmhouse kitchen, Tony played the camera recordings on his laptop. So far, all was well – just eerie black-and-white images of the two adult curlew changing shifts, hidden in the grass.

To me, that concealed nest and its eggs were strangely beguiling, and deeply affecting.

◎ ◎ ◎

There was one more visit with the ornithologists to a nest, this one in a vast field under the shadow of Bromlow Callow: a distinctive circle of pine trees on the summit of a hill, visible for miles. The Callow is a way-marker, part of an ancient trackway that dates to the Stone Age, used by those navigating the land as they travelled for trade. It was a cattle-droving road too, and I wondered about the number of curlew that used to come in the spring to these blackthorn valleys and hills. What would the drovers have heard as they camped up at night, or moved the cattle onwards? That indescribable bubbling, rising, whistling, haunting call of scores of curlew would have been stitched through their soundscape, and taken for granted.

At a quiet crossroads, we got out of the car, gathered the gear and set out to walk the perimeter of a field under a blue sky cruised by billowing towers of cumulus. I knew the routine: walk in silence, intruding as little as we could. The male curlew flew up from the nest somewhere out there in the long grass and began beating the bounds of the hedges and trees around the field edge, shouting a warning to its mate: *courlie! courlie!* David and I continued walking in. The nest camera came into sight. We slowed down. Suddenly, David dropped into a half-crouch. I copied instinctively. He put out a hand towards me, indicating 'stop!' Something began to stir. Materialising out of the long grass, the female came up like a ground spirit. Here she was, so close, this ethereal creature, with that eccentrically long, elegantly curved bill, feathers dappled brown and cream, flecked with rivulets of umber, her gull-sized body pushed up on stilt-like legs. Inside the surrounding white ring, her dark eye watched us watching her. Then she unfolded her wings to reveal the pale speckled underwings, and took to the air. This proximity, this encounter – I understood why sometimes people say, after such moments, that it was like watching in slow-motion. Up she flew, across the clouds, silhouetted in smooth, determined flight, *Numenius arquata*. *Numenius* from the Latin, named for the new-moon curve of the bill; *arquata* from the Greek, for the wings curved like an archer's bow. Travelling across the clouds she cast her curlew spell, her voice a tone poem.

This was the first nest to go: raided by foxes, caught on CCTV.

◎ ◎ ◎

Four more times, I travelled to Shropshire. Word had got out, and folk travelled in from towns, villages and hamlets from miles away – an enthusiastic and melodious bunch – to sing about curlews.

We sang an Icelandic curlew song, and Mary had set a couple of my curlew poems to music. The days spent singing with the choir were completely joyful. Ben put up a hide at the edge of the field at Jill and Bob's farm for taking close-up photographs. Bill ran curlew lantern-making workshops for families and, for our final evening, had made a flight of seven curlew, uncannily like the real thing, constructed from thin willow layered with white tissue. Inside each one Bill had fastened tiny solar-powered LEDs that came alight as darkness fell. The number seven was significant because of the Shropshire folktale of the 'Seven Whistlers': when six curlews find the seventh they've been searching for, this will mark the beginning of the end. No doubt conceived at a time when curlews were plentiful and taken for granted, the tale is a folkloric attempt to reconcile death. And it is all the more prescient, given the dire situation that curlews themselves now face.

Over the weeks of the project, Amanda kept us posted with developments. This year again, twenty-one nests were being monitored. But one by one, they began to succumb to the nocturnal visits of predators, and the number of viable nests began to fall, almost it seemed, by the hour. The eggs in the nest at Jill and Bob's farm hatched, and the chicks developed into fledglings. We all felt a sense of anticipation mixed with anxiety: were they going to make it? One morning, Tony found an animal trail invading the grass, but the birds were still there. Having been there and seen the eggs for myself, I felt a strong sense of connection with that nest, and had kept the picture of it in my head over the weeks. However ineffective a method of support it was, I willed those curlew youngsters to survive.

One of the project volunteers laid on a breakfast, then a bunch of us – conservationists, ornithologists, people from the local wildlife trusts, from Natural England and the RSPB – took a walk along the Stiperstones Ridge with Mary Colwell who was passing through on her 500-mile walk from the west coast of Ireland to the east coast of England, undertaken to highlight the shocking decline in curlew numbers in both countries. In Ireland, Mary found that peat extraction as fuel for power stations has, quite literally, removed curlew nesting grounds from the map. In Sligo, at the time of writing, only one pair remains. This is local extinction, happening now. In Wales, Mary met people who had come to the realisation that they'd not heard curlews arriving inland at all this year, that whole swathes of the land we think of as true countryside – those patchworks of farms amongst hills – were now blank places where curlews no longer 'hung their harps over the valleys.'[7]

We stopped for a break at Blakemore Gate Cottages, from where the border country beguiled and faded to haze. We drank coffee from flasks in the yard while we had a mini 'curlew summit'. What, if anything, was to be done?

Here in the borderlands, the numbers of ravens, red kites and buzzards have all increased on the back of protection. But where is the protection for curlews? The Landscape Partnership offers subsidies to farmers who enlist in the curlew restoration scheme; however, no laws or requirements are laid down by DEFRA (the Department for Environment, Food and Rural Affairs) – everything happens through goodwill. But the ask is straightforward: simple commitment to not rolling or chain harrowing the fields after a certain date when incoming curlews may have laid eggs, and not cutting the grass until mid-July when any curlew young are fully fledged. (I talked later to one Cumbrian farmer who said, when I asked about the practice of rolling and chain-harrowing the ground in spring, 'We know all about that – May Murder we call it').

A few of us had been invited to lunch by a family whose farm lies under the Stiperstones, where the land falls gently down and rises again towards that other whaleback Shropshire hill, the

Long Mynd. As we walked towards the farm, a single curlew voice was caught on the breeze coming, tantalisingly, from the furze and scrub back up by the path we'd just walked down. At the Hollies, three generations farm together: father, son and the son's seventeen-year-old daughter. Their wives hold down jobs elsewhere. We ate roast lamb from Tesco and talked curlews.

'I think we hadn't realised there were fewer and fewer of them coming in,' the older farmer's wife said. 'It's happened so gradually. Years ago, we took them for granted. But I think we've only heard one this year, down in front of our bungalow.' She also told me how the ravens come for the lambs. 'I had one last week, tried to keep the poor thing alive, but it wasn't any good. I just kept it warm until it died. The ravens take their tongues, their eyes and their back end. It's a terrible thing.'

'Make it easy for us,' the son said, 'make payments for not rolling and cutting. That way you get everyone on side.'

Is that what we should do? Pay the farmers to do what's right, and have no control over those that won't? And what is the ultimate price for ever-cheaper food? Part of the answer is this: the loss of some of our most iconic bird species. We need to ask ourselves, is this a price worth paying?

Voluntary schemes such as the Shropshire's are pin-pricks of hope against a wider background of loss. Curlews have become extinct across huge swathes of the southern UK. Current agricultural practices provide little, if any, sense of connection with nature. Hedges are grubbed out, habitats destroyed, and birds like curlews and lapwings reduced largely to a northern phenomenon. This is what happened to the corncrake too – that rasping sonar reduced and reduced again to just a few fields in a few Scottish islands. Agricultural land is often, though not always, managed by contractors who come in to roll, chain harrow and cut the grass, and they, and many farmers, have no awareness of nests, or are simply not interested. Ground nesting birds become collateral. Curlew are long-lived birds, some living to thirty years, and there is a very real fear that they may be subject to sudden colony collapse after attempting and failing to breed over decades.

◎ ◎ ◎

We had our final celebration evening at the Norbury village hall. Over a hundred people came from that highly scattered and rural community. The 'curlew choir' sang their curlew songs. People read poems they'd written about the landscape and talked about what the curlew means to them. At dusk, we proceeded up the darkling lane, curlew lanterns held aloft and bats beating their aerial pathways amongst them. We walked to a field where Bill's Seven Whistlers, ghostly white, rose in a stationary line, one above the other, from a small black water lake, whilst ethereal music and curlew calls played over loudspeakers.

◎ ◎ ◎

Another of Shropshire's ornithologists told me that at least thirty-five million (some say fifty million) non-indigenous pheasants are at large at any one time in the UK, released by the shooting industry. He told me that this unnatural bounty provides everyday ready-meals for foxes, and as a result of this, in some places, fox numbers are at an all-time high. Foxes take anything that presents itself, and curlew eggs, chicks, and fledglings are typical – and easily come by. This has been eloquently evidenced by the Partnership's monitoring. However reluctantly, after spending time in the Shropshire hills, I faced the inevitable conclusion that the control of foxes is one part of the key to curlew survival.

There seems to be, though, little public appetite for the acceptance of predator control, given the ongoing debacle on badger culling. I wondered if conservation organisation membership would diminish if the imperative for control were made public in their magazines. And TV programmes, *Springwatch* and the like, don't help, as they rarely engage with the grim reality and complexity of our relationship with the land. Me, I don't need my countryside wrapped up and cosy, a place where everything is a matter for wonder and nothing is political. I've watched curlews looking for their fledglings the day after the contract mowers came.

◉ ◉ ◉

The debate on the illegal persecution of hen harriers and other raptors on grouse moors has become highly politicised and polarised – conservationists on one side, estate managers and the shooting fraternity on the other. Raptor Persecution UK, and high-profile naturalists Mark Avery, former head of the RSPB, and Chris Packham have demanded the banning of grouse-shooting, believing, apparently, that all estates carry out the persecution of raptors.

Hen harriers take grouse chicks. Ravens take lambs. Foxes, badgers and ravens take curlew eggs and chicks. Whose job is it to decide which animals are protected and which are not? Can we really sit back and allow the curlew's haunting call to only exist in recordings, as yet another potent symbol of loss, and one that snags on memory and our shame? Is a hen harrier really worth more than a curlew? Who decides? It comes back to this.

Yet there *are* moors which are well managed, where raptors appear to be tolerated, and where, crucially, birds like the curlew, golden plover and lapwing are thriving on the back of predator control. (With weasels and stoats largely absent, however, rabbit numbers have to be seen to be believed...). This though, is the trade-off in action: manage predators (excluding illegal raptor destruction), and wading birds will breed successfully. Try telling that to the hen harrier campaigners, and they don't want to know.

I am, always have been, and will always remain anti-hunting and shooting. But Mary Colwell told me about a grouse moor in Yorkshire and put me in touch with Tom Orde-Powlett who manages the shooting above Bolton Castle, and Tom invited me over.

We drove up onto the moor and into a mist that pressed near, obscuring any views. Sometimes it shifted, offering tantalising glimpses of a wider, and for me, unfamiliar landscape. Though we couldn't see far, we did see hundreds of wading birds: first one curlew, then another and another, casting their sibilant calls over the land, their strange silhouettes passing across the drear clouds. There were yet more curlews, golden plovers, lapwings, grey partridges, ring ouzels; Jane Eyre would have felt right at home. Compared to the devastated Shropshire borderlands, in terms of successful wading birds, this was Eden indeed.

Tom set up his telescope and pointed out curlews perched on fence posts, keeping their eye on youngsters exploring the ground around them, stepping in and out of view in the long grass. They were like birds designed by committee – a fluffed out puffball body from which the neck and head protruded, legs like articulating cranes. Higher up the track, we came across lapwings and their fledglings, like fluffy Christmas puddings on matchstick legs, and Tom spotted several adult curlews wearing leg rings, birds he had helped to ring last winter, working alongside the British Trust for Ornithology.

I returned to the moor many times, constantly asking myself if I was allying myself with 'the enemy.' This, it has to be said, was uncomfortable territory for me. I was only too aware of how I was caught between the two worlds of grouse management and conservation, yet it was absolutely necessary to see the debate from both sides. A grouse moor is without doubt a managed landscape – one that is problematic for some in the conservation world. But over the breeding season, there are so many curlews, their heady, ebullient calls effervescing onto the moor in every moment of every day, the warning calls marking out all those youngsters below – youngsters that are thriving – until you almost find yourself thinking, *not another damned curlew.*

So not every grouse moor in the UK is managed to the destruction of all habitats. Not every gamekeeper is involved in the business of killing raptors and destroying satellite tags – though clearly there are those who are, taking it upon themselves to capture hen harriers, golden eagles, owls and buzzards by the most vicious means and destroy them – God knows how they live with themselves.

But just suppose that grouse moors are the last habitats to sustain our final ark populations of the astonishing curlew; well, I think I can live with that.

Five

THE AIR IS
FULL OF BIRDS

April 6

The season's first swallow, seen whilst driving home from the other side of town, flitted raggedly above the traffic with that characteristic lift – one moment skimming the tarmac of the road and the next spinning through the air and over the buildings.

Two weeks ago, the first lambs arrived on the fell, lying on the ground like remnants of snow. Within a day of being born, they took off in little stuttering bursts to greet each other, and after a couple more, were running and jumping, careering about the field in short-lived bursts of energy.

April 7

In the grip of a gale coming in from the west, rooks lifted from the cliffs underneath Scout Scar. Their black forms were snatched immediately away by the updraft, and I watched them pull their wings tight to their bodies before releasing them again, travelling half a mile in mere seconds, ducking and diving through the wind's wild pockets.

◉ ◉ ◉

In the garden, greenfinches dazzled and the chattering classes of goldfinch attempted to take over the seed feeder outside my study window. I love the shenanigans of small birds and the subtleties of their articulation – the repetition of phrases delivered convivially or with an underscore of irritation, perhaps because of someone else getting to the seed before them. These avian conversations enrich my work, my home. Every now and then, there's some new song to tune in to – the sweet dunnock singing companionably, or goldfinches holding high-pitched conversations up in the silver birch. In the grander scheme of things, it might be an unremarkable event, but the birds' daily rituals nourish me, keep me connected to the world outside.

A new sound from a pair of siskins on the feeders, like new arrivals at the ball, the male all dressed up in his yellow waistcoat, the eye of the more petite female tuned to the garden. When a goldfinch approached, the female siskin leaned forwards on her tiny legs, cantilevering out over the feeder post to see off the goldfinch with her frazzling *tzeet, tzeet* call before feeding again as if there were no tomorrow. I walked slowly towards the window, stopping just half a metre away from her, only the glass between us, and absorbed each detail of her tiny body: the pale yellow glow above the wing, the anointed yellow line above the eye.

When other birds came too close, the female flitted into the air, using her body and wings as a barrier between herself and the food. The goldfinches, larger by half at least, were no match for her. They zipped away up into the birch to wait for another chance. Oh tenacious, tiny siskins.

This little finch weighs about half an ounce, no more than a small handful of peanuts, and is another relative newcomer to our garden. In the past, siskins were kept as caged birds because of the sweetness of their song. According to Francesca Greenoak,[8] the siskin has been referred to as 'aberdavine', 'blackheaded thistle-finch' and in Cheshire as the delightful 'golden wren.' Because of their high-pitched '*tsy-zi*' call, in Sussex they were known by the onomatopoeic, if mundane appellation of 'tea leaves'.

April 8

A pair of jackdaws floated above the traffic and the rooftops, travelling towards the fell. One carried a twig in its beak, held forth like a divining rod to foretell the best place to make a nest.

The jackdaws circled the pollarded sycamore at the bottom of the fell. Then, with nothing more than a few subtle flexes of their wings, they returned, landing on the chimney stack of a neighbour's house. They repeated this circuit again, but from somewhere on the roof it appeared that the second bird had acquired a new, more complex twig, complete with the tracery of finer branchlets and buds.

The pair took off and landed on a more distant chimney stack. This time, they deposited the sticks inside the red ceramic chimney pot.

No other bird has such a love affair with the humble chimney. The filthy outlets from our fires and wood burners are to them the best location to make a home. Their preference is for large Victorian chimneys, which are more spacious and have ledges inside them – perfect for nest construction. Jackdaws are particular about the kind of twigs they use, too: they must be just springy enough to give the right amount of resistance. Building stick layer upon stick layer inside their chosen sooty ledge, they form the scaffolding of a U-shaped nest. If the chimney is too modern and smooth, the sticks may fall and the nest will be abandoned in favour of something rougher, but if a Victorian chimney is unavailable, an Edwardian one might do very well – something we experienced first-hand ourselves.

We had lived in our house for a couple of years when, in the very early hours of a spring morning, I heard rustlings and faint voices coming from the wall behind my head. Each morning, as the daylight began to break, the stirrings would begin, and my sleep for the night was over. As spring drew on, the voices grew louder.

We pulled our bed away from the wall, from where a fireplace had once been, and, having removed the brass plate air vent, we began to chisel out the bricks one at a time. Eventually we'd opened the old flue up to the light in the room. The mutterings inside the chimney became unequivocally louder – and uncomfortably close. Bits of twig began to fall out from the hole. My husband Steve put his face as close as he could to peer into the void, and at that moment a juvenile jackdaw emerged like a wraith into the bedroom, shooting past the tip of Steve's nose. It landed on the foot of the bed, crapped, then flew through the open door into the smallest bedroom at the back of the house – with me in hot pursuit. Perching on the bedhead, the youngster squawked, flapped, looked daggers at me, and ruffled its black-taffeta wings in abject umbrage. Clearly lacking any sense of gratitude for its release, it crapped again before flying out the open window.

Then Steve shouted, 'Another!', and I ran back in time to see a second youngster shit on the duvet before following the escape route pioneered by its sibling. I looked out to see one of the fledglings on the roof of our garden shed, the other on a branch of the young silver birch. Their heads turned from side to side; no doubt they were reconnoitring their strange rite of passage out from the sooty blackness of the chimney into a world of light and weather, of trees and gardens, of other jackdaws and other birds, beholding for the first time their place in the colony, in the air, in the world.

Afterwards, we summoned the chimney sweep and had the redundant chimneys capped. I slept.

April 9

I was at Caerlaverock again, stopping off on a trip to visit friends who live deep in the Dumfriesshire hills. We'd journeyed north, my friend Fiona and I, following the coast road along the Solway. The incoming tide sparkled beneath a sky of pale blue that faded almost to silver in the upper atmosphere. There were few clouds. Gulls drifted on thermals along the edge of the sea.

◎ ◎ ◎

In the Peter Scott hide – the one with the huge plate-glass windows and the view out over a pool of black water – we watched last year's newborns, now juveniles. Last summer's whooper swan cygnets had almost reached adulthood, distinguished by dirty brown patches on their wings and necks, as if they had just a moment ago bathed in silty water. I thought of their journey south from Iceland, travelling as they do in family groups, sometimes accompanied by singleton juveniles from previous years, and how, any day now, they would travel again towards the north.

We left the hide to wander Caerlaverock's hawthorn avenues. The first leaves were coming in, buds tinted pink, and it was as if we were walking in step with the season. The hawthorn branches formed a tunnel at the end of which we could see snow on the Cumbrian hills beyond the tide-filled Solway.

Approaching the hide door, a small boy of about four years of age shot suddenly outside. Inside, a family group were packing up binoculars and cameras.

'I think one of yours might have escaped,' I said.

One of the men came over to us, pointed out the window.

'See on that strip of grass? A couple of deer for you.'

And there were. On a thin strip of land jutting out into the filling tide, two roe deer were cropping the grass, the sea sparkling behind their heads, their ears upright and still. Through the binoculars their tell-tale white rumps showed; they were no more than a quarter of a mile distant.

Herons stalked the shallow sea, cantilevering out over their own feet. One stabbed down into the water, caught a fish and took off to drift like a parascender, landing in a new position only metres away. A solitary lapwing dived at the heron, then again – and again. The heron bobbed its head with each pass, though assumed an indifferent air. A second heron passed through – an animated drawing by Leonardo da Vinci sprung to life. It landed on the sea margins, all yellow beak and ridiculous Meccano legs.

A singleton shelduck cruised past, gathering with a dozen or so more on the pool north of the hide. In front of the hide the saltmarsh was subsumed and became sea. Only narrow strips of grass remained, on which mallards and teals lay sleeping or preening. Then we heard the geese. Layer upon layer of barnacles passed over from west to east, moving inland and calling, calling.

In 1948, barnacle geese numbers were falling off the scale; a mere three hundred overwintered here on the Solway. But encouraged by Sir Peter Scott, the formation of the National Nature Reserve in 1971 guaranteed protection. The increase in numbers was achieved by simply allowing the geese to spend their winters here undisturbed. These days, some thirty-five thousand arrive in the autumn months.

In April, the barnacle geese begin to head north to their summer breeding grounds in Arctic and inhospitable Svalbard. By the end of the month, the fields no longer resound to that call of the far north made manifest.

Across the Solway, Skiddaw and Blancathra were at their sculptural best, as if the sky had carved the mountains out from itself early that morning. On Cumbria's coastline, buildings shimmered through a rising heat-haze. Out west towards the Irish Sea, steel-grey clouds formed along the horizon. The sea sparkled and shone.

Looking back again towards the grazing deer, it seemed that now only one remained. But looking again, I found the other, now lying down and camouflaged entirely by the sward, revealed by nothing more than a pair of occasionally twitching ears, silhouetted against the glimmering water.

We tore ourselves away from the deer, the sea and the mountains, the herons and the lapwings and walked back underneath the hawthorn arch whilst barnacle geese passed overhead almost continuously. We heard their bittersweet call as they gathered in vast flocks on the low-lying fields. I imagined the geese sensing the call of the north, waiting for the moment when the urge to migrate became imperative, no longer to be delayed. Then the skies and the fields around Caerlaverock will no longer ring with the clarion sounds of the geese until their return next autumn. I tried to imagine the silence, and found that I couldn't.

April 10

Another day of sun and blue sky. We drove the coast passing through New Abbey, and glancing over to the ruins, glimpsed the remaining tracery of a sandstone rose-window against the cerulean hue. We'd arranged a rendezvous with friends at the RSPB Mersehead nature reserve and walked with them to a hide overlooking a lagoon. In a corner of the room, a red-tailed queen bumblebee frazzled against the glass. I took out my phone, opened the case, and holding it against the window, scooped the bee up. Another second, and she was free. I sat on a wooden bench and began to tune in to the bird calls, to the enthusiastic whistle of wigeon, the softer tones of pintails and the crow-like *craa, craa* of scaup. Birds meandered, slept on islands.

An urgent whisper from the other end of the hide – Roseanne waving me over urgently. Something on the water in front of us, swimming on its back. We '*oohed*' and '*aahed*' and squealed almost silently whilst the creature turned and swam and dived and resurfaced before our eyes. It was a water acrobat swimming through blue and black and silver. It was an Archimedean screw, a sinuous machine that rolled and rolled for the sake of rolling, oblivious of everything other than itself: otter. Then that final moment – the sinuous tail suspended above the water for just a moment before it too slid beneath the shimmering surface. Yet we still saw it, the imprint playing out on our eyes.

April 11

In one week, our single pair of siskins has increased to ten or more, the seed feeders visited increasingly by these vivacious little birds.

Washing up in the evening, I looked out to a frenzy of fiery siskins on the feeder beneath the clematis. They gathered on loose stems that bounced lightly beneath the small weight of them as they waited for the opportunity to feed. I went outside, and it was like lighting a fuse – the siskins fizzed into the sky, their intense colouring and furious speed of travel turning them waspish; like fireworks.

◎ ◎ ◎

The blackbird's full seasonal song has arrived. Every evening, the male's nuanced music plays from his song-post at the top of the Scots pine. Described by Victorian poet William Earnest Henley in his poem 'The Blackbird'[9] as like the playing of a box-wood flute, this evening song is the blackbird's best, its most complex. It makes me stop and listen every time.

April 19

The first crow leaned out over the edge of the Scar like a sailor contemplating the depths from the prow of a sailing ship. The second crow, just feet away, strutted to the edge and leaned out-wards from the rocks in imitation. The first began to ruffle its wings in anticipation of flight, and as if on some hidden sig-nal, the pair launched themselves almost simultaneously into the shadows towards the trees and the rocky screes below, dropping away from sight. I walked to the place on the edge from where they had scrutinised the valley, but they had been spirited away.

Earlier, as I'd walked up through the woodland, two blackbirds welcomed the morning with lyrical chatter and song, the first high in the tips of an ash tree and the second somewhere unseen on the far side of the narrow, wooded valley.

The leaves were yet to come in.

Rounding the path onto the Scar itself, the view opened out over the rolling hills rising from the long plain of the Lyth Valley. The land then gains height, growing in bulk towards the mountains.

Down in Brigsteer Woods the voices of birds lifted into the clear air. The loudest of all: the blackbirds and thrushes.

◉ ◉ ◉

At Oxenholme Station, waiting to wave our eldest off on his first big trip abroad; later that day he was flying to Japan. We made small talk, as you do when waiting for a train. On the platform, not three metres away, was a flotsam and jetsam of hefty twigs, sheep's wool, grubby paper and old string.

The station was under siege; jackdaws peered down from the wrought-iron structure of the canopy. They pulled at what looked like clematis stems but we soon realised was redundant electrical wiring. In their hapless nest-building ventures, twigs rained down from above. A jackdaw flew up and disappeared into an iron column, dragging a twig inside after him, though one end remained jutting out from the hole at a jaunty angle. Another gang of them were busy pulling at something down on the middle of the track – the remains of a kestrel, though how it had ended up there, God only knew.

At 10:12am the train pulled in. We hugged and laughed and wished Cal a fabulous trip. We waved goodbye, and as the train pulled out on its journey south, I noticed something protruding from a hole above the station guttering – the wiry black end of a toilet brush. Those poor jackdaw babies – born into such a world.

◉ ◉ ◉

The clematis had begun its great push forward into spring. It was greening up, the leaves and growth dense, compact, and beginning to suppress the view through its twiggy winter structure into the bottom garden. At that stage in the year it was almost possible to feel the sap rising, the life-force insistent and moving.

It was shirt-sleeves weather. I sat in the garden eating lunch, lulled somnambulistic by the heat of the sun on my head. I could hear the small pine cones of the Scots pine expanding in the heat, popping and crackling under the sun.

After lunch, I walked the dog through the meadows along the River Kent where small, wild daffodils were fully open, drinking up the sun and showing off their Lent lily faces. On the opposite bank, inside Beckmickle Ing woods, a faint, pale yellow radiance of daffodils.

It was here that we made one of our first explorations, with friends, one hot July afternoon in 1995, shortly after we moved back to the west – a picnic on blankets under the shade of old ash trees. Our friend Brian waded straight in, paddling, stumbling and grabbing boulders for support until he arrived mid-river and sat in the flow of a small waterfall, from where he began to sing at the top of his voice. That's the negative ion effect for you.

Later, we explored the river's edges, Brian turning over flat rocks and sometimes, quick as a whip, catching something in his hand: our indigenous white-clawed crayfish. Slowly uncurling his fingers beneath the water, we watched, along with wide-eyed two-year-old Callum, as the crayfish kicked its antediluvian armoured tail and was gone, obscured by small clouds of sediment as it buried itself beneath another stone.

April 20

My study is a small building at the bottom of the garden with two windows looking out onto the lawn and the back of the house. In the adjacent north-facing wall, a third window offers a prospect over the four neighbouring gardens and toward the top of Kendal Fell. The fourth window, immediately in front of my desk, affords views of the Kentmere hills rising above the top of next door's garage. Keeping an eye and an ear on the business of the garden birds is easy from here – and a common distraction. The cock blackbird comes frequently to land on the garage roof a few feet away from my computer, always with that elegant tip forward and immediately applying the brake of his flicked upright tail feathers.

Over the top of my computer screen I see him in profile, his head inclined towards me, hardly any distance between us. I stop work, look at him, and he in turn looks at me. What is it, I wonder, that is understood in these moments of connection? Do the blackbirds recognise me as I do them? Do they know that I am the one who clucks softly at them whilst gently throwing raisins or cranberries towards them as they forage outside the kitchen door? Do they have any concept that my weak attempts to replicate their voice are a form of communication? And do they comprehend that this territory is shared, belonging equally to us both? I would love the insights of this knowledge, even for the briefest of moments.

April 22

At Oxenholme station, waiting for a train to the south. I bought coffee from the coffee van on the platform. The jackdaws were not in sight, though I heard them *chack-chacking* up above in and on the roof.

'They're a flipping nuisance,' the coffee man said, adding, 'He's just swept all the mess up again,' nodding towards the agent in the ticket office.

I remembered all that fallen nest material amongst the pink suitcases, leopard print clothes and peroxide blonde hair of the women waiting for the train the last time I was here.

'They bring someone in with a rifle – very early on a Sunday morning – keep the numbers down.'

'Ouch,' I say, and not because of the coffee steaming in my hand.

April 26

Planted out as a youngster once it had grown too large for its ceramic pot, our deep-red Japanese maple was bursting with pendulant leaves resembling bat wings. Over years, it has matured into a small tree with an open structure and branches that offer a bird room to move about and shelter in whilst keeping an eye on the garden.

So much for spring. A slew of snow showers fell from raggedy clouds. They formed and dissolved, leaving the hills dirty-white after they had passed through. Four seasons in one afternoon – rain, sudden cold winds, sleety snow, then stillness and warmth. April: doing its thing.

April 27

Walking home along the River Kent after a visit to town, swallows and martins clicked and twittered and water-skimmed above the river. I watched the dance of them, trying to follow just one individual bird, seeing it touch down on the water surface for a split second, taking some invisible insect or drinking on the wing and flitting upriver amongst dozens more of its kind. An animated flutter on the opposite bank caught the corner of my eye: three blackbirds – two males and a female, the female pursued by both males who beat at each other face to face, wing to wing. In the midst of the fracas, the female slipped quietly away.

April 28

By mid-morning I was back in bed: migraine. I slept fitfully until late afternoon, waiting for the wonder drug to kick in, occasionally aware of birdsong drifting inside. At some point, a blackbird took centre stage, his aria accompanying me back to sleep.

I dreamed a vivid and memorable dream – a rarity for me:

I am at Loch Don on the Isle of Mull, standing amongst giant red sandstone boulders and surrounded by the rounded red cliffs of a gorge where a river falls down and pours itself into the sea loch. There are voices close to me, though I can't see anyone else. Then, silently, I begin to move upwards. My invisible companions and I rise into the air and I look down at the red rocks moving further and further away. The other two voices squeal with delight. One – an American – shouts, 'Oh man!'

We soar over the sea. The air is full of birds – guillemots and razorbills and something else that flies so fast it is difficult to identify. We move low over the water, skimming the surface and then up again, and I realise that this is a swallow's view of the world.

A puffin, resting on the milky blue surface of the water, comes into focus, followed by another, and another. 'Puffins!' I shout. We rise into the air again then a voice calls, 'Look – look!', and a black shape below us surfaces and rolls away again into the opaque water – a humpback whale.

We return to the red sandy rocks where I discover that my companions are presenters from an American YouTube Channel. One is Chinese-American and wears glasses. The other says, 'Let's do it again', and as we begin to rise up, the half-Chinese guy says, 'I hope we have enough fuel…'

At 4:30pm, Fergus arrived home from school, came upstairs to see me, kissed me and, having offered to make me a mug of tea, went downstairs where I heard him tell his father to make one for me. Revived by tea and biscuits, I looked out of the window at a world transformed by snow.

On the roof of the house beyond the end of the garden are six chimney pots arranged in two rows of three. Surrounding each pot is anti-jackdaw wire, and on the top of one of the pots, a pair of jackdaws, inspecting its interior. I fetched the binoculars. One jackdaw perched on an upright TV aerial, the other on a horizontal. A third jackdaw emerged from the black pot, exiting through gaps in the wire basket. Perhaps an early juvenile, this bird was all fluffed-out feathers and had a shorter bill. On an unseen signal, the two adult birds dived into the air, and a few moments later, the juvenile followed: the Addams family, with wings.

Beyond the rooftops, the small wood on Kendal Green was coming to life. Two cherry trees glowed pale pink, fringed with blossom, their slender trunks angled slightly away from each other. The westering afternoon sun found a holly and gifted it shadows and light. A larch tree, cones adorning the upper branches. A birch, with a purply-green mist of new leaves coming in. Ash trees too, and something smaller, lime green. Someone had lit a bonfire. Smoke wreathed and billowed, passing in front of the wood, bringing it into and out of focus. The uniform clouds began to break open. Above them, patches of cerulean blue.

The view from this room is always my consolation after the damned wreck of a migraine. I survey the fells through the binoculars, noting the washed-out line below which only rain has fallen. Above it, there's snow on the roofs of the houses at Garnett Bridge. A pair of parallel dry stone walls border the narrow lane over to Bannisdale and in between them, the faint markings of tyre tracks. The Whinfell Ridge glowered underneath thick cloud. On its flanks, the frosted forestry plantation was like the dense, dark pelt of an animal in snowfall. Three gulls worked the air. Beyond, a pair of buzzards soared over the fields.

Six

UNSTOPPABLE, BRILLIANT SPRING

May 1

Rain all day; typical Cumbrian bank holiday.

May 2

A wet morning gave way to sun and scudding clouds. I drove the back road to Staveley and walked through Beckmickle Ing woods where the River Kent poured on towards the fields of Burneside. The river was peaty and snowmelt-heavy. It ran over boulders and dropped from rocky ledges, sunlight turning the thickened cascades the churned pale-yellow of clotted cream.

Bluebells. I love the way things come in and, even though you know they're on the way, they still take you by surprise, like meeting an old friend after months apart. The flowers were not yet fully developed, but amongst patches of sunlight on the floor of the woods, that resonatory blue was beginning to send its unparalleled beauty into the world. Wild garlic was beginning to emerge too, and the white stars of wood anemones. Up in the tree canopy, new leaves were forming, bringing the magic of new green, the hawthorns the limiest, brightest green of all. Wild honeysuckle twisted around the stems of young beech trees, trailing down from branches over the path, as if asking to be gently brushed aside.

The remains of ancient coppiced hazel trees create an intermittent border at the edge of the riverbank. From one original tree, broad beams of immense girth can form, growing horizontally, and springing up from this bulky base grow the trunks of many more hazel trees of varying ages and thicknesses – trees sprung from trees. Some are full-grown almost to maturity, and each time I see them, the image of a many-masted galleon comes to mind.

Eventually, the footpath swings away to climb uphill and re-joins the narrow road. At the turn in the path, someone has made a half-hearted attempt to close off the way into the far corner of the wood with a low stack of timber and the thinnings of trees. I clambered over, the dog running on in anticipation of the opportunity to paddle. Here, the wood assumes the atmosphere of a lesser-known place. A dry stone wall comes to a tumbled end, and a barbed wire fence plunges deep into the river, to keep cattle from the fields beyond the wall out of the wood – and perhaps also people like me, out of the field. In a dry spell and with the river low, there's a small pebble beach. Here, I'll sit and idly chuck pebble after pebble up or downstream, the dog charging about enthusiastically in the shallows, chasing, though not very often finding them.

The undergrowth of the riverbank was spangled with the stars of wood anemones and here is the greatest tree-galleon of them all, its great keel masted with thirty-three trunks that surge upwards towards the light, and more gaps and crevices where others have rotted away. This is no mere tree, but a leviathan of the woods; what river-songs and tales it could tell. I think of it as anchored, waiting for the tide to fill, to launch itself into the current and sail downstream towards the sea.

❂ ❂ ❂

Snow showers brushed the hills, spinning down the valley of the Kent from the north, blown along by rapidly shifting weather.

May 3

How to see swifts arriving back from Africa: sit on the sofa with a morning mug of tea, day-dreaming; look up through the window, and think, 'They should be here by now...' At which point, a single swift wrote its brief arc of wonder across the sky.

Later, walking the dog up the field onto the fell, the ground was dotted with black and splashed with yellow – jackdaws hunting for worms and buttercups with their full faces open to the sun. Yet more snow on the mountains, blown in from the north in chaotic, fast-moving clouds. Icing sugar dustings on the lower fells.

May 4

Drinking coffee on the terrace overlooking the River Kent at the back of Wilf's Café. For the uninitiated, Wilf's is legendary. Cyclists, walkers, kids, dogs, babies, and grandparents are all here, rain or shine – and a new kind of family had discovered the delights of this riverside setting, too. A friend had let me know of their arrival.

So we met, and sat and talked, indulging in tea and scones with jam and clotted cream on the terrace whilst watching the new-comers – a pair of adult dippers that zinged upriver like small, pied missiles. Turn by turn they raced upstream, diving into the shallows beside a reef of shingle, emerging naiad-like from beneath the water, and spiriting themselves once more downstream. After the brief respite on the upper wall of the fish pass, they zipped up to a cavity in the stonework where a pair of youngsters popped out from the darkness, like figures in a cuckoo-clock, and visible for only the three or four seconds it took for the adult to pop the caddisfly larvae expertly inside their apparently insatiable gapes.

Dippers are one of the star performers of the bird world. Frequently noticed as a flash of movement from the corner of an eye, they're propelled on a blur of quick wings as they zoom up or downstream, banking at river bends like low-flying daredevil pilots, all goggles and white scarves trailing. Resembling a chunky, over-sized wren, their livery is smart: a dapper bib of white, the head and lower chest the richest chocolate brown, smudged to an inkier palette over the wings and tail feathers. I have heard a male dipper's song in the early spring, the melodious sonata underscored by, but overriding, the river's plunge over the weir beside the incongruous modernist flats at Cowan Head. Roused from some train of thought, I heard that sweet combination of wren, blackbird, young blackbird and robin.

Unsurprisingly perhaps, the dipper's name derives from the species' characteristic habit of bobbing up and down mid-river, their favoured rocks splashed with tell-tale signs of white. Curtseying on and on, like a Japanese greeting, they survey the river margins before taking off with that characteristic whirr of wings. Both the tail feathers and wings are short, and are used almost as paddles, helping them to propel themselves forward along the riverbed. Their eyes possess the peculiar and extraordinary ability to alter their lens curvature, giving them exceptional clarity of vision underwater and enabling them to hunt out their favoured caddisfly larvae, mayfly nymphs and minnows.

Tucking into our much more easily-come-by scones and cups of tea, we watched the dippers catching a seemingly endless supply of food on a stream of continuous journeys between the nest above the fish-pass and the upstream riverine supermarket.

◎ ◎ ◎

A week later, returning to the café, the nest above the weir was empty, with just tell-tale traces of dry grass protruding from the small dark hole in the wall. But then, just upstream, three dandelions along from the top of the fish pass on a rock protruding from the water: a juvenile, now established out in the big world of the river, assuming the habit from which the species came by its common name. There it was, dipping. It had not yet acquired the full, smart uniform of adult plumage, its bib being dowdier than the adult's dinner jacket evening attire. I scanned the river for an adult; nothing. The youngster, though, was well masked by the grey Cumbrian river rocks.

Then off it went, whirring upriver to the island of shingle where we'd seen the parent birds hunting for food. And this young dipper dipped, half underwater and half out, its back visible above the current as it walked, its bright eye surveying the dark gaps between the stones while the river ran on and on, singing its watery song. Seconds later, the juvenile whirred back to the stone below the dandelions and at the same time, an adult dipper flew in from the far bank, where, no doubt, it had been observing developments: *Kid – you done good.*

It seemed that of the pair of young dippers in the nest, only one had survived. But I wondered if perhaps the other was out there somewhere, dipping up and down on a rock in the middle of the river, catching the corner of someone's eye as they walked along on a path between the trees.

◎ ◎ ◎

Afternoon: my study door open, sunlight pouring inside. The dog lay across the doormat, feet twitching in dream-memories. Swallows chirred and gossiped as they sketched abstract patterns above the gardens, and goldfinches engaged in animated conversations. The mountains were printed clear on sky. White cumulus clouds sailed towards the east.

◎ ◎ ◎

Evening: washing the dishes, the back door open for the first time that year, there came the sound of swifts reeling over the houses. The dishes would have to wait. Scanning the sky, it wasn't long before they passed again, eight of them hunting over the rooftops. That high-pitched, joyous whistling screech is, for me, the quintessential sound of summer.

May 5

In the early morning, the hills, houses and gardens were bathed in an ethereal yellow glow. By 7am, bands of cloud had filled the sky, that lucid-weather moment passed.

Walking into the garden, it was as if overnight, the place had sprung to life – as if one moment it was still winter, and the next, everything was pushing headlong towards summer. Every year, the pulse of the season's growth takes me by surprise. Clusters of herbaceous border plants had gained bulk and height; foliage aplenty for the dunnock and her fledglings to hide inside. The high-pitched demands of the youngsters emanated from underneath the crowding spears of *Rudbeckia,* the parent bird keeping close by. I planted out the sweet peas and, digging, began to cull strands of the damned ground elder. Inherited years ago with a new batch of topsoil, it is the bane of my summer.

Talking with our neighbour Laura over the garden wall, I became aware of an oscillating beat, like a current of electricity, sounding in the air above the gardens. Two goldfinches, tawny chest to tawny chest, wings thrashing at each other, rising and falling and locked in frantic fluttering. Then suddenly it was over, and they disappeared over the gardens. Springtime testosterone is clearly on the rise.

After a strangely mild winter, our garden pots and planters were unusually late to flower. But now at last the moody, deep purple-black tulips, Queen of the Night, were at their opulent best. The creamy double narcissus too, and, at the end of the garden, the *Magnolia stellata* in full flower, starry-white, pale flushed pink.

May 8

A blackthorn spring, temperatures fluctuating wildly. Snow a week ago and now shirt-sleeves weather. I took the strimmer to the allotment grass, and then, as a reward for my labours, cycled out to Staveley in unexpected heat, the temperature gauge registering 26°C by lunchtime. I stopped to take photographs of bluebells and the white stars of stitchwort in the hedgerows. Over the mossy, shaded walls, deep in Beckmickle Ing Woods, the long-awaited blue was diffracted between the trees. Sunlight pooled, turning the ground lapis. The full blue hum of spring had arrived.

May 9

The male blackbird rocketed out of the clematis as I walked down the steps, almost touching my ear with the tip of his wing. I recognised this behaviour: he wanted to let me know that something was at stake. Up there, in amongst all the new green serrated leaves, was the narrowest opening, just space enough for a bird to pass through into the darkened interior.

Since first light the blackbirds had been building a nest. I felt blessed that they had once again chosen our garden as their place to raise a family. Last year, the chicks fledged from somewhere else in the green tangle of gardens during a heavy downpour. For two whole days of monsoon, the adult blackbirds whistled that high-pitched, unsettling, descending contact note. Of the chicks, there had not been any sign.

◉ ◉ ◉

An evening walk in Dorothy Farrer's Wood, one of the ancient woodlands of the River Kent's borderlands. Here, three distinct areas of woodland merge: Dorothy Farrer's Spring Wood, Spring Hag, and Mike's Wood, each bordered by dry stone walls reinforced with deer-proof fences. A series of gates gives access from one area to another, creating the impression of walking through a series of woodland rooms.

I parked the car and walked the path across the field under a high bank of cadmium-yellow gorse. In the top corner stands a centuries-old oak. In recent winters, two of its far-reaching boughs had fallen and now lay crumbling amongst accumulated leaf litter. Just beyond the oak is a tall, narrow wooden gate set into the wall. I pushed it open and stepped inside. Close the gate quietly, and you become part of the wood's world; let it bang shut, and everything knows you are here.

A small stream runs across the path immediately inside. In wet weather, it runs wide and there's little choice but to wade through. That day though, the stream was a lilting beck immersed in woodland shadows and seams of rippling light. I crossed over, stepping from stone to stone. These woods are beautiful at any time of year, but in spring, they come into their own; hence the inclusion of 'spring' within their names. Rounding the next bend in the path, the rising wooded slope ahead was luminous with the intense, unparalleled cobalt of bluebells. A slight path had been forged through the flowers, and as I walked, the scent rose from the ground, drifting on the evening air like a woodland spell. Evening sunlight streamed onto the trunks of trees. Where the light pooled or fell slantwise across the bluebells, the woodland floor was transformed into pink or silver, striped slantwise with tree shadows. Slopes and slews of blue – the blue of memory, of distance. Throughout the wood, woven everywhere, the almost phosphorescent green of new leaves. Oh, unstoppable, brilliant spring.

◉ ◉ ◉

Another tall, narrow gate, and beyond that, Spring Hag Wood, its lower slopes swathed in the white of wild garlic. The wall between Spring Hag and Dorothy Farrer's is the demarcation line – bluebells to one side and garlic on the other. The pungent scent of the garlic lifted, saturating the air as I climbed the winding path. At the junction of this path and the next were two vast stacks of timber, the sorted lengths cut from winter's fallen trees. Ahead, the rising ground was awash with yet more blue. The sun lowered, and before it fell behind the western fells, I stayed awhile, watching the very last of the brilliance lighting the bluebell floor of the wood.

I turned left, following a little-used path between the trees to a black metal gate. I pushed it open and passed through into Mike's Wood. This path is less distinct – far fewer people walk this way. The woodland here is open, newer, with young coppices of hazel protected by rough fencing of hazel hurdles. Here were sweet cherry, or gean, in faded inflorescence, and elder coming into flower. The grass had already grown high, unimpeded by human track-making. It was woven with nettles and thistles; another few weeks and the path would become subsumed, impassable. As I walked, pale, tiny moths emerged from the long grass in little swithering journeys. A blackbird surfed swiftly through the undergrowth, *chack-chacking* its alarm call, landing somewhere deep in a hawthorn. Overhead, clouds began to gather.

Another dry stone wall rides up the crest of a large, craggy outcrop of rock. The crag has sheer faces of stone and greasy, moss-clad shelfs and slopes. Built in such an awkward, gravity-defying place, it's as if the people who constructed it were showing off. How many times, I wonder, had the structure fallen before the right angles were found and the layers of stone could grow?

The outcrop itself, even without the wall, makes a natural barrier to the next woodland room. The wall was moss-covered. It descended the crag, dipping down before it rose up again like a green roller-coaster. In the wall's midst was another black gate. I went through into a small, steep, bluebell and bramble-filled enclosure, and as I entered, a buzzard crashed out of its perch close by, close enough for me to see its marled wings skim through the canopy and disappear. There were young oak saplings, and two ash trees growing out of the craggy outcrop itself. Somewhere nearby a robin sang songs of winter. The place had the feel of both ancient purpose and no purpose. Why close off this small area within the wood, especially given the cost of building such a wall?

The black gates, though, are one of Lakeland's best kept secrets. They follow the route of the Thirlmere to Manchester Aqueduct, put in place to allow maintenance staff access along the length of the structure so it can be inspected, to hunt down leaks or make sure that no-one is attempting to build on top of it. I have inside information: a friend's husband is not only involved in maintaining the aqueduct, he is also a self-confessed aqueduct nerd. I wrote to him for information and received the following explanation:

> *The black gates mark the centre line of the aqueduct which lies directly beneath them. They're installed at every boundary crossing between Thirlmere and Manchester. If there are different land owners on either side of the gate then they are locked, if it is the same landowner they are without a padlock.*

He also sent me a picture showing the line of the aqueduct as it tunnels beneath Craggy Woods – just half a mile further up the road.

> *The picture shows the gate adjacent to the River Kent in Staveley looking up towards Craggy Plantation. The tunnel, which is 375 yards long, starts from where the gap in the trees stops. When the aqueduct was drained for maintenance a few years back, we measured the tunnel – it is 7'6" in diameter. The aqueduct was completed in 1894 and is still in use today – largely unaltered. There's even a Thirlmere gate-spotting society – if you're interested.*

Well, who'd have thought…? At home later, I'll admit it, I checked out the black gate-spotters' website and found an in-depth survey of this land-locked, watery phenomenon: that the gates pop up in unexpected places or can be missed entirely, hidden amidst overgrown hedgerows or in difficult-to-access locations. 'Hence a passing surveillance unit may be pardoned for overlooking the odd one. There are other reasons not so excusable like loss of concentration, seeing a pub, seeing a female cyclist, or simply forgetting why you had set out in the first place.'

They also note worrying anomalies, such as certain gates not appearing in their mapped locations, and express concern about why this should be, speculating that the gates may have been hijacked for some other purpose: 'Not until these anomalies are investigated will there be any hope of a rational explanation. This matter is the subject of future research.'

◎　◎　◎

Set in the opposite wall of the enclosure: the next black gate. I walked through. From there, the path became indistinct and seemed to disappear altogether. I studied the ground. It seemed as if the path through the woods led only to the walled enclosure and no further – though I knew there was a way through. The trees crowded close, the ground dropped precipitously away, and the light was fading. I brushed past holly leaves as I pushed on. A long, sloping slab of dry rock. I stepped onto it, but my feet shot out from under me; I fell, and carried on falling, slithering down the greasy surface until coming to an abrupt halt on a ledge of earth. My backside hurt, but it was more my pride that suffered. Several things happened at the same time. A late blackbird piloted itself away, alarm calling through the wood. Then a movement in the undergrowth: a rough, snuffling, shuffling presence pushing away through the low-growing branches and new bracken. And at my side, like *Alice*, a cavernous hole in the earth, dug from underneath a moss-covered boulder. I stood up, and dusted myself off. There was another tunnel, and another, then more between the gnarled and spreading roots of a beech tree. My closest encounter with a badger, and I'd wrecked it, frightened the creature half to death, no doubt. I continued, picking my way through the trees and down the steep slope with more concentration through the now tenebrous woods.

May 11

The male blackbird was constantly at work in the garden. He foraged, then slipped back into the nest in the clematis and out again, flitting across the grass. There was a quiet intensity about him.

Later, washing up the dishes, I watched him hunting for snails in the other clematis that winds and spills over the dividing wall between our garden and next door. He'd found a treasure trove of tiny yellow snails, a true blackbird delicacy. Our eyes met. I opened the kitchen window and pinged raisins and cranberries towards him, which he took, one at a time. Silently, we acknowledged each other's presence.

May 17

Spring segued riotously towards summer. The shift of the season was in every new leaf, every tall spire of blue in the garden. The corn cockles had begun to fall over themselves, spilling onto the lawn. In the big planters, the Queen of the Night tulips had opened themselves flagrantly, extending back upon themselves in the final throes of shameless decadence before they began to fade. The last of the narcissi, the pheasant's eye, were open and simply beautiful. In the corner where one day I plan to make a small pond, the golden-leaved Japanese maple pushed its serrated leaves out into the world. In the border, the purple allium burst in time lapse, out from their green-striped paper cases.

May 18

A mid-afternoon walk on the fell. Inside the mazy leaves and branches of the mixed hedgerow, in the rowan and oak, cherry and lime and hawthorn, birds were at work. A tree sparrow dangled an insect morsel from its beak. Great tits sang 'teacher, teacher' and a male blackbird stood proud on the extending branch of a young oak, uttering that soft, contented cuck-cuck call quietly, and to himself.

As ever, the dog reached the stile over the wall and moved off into the dense tangle beneath the Scots pines. There had been more, but the tallest had succumbed to a storm some years ago. I remember lying awake that night, unable to sleep for the sound of the wind slamming into the end of the house. The gale had come, unusually, from due south, and every gust racketed against the exposed gable wall. I remember, too, that I'd thought about chimney stacks, and how strong they were – or weren't. With the storm at its height, a sound like a gunshot ricocheted into the early hours, and I knew instantly that one of the big trees on the fell had given in to the pressure. But which one?

In the calm of the morning after the storm, I had gone up to the fell to investigate, finding one of the Scots pines lying broken-backed over the wall, and all sizes and shapes of wall-stones tumbled around and underneath, spilling away down the slope of the field. The newly exposed and splintered wood of the tree was healthy; there was no sign of disease, but nevertheless, the wind had been powerful enough to split it apart. Imagine the pressure needed to snap a mature tree in two. It took days for the tree to be cut away from the path, and it will take years for it to rot away in the field. As for the wall, it has since been rebuilt.

◉ ◉ ◉

Above the Scots pines, there's a meadow, a meeting place of the many pathways that wind up onto the fell from the town below and from Serpentine Woods. Wooden seats are set at intervals, offering a grandstand view over the allotments, over the rooftops and chimneys to the Whinfell Ridge and the valley of the Kent, and on up to the mountains. In mid-May the meadow is awash with pale yellow cowslips and low-growing spikes of early purple orchids, yellow-rattle, buttercups and the little blue pagodas of bugle. Come in the early morning or evening, with the sun low in the sky, and the grasses and wildflowers glow, as if the earth itself emitted light.

I walked the disused tramway towards the old quarry, the place from where limestone was hewn for the building of much of the local housing stock. It's likely that our own house was constructed from it. I like this, the sense that we live in a house that has a direct connection back to the fell. The small amphitheatre of the quarry has returned to nature – orchids brighten its edges, and on the rocky ledges grasses and celandines grow. Ash and hawthorn line the path, and from up in the foliage came the small conversations of whitethroats, calling and responding. I listened in. One of the birds broke cover, its white throat defined against the fresh green leaves, pale underbelly pulsing as it pushed out its song – fresh and optimistic as the spring itself.

My reverie of small birds was broken suddenly by the raucous *craa* of a crow. Over the higher ground, a single corvid was mercilessly mobbing a buzzard, and as it did so, uttered a continual rolling, guttural call with the timbre of a worked-up football fan. *Raaraaraaraaraa* – on and on. The buzzard ducked, resembling someone diving away from of a bothersome wasp. Finally, the buzzard was clear of what the crow clearly saw as its own territory, and soared away over the edgelands of the fell.

Down below, in the fields, the ewes were at their bedraggled worst, fleeces hanging in filthy dreadlocks. After one of the wettest winters on record, they were grubbier than ever. One of them trailed a length of briar garlanded by snatches of wool. She'd be glad, I thought, to be rid of it all, to be reborn through shearing. It was only a matter of weeks to go.

The lambs could only be described as fat, their coats all dense and springy. Walking ahead of me, their rear ends bumbling along, they resembled a small country bus navigating an uneven lane.

Tramping past the hedge again, a juvenile blackbird lit onto the wall by the allotments, its breast that subtle melding of browns and reds and golds. Crossing the road back to the house, a squadron of goldfinches fizzed overhead.

May 19

The distinctive, tiny, discordant chirring of new voices from the nest in the clematis. The cock hunted from the early morning, continuing all day and into the evening, working the earth of the border underneath the escalating plants.

May 20

After a brief shower of rain, I watched the cock, head to one side, as if he were listening for the minute tunnellings of worms. More than once I've seen him pulling small rubbery bodies from the earth before zipping up to the nest – and out again.

May 23

On days of fewer clouds and high, celestial blue, the piercing voice of the swift travels faster, reaching the ground with greater eloquence than on a day hemmed in by cloud. After a morning dominated by shopping and chores that never seemed to end, I sat in the garden with a mug of tea, the dog lying flat out in the full sun, occasionally retreating into the shadow of the clematis archway.

It was just a few days post-hatch, and the chicks were keeping up an almost constant chirring, demanding food. I'd taken to standing beneath the clematis to listen in, hearing three different voices. The blackbirds worked in shifts; from the windows of the house I kept an eye on their constant foraging. As one bird swooped up into the nest, beak garlanded with insects, the other dropped out and flew low over the lawn, leaving the garden with a final banking turn past the black, metal sweet pea frame and between my study and the neighbour's garage.

Beginning on the top branch of next-door-but-one's weeping birch, the blackbird's new habit was a short flit to the viburnum, its white, pom-pom flower heads about to burst, then a short drop over the fence and into the garden before rising up to the nest, disappearing with a brief flurry of wings. Each time food was brought to the nest, the chicks' voices rose, becoming the small, whirring crescendo that only ceased with the delivery of more. Seconds after the food-bringer departs the nest, silence.

◉ ◉ ◉

Over the mountains, a mackerel-back sky. Above the town, clouds like rovings of cleaned sheep's wool, slowly drifting apart. The upper cloud layers were super-lit by the lowering sun, soft grey underneath.

An evening saunter with the dog to the Green. At the bottom of the lane, the songs of two birds filled the air. Having taken up residence on chimney pots on opposite houses, a song thrush and a blackbird were taking it in turns. As each song was delivered, the other bird appeared to listen, head to one side, each apparently captivated, entirely, by the other's psalm. The thrush's music was all invention and repetition, the composer seemingly delivering a series of lyrical thoughts as they materialised. Here was optimism, exuberance, short bursts of song that sparkled, or that insisted, the slowing beat of rallentando, ambivalence and insecurity.

The song of the blackbird, meanwhile, was more lilting and interspersed with lyrical exaltations. As the naturalist and ornithologist William Henry Hudson had it, writing in 1913:[10]

It is this delicious song of the blackbird – a voice of the loveliest quality, with an expression derived from its resemblance to a melodious, brightened human voice, uttered in a leisurely and careless manner, as of a person talking sweetly and mingling talk with snatches of song – it is all this combined which has served to make the blackbird a favourite and more to most of us as a songster than any other, not excepting the nightingale.

Listen: now the brio of a high-pitched, ascending xylophone scale – all delivered in less than a second, and I am unable to keep up, or to distinguish or record to memory each single note. Now the briefest tone of impatience – *come on, come on!* And now, perhaps, the loss of someone close. Here, a fractious child. Now the diminutive zing of something almost inaudible. In a male blackbird's full seasonal song, what I hear over and over again is the asking of questions – an uncertainty of song, if you like, as if the bird is questioning its own mortality. And simultaneously, with the artifice of a minor key, arrive the deepest, most affecting qualities of melancholia. How could we not connect – to this?

I am in no doubt that it is the presence and the song of our ubiquitous blackbirds that offers us a sense of hope, and of rebirth. The notion of being able to pull ourselves back from the brink of irredeemable change, and the ability to accept, if only for a few moments, that we are all in this together: that we are in our very essence, connected, and part of the whole.

On some hidden signal or interference, the blackbird jibbed away over the gardens; the performances at an end. The dog, bored with waiting, had disappeared into the wood. I turned to follow. The sun was setting in the gap where the lower fells meet the rising ground of the Kentmere mountains. Before sinking away below the rim of hills, the last minutes of sunlight flared gold on the white-painted houses.

Later that night, reading in bed with the curtains and the window open, by the quiet glow of the lamp, the song of a late blackbird drifted inside from a rooftop somewhere close to; a private oratorio – of faith, of joy and of hope, of all the losses of all the world, melting away with the last of the light.

May 25

The chicks were silent, and there'd been no sign of either adult bird for some time. I listened from below the clematis arch: nothing. My reaction, I recognised, was almost one of panic.

Later, pegging out the washing, a sudden swish of wings. The cock swooped into the garden and rose up into the nest, the female dropping out immediately and winging her way over the gardens. The chicks' small voices rose again into the morning.

I went down to stand with my back against the shed's blue-painted wood. I wanted to watch the action. The hen was on the top of the neighbour's weeping birch. I knew she had seen me; she missed nothing with that keen eye. I squeezed myself further into the corner between the shed and the wall.

Cal walked down the garden.

'What are you doing?' he asked, with just the slightest suggestion in his voice that I might have lost the plot.

'I'm watching the blackbirds. Come and join me?'

He squashed in beside me and after a minute of stillness, the female swooped back into the garden and up into the nest, the cock instantly dropping away, banking and swivelling out of the garden and down the lane.

'Cool,' Cal said, and went on his way.

◉ ◉ ◉

The door to my study was open and the afternoon's warmth poured inside. Mrs Blackbird was outside – I knew this from the signature *tap-tapping* as she cracked open a yellow snail on the paving stones. My work was punctuated by the intermittent contact of shell on stone. Occasionally, I caught her eye – or she caught mine.

May 26

The female blackbird was in the top of the weeping birch, softly calling '*cuck cuck...cuck.*' She uttered it softly, persistently, contact calling the fledglings. It was, I supposed, her way of telling the chicks about the world outside the nest. 'I'm here, out here,' she might have been saying, letting them know there was more to the world than their soft cup of twigs and grasses and the tangle of deeply filtered sunlight – that soon they would be out here, with her.

◎ ◎ ◎

The chicks' response to food has changed. As the adult birds arrived at the nest, instead of the usual chaotic chirping, the youngsters now sing in unison. The sound began softly, rising in cadence and volume as each morsel was presented. Then, as each parent flew away, the miniscule music became discordant and faded quickly away. Later, pegging out more washing, I heard the chicks again. The cock bird had just flown in, and the voices rose and synchronised. The sound is repetitive, whirring – the pulsating tone of a piece of clockwork – as if someone was turning the handle of a delicate Victorian automaton.

As I worked my way along the washing line, the hen uttered her soft, new call from her perch in the birch tree, her feathers fluffed out as if to keep warm, wings held away from her body slightly. The clucking continued, each sound formed by a pulse from her throat. She launched from the tree down into the garden and up into the nest, and the whirring, chirring song lifted into the air again. I moved to the corner by the shed. The dog came out of the house, and from her position at the top of the steps, looked at me with her head to one side. I pointed her to the ground and – eventually – she obliged. She didn't take her eyes off me, didn't see Mrs Blackbird leave the clematis. This time, avoiding the possibility of attack from a dog who hasn't the faintest idea of the life above her head, she emerged from the back of the archway, from where she flitted away.

May 27

Reading in the garden. The hen has a new route of entry into the nest. She wings in from a neighbouring tree and lands on the lawn. From there, she propels herself onto the top of the folded clothes dryer, *clank*, and swoops up into the nest. *Chirrrr chirrrr chirrrr* go the chicks. Out she comes, *clank*, onto the top of the clothes dryer and down onto the lawn where she begins hunting for worms.

The pattern continued for the rest of the afternoon: *clank, chirrrr chirrrr chirrrr, clank*, silence. Over and over. I watched her working her way through the planters on the garden wall, then dropped to the border. She worked the soil through the tall stems of the bursting purple globes of allium. Later, she was up in the birch tree again, silhouetted against white cumulus clouds. A breeze pushed through the trembling wands of new birch leaves. They moved light as air.

The hen observed the gardens, constantly clucking. The strengthening breeze pushed at her feathers. She resisted the wind pressure, recalibrating her balance with the slightest shift of her weight. She flew up to the lower edge of the house roof, and from that increased elevation seemed agitated, flicking her tail and adjusting her sightline by continually shifting her feet.

◉ ◉ ◉

Eating lunch in the garden. The hen landed on the wall between two plant pots, cocked her head to one side and looked directly at us, then flitted into the clematis. The cock had been absent for hours, and the hen was spending less time in the nest; she was now much more often up on the birch scanning the sky. I told Cal that I'd not seen the male blackbird for ages.

'He's probably in the pub,' Cal said.

A short time later the cock stormed back into the garden on the tail of one of the neighbourhood jackdaws, his body swivelling like a fighter plane and delivering a crescendo of blackbird indignation. The jackdaw jinked away. The blackbird landed in the lilac tree over the fence and, with his distinctive staccato crowing, proclaimed himself Lord of the Garden. The jackdaw, meanwhile, had gained height, banked around the chimney pots and sensibly headed home to his roost in the sycamore down the lane.

May 31

After a few days away from home, we returned to find the nest silent. I feared the worst. If I'd missed the fledglings emerging from the nest, I would be sorry, with a sense of having missed out. In previous years, the fledglings had often made their maiden flights in the early hours of the morning. Only once had I managed to witness their moment of embarkation, the immature wings used for the very first time, the half-floating, half-frantic trip to ground level, the scurry into undergrowth. That year the youngsters fledged during a period of insufferably heavy rain. The adult birds' high-pitched, piercing *tseee, tseee* contact call made a high-tensile backdrop to my life – to the washing up, the making of beds, carrying in the shopping – and it lasted for days.

Somewhere close by, there was a fledgling; I could hear the piercing parental contact whistle, delivered once, loud and assertive, for the first time this season. And then, there came a response: the fruity chirrup of a fledgling somewhere in amongst the dense foliage of the border.

◉ ◉ ◉

The clematis is guaranteed to be at its showiest, most glamorous best in the last week of May, when we are often away on holiday. This year though, everything was late, and as we set off for our week away, just one or two white flowers adorned the greenery, emerging like first stars across the evening sky. Returning a week later, unpacking the bags upstairs, I looked out of the window to a galaxy of flowers spiralling over the archway, across the trellis and over the wall. In the garden next door, the creamy-white snowball heads of viburnum flowers are a decadent riot of white, and beyond that, white lilac: '*whitefulness*', as my husband says.

Seven

GARDENING WITH BLACKBIRDS

June 1

'Here come the red kites,' Steve said, after putting leftover food on top of the garden wall. Then he stood at the kitchen window, counting the seconds until the jackdaws arrived.

It's his homage to a red kite feeding station in the Galloway hills, a place we'd once spent an afternoon in the company of these aerial acrobats. The farm advertised itself as a feeding station, though I'd not anticipated quite so many; as we pulled into the car-park, eighty or more kites were circling above like aircraft in a holding pattern. In the viewing hide, an RSPB warden was on hand, talking about the successful kite reintroduction programme, and how their presence in Galloway was due to careful planning, consulting farmers and landowners – doing the groundwork to make sure the birds had as great a chance as possible.

In the wild, kites are scavengers, specialising in taking anything old and dead rather than hunting live prey. In contrast to the Galloway scheme, a more recent kite reintroduction attempt in south Cumbria failed to undertake the same degree of planning and outreach; within days of release from Grizedale Forest, three kites were shot or poisoned thanks to age-old prejudice.

In Galloway, the pioneering farmer came out of her house hefting a bucket. Her long grey hair was tied in a knot, and she had on an apron and welly-boots. In the field below the hide, she began to throw finely chopped chicken onto a wooden platform, as if in preparation for some obscure ritual. The kites swooped in to feed in a hierarchy of seniority, younger kites waiting until last. Once the food had been taken, the raptors melted away into the heather-topped and forested rolling hills. I watched until my eyes strained to see the last one disappear. Two quid a car and a spectacle to remember – there's farm diversification for you.

In the ordinariness of our semi-urban garden, the jackdaws also feed by hierarchy, but co-operatively too, taking a share and moving on. Most days there are jackdaw scouts watching from up on the chimney pots, waiting to spread the word if food appears anywhere within the radius of their all-seeing eyes – *ak-ak, aak, ak-ak*. Once though, a jackdaw got it badly wrong. Steve had put a scatter of crumbs on the wall as usual. One of the clan – presumably a juvenile – must have arrived ahead of its turn. Another, seemingly more senior, jackdaw flew in and wasted no time in mugging the first, pinning its back to the wall by standing squarely on its legs and proceeding to stab murderously at the youngster's chest. Left with little means of retaliation, the victim was reduced to weak and unsuccessful attempts to jab with its beak at its assailant. We looked on, horribly fascinated. Once the lesson had been dealt, the recalcitrant bird was set free to retreat to a nearby chimney pot where, wings ruffling in indignation, it licked its wounds and looked around to see who, or rather how many, had witnessed this act of avian punishment.

◎ ◎ ◎

The rain began at midday, building itself into a deluge through the afternoon and on into the evening. By 9pm the sky had assumed a drab colourlessness, in sheets of deep dark gunmetal.

Then, just as it seemed as if no more rain could fall, the pulses increased, lashing down in wave after wave of intensity. It was as if someone was pressure-washing the windows – oh, flaming June. Worrying about the blackbirds, I kept looking out to the garden, wondering if the fledglings would survive the downpour, about the permeability of immature feathers.

Half an hour later, reprieve; a sudden shot of light from behind the cloud layers. And the sun emerged, all watery-edged, a glowing, oscillating glitterball of gold in the few moments before it lowered behind the fell.

June 2

Walking into town, during a moment's break in the traffic, a brown leaf fluttered down onto the white line in the middle of the road. But no – not a leaf – an ancient fairy-tale character shrugged into a ball of feathers, hunched and crabbed. A blackbird fledgling, squatting on the central line. Scanning the road for cars – all clear – I walked towards it. Reaching out my hands, a single squeak of protest emerged from its petulant gape, then the youngster lifted itself into the air and with a few faltering wingbeats made the relative safety of an adjacent garden, where it manoeuvred itself underneath the herbaceous border. Then a cock blackbird dived in from the field on the fell, banking and swooping down to join his young charge. The traffic resumed; oblivious.

◎ ◎ ◎

Weeding the dense garden border below the dry stone wall, I was busy pulling out the winding nuisance of *Convolvulus* and grappling with ferns that had taken root in cavities between the stones. Head down, trowelling away, I sensed the hen blackbird buzz close, close enough for me to feel little bursts of air disturbed by her wings. Then she did it a second time, and I felt her feathers ruffle the top of my head.

She landed close by – close enough that I could have put out a hand to stroke her glossy, umbered wing; if only she would let me. Ever the opportunist, she was gardening herself, waiting for a turn of worms from the soil as I worked. Trowelling away, I scooped and gently cast a pile of earth towards her feet. Unfazed, she picked out the worms, then slipped silently into the undergrowth. From inside, from underneath the brushy stems of *Spirea,* the slightest of sounds: a fledgling, hidden.

◎ ◎ ◎

'Come and see this,' Cal called. 'There was a blackbird with a worm dangling from his beak on the garage roof, then he flew down onto the fence – that's when I saw the fledgling.' He was beginning to get the blackbird bug.

Next door, hunched on a piece of old trellis tucked away at the back of a shed, a fledgling eyed the sky. Nut-brown plumage, tinged with notes of red, and lighter again on the chest. Blackbird youngsters, at this stage, are indistinguishable male from female. The youngster turned its head, its juvenile gape beginning to morph into the beak of a mature bird. With the beak tucked into the downy feathers of its back, the fledgling promptly went to sleep and, with no more sign of activity, Cal and I returned to work.

From somewhere out in the gardens, I heard the staccato delivery of an adult blackbird venting his ire. Ten minutes later, the cock appeared on the garage roof and hopped down towards the fledgling, offering it the gift of a worm. After the adult flitted away, the juvenile rose and stretched, revealing tiny legs amidst the ball of its body, before settling again into the nest of its own feathers.

I'd not seen the female for two whole days. Had it all begun again? Was she sitting already on a second clutch of eggs? I lived in hope.

June 3

The hen blackbird quick-stepped across the lawn into a corner of
the garden, underneath the clematis. Moving towards her softly, I
noticed at her side a fledgling. Together they moved further into
the undergrowth – or rather, they melted away; at this time of
year, and with young to watch, blackbirds possess this great ability
for being highly visible and proud of it – but also to disappear:
here, not here.

◎ ◎ ◎

A slight chirruping from the trellis in next door's garden. On
a horizontal branch underneath the lilac: a blackbird fledgling.
Hopping along, it flicked a short, stubby tail, checking out the
differing angles of its expanding world. A thrush, last seen crack-
ing small yellow snail shells on the garage roof, landed in the top
of the lilac, closely followed by the cock blackbird – chest pushed
out and flaunting his supremacy. He moved closer to the thrush,
who, obligingly, in no mood for argument, flew away. Father and
offspring spirited themselves into the white lilac.

◎ ◎ ◎

Cycling home through Burneside, an out-of-season curled leaf
fell from an over-hanging branch and trembled down onto the
road: another hapless fledgling. I stopped to usher it back into the
safety of the hedgerow. Suddenly, the world seemed full of danger.

June 8

Something was up. It was eight in the evening, and the hen
bird was in the top of the birch tree, alarm calling in rising
staccato: *cluck cluck cluck cluck cluck cluck!* In the garden across
the lane, a blackbird prinked unseen: *pink-pink, pink, pink, pink,
pink, pink-pink!* Gradually, the sounds faded. I walked down the

garden, and the female clucked softly from the interior of the mock-orange. Our eyes met. Silently she hopped onto a lower branch. She was in profile, her head tilted downwards, and one eye fixed on me, framed by the motionless heart-shaped leaves and white flowers.

For the third evening in a row, all was utterly still. Clouds broke apart revealing seams of intense phthalo blue, orange and pink, charged with light as the sun fell into the west beyond the rim of the fell. Squadrons of swifts performed aerial manoeuvres against the sky, scattering their piercing, thin and hard-wired whistles through the tranquillity.

June 11

Someone had pulled the clouds into long, thin hanks of wool, cross-hatched by vapour trails. I was running again – or kidding myself that I can. Up the fell early before the heat kicked in. Hot already and only ten past eight in the morning.

The Coniston fells ranged along the western horizon, the hook that drew me onwards: Coniston Old Man, Wetherlam, Brim Fell and the climbers' territory of Dow Crag, all old stomping grounds from my Ulverston days. I've walked every path on the range and climbed the Old Man and Dow Crag fifty times or more. Once, on midsummer's eve, I walked up to the summit of Dow and had the place to myself. I stayed for hours, watching the gradual dimming of the light, the landscape's edges losing focus as the sun eventually sank in the north-west and was inevitably lost below the Irish Sea. Swifts and swallows winged past on nocturnal hunting missions. They gave my evening a tangible grace and, in their presence, I found it hard to leave. Time faltered, slipped on, and I walked down the mountain in the never-quite-darkening night.

◉ ◉ ◉

In the big field on the way to Cunswick Scar: Friesian bullocks, all nosy and bolshie. Sometimes I try to make contact with them, touch a nose before they draw back again. That morning they jostled after us, following me and the dog to the gate, all bunched and shoving together as I extended my hand, while the dog – the one they're really interested in – had gone on ahead, oblivious.

Walking the common on a day when the gorse, the hawthorn and the blackthorn are blossoming, I think of the opening sequence of Adam Foulds' novel *The Quickening Maze*, in which the young John Clare is sent out onto the heath to collect firewood. Instead, he finds himself drawn on into nature, further than he had ever been, past stands of gorse that shifted minutely in the breeze, walking into unfamiliar territory and being, for the first time, quite alone.[11]

And though my shadow has been to this place many times, there is always the quiet thrill of being lost within this natural world. Of being drawn on into it.

Somewhere above the fields to the south, a solitary lapwing worried the sky. And with the lapwing comes a reckoning. As a teenager walking or riding the lanes between our house on the edge of Ulverston and Birkrigg Common, most expeditions were accompanied by vast, wavering flocks of lapwings. They lifted from the fields as I passed, so numerous they transformed the sky: black-white, black-white, black-white in wavering, idiosyncratic flight. Bending and flexing their wings, they beat the air out from underneath to propel themselves forward. Sometimes you can hear it, the Doppler effect, as they circle around and back, the rasping, rolling *pee-witt!* call lending them an air of permanent surprise. But lapwings are another previously abundant bird now on the red list of endangered species. For me, they're birds to write home about.

Ahead, above the path to the summit, a pair of crows mobbed a buzzard, and I wondered if it might have been the youngster I'd encountered on the fell back in the early spring.

As I moved onwards over the rising ground, the birds vanished below the northern rim of the Scar. A few minutes more and I gained the summit cairn. Some ten or fifteen feet at its base, the circumference decreasing through an untidy mound to a rubbly pinnacle, the cairn is made of limestone cleared from the ground, and glows silvery white; even on dull days it can be seen from miles around.

The air was soft and easy. In the south, the bay was half underwater and half not. On the far horizon, the sun set the sea all a-sparkle. I turned full circle, the mountain tops clear, etched pale against the sky from Black Combe in the far west to Mardale Ill Bell in the north-east. Lying down on the earth and shielding my eyes from the brightness, I scanned the sky for larks. When I found them, I closed my eyes to better hear them.

Walking home through the small wood underneath the fell, the moon was risen into the morning, nested in hawthorn blossom and cerulean blue.

June 16

A young blackbird on the garden path next door. With the neighbours away, the blackbird family was exploiting the lack of human activity. From the path beyond our fence, one of the youngsters regarded me by turning to look over its folded wings. Her tail almost full length, she wore it like the train of an evening gown, spread out on the pale ground behind her.

Coming home from town through Maude's Meadow, some twenty blackbirds foraged for worms in new-mown grass. The further into the park I walked, the more blackbirds I counted; all those mouths to be fed. Reaching Fellside Lane, the pavement was at tree-canopy level, and from deep inside the web of branches came the unmistakeable discord of blackbirds in high dudgeon. They flitted restlessly through the branches, *tak, tak, tak, tak*. Then came the rattle of magpies: killers on the prowl.

◎ ◎ ◎

The young blackbirds were becoming bolder and spending more time out in the open. They had a new call – fruitier, a sweet chirrup, like sucking air in through top teeth with the cheeks drawn in. I practised imitation.

The cock bird was down on the lawn, all three of his brood hurrying after him. Still no sign of the female; perhaps she is sitting on eggs. So this was to be a good year – one with two or even more broods. In a favourable year, blackbirds will lay up to five times, and usually in the same nest. It made me tired just thinking about it – all that new life to nurture. I wondered how many blackbirds have fledged from the sanctuary of our clematis since it was planted back in 2000.

Unable to resist, I fetched the step ladder and climbed up to investigate. Gently parting the tangle of leaves and stems, white pollen smoked out from the last of the clematis flowers, and the female shot out past the end of my nose, disappearing over the gardens. I retreated, chastened and guilty. I sat on the step. Five long minutes later, she reappeared. But she wasn't stupid; she entered the garden and lit onto a branch of the Japanese maple. Above her, up in the tall birch, a huddle of jackdaws fretted, *chak-chak, chack*. With the young blackbirds' newfound confidence, no wonder the cock bird continually led them back into the undergrowth. Like the child-catcher from *Chitty Chitty Bang Bang*, the jackdaws were angled forwards, studying the garden below, all black feathers and enormous beaks.

The female waited, silently, in the maple. I clapped loudly up at the jackdaws. Lifting their black taffeta wings, in moments they had spirited themselves away. The hen flitted back inside the clematis. Just yesterday, Steve had been up there on the step ladder, clipping away for ages, getting rid of the ever-expanding clematis stems that twine and grow and reach towards the light.

⊚ ⊚ ⊚

The plants were quickly taking over. The *Ligularia, Crocosmia Lucifer*, black-eyed Susans and delphiniums needed lifting and dividing, but overcrowding makes good cover for young birds, and shelter from hungry magpies.

Pink and white foxgloves were beginning to emerge, budding open from the base of their spires as they gained height, becoming bee-dreamed towers. White ox-eye daisies spread, as is their wont, needing to be shown who's boss. I loosened and lifted clumps of them, compacted root systems riddled with damned ground elder. Year after year we've dug and dug, and even though there's satisfaction to be had in pursuing the burrowing root systems, even though we've uprooted every shred of evidence, it persists – and worse: it is extending its range year on year. Any amount of effort is met with the sight, a few days later, of new pale green leaves pushing up again, all innocence and impertinence.

At the far end of the border, I dug and pushed and pulled with the spade and fork, fighting the obstinate root system and eventually pulling out the rampant squanderings of a lily. It had had its chance, been there for years, and every year it pushes up vigorously, then fails once again to flower. Mixing compost into the soil, and throwing in manure for good measure, I watered the earth and planted out marigold seedlings; they wouldn't let me down.

Still, the summer wouldn't fully come. At afternoon's end, clouds like Hokkaido waves broke over the Kentmere mountains. Closer in: clouds all downward swags, foretelling precipitation. The forecast was for rain. The caustic stink of barbecue lighter fuel was on the air; there was optimism for you.

June 17

Underneath the wooded fellside, in the overgrown path, the morning's peace was broken by the sudden upsurge of bird calls. Blackbirds, and what sounded like youngsters too, their voices building rapidly and remaining elevated, on high alert, as if many nests and bird families had all been flung into panic. Whatever it was that provoked alarm remained unseen, somewhere amongst or above that complicated tangle of branches. Then, a nanosecond-long sighting of the marled, chestnut-brown back of a bird of prey, breaking cover above the trees. The predator circled, swivelling artfully above the burgeoning growth, flickering in and out of vision. The chaffinches' and wrens', the blackbirds', the tits' and the whitethroats' protests gained momentum, turning cacophonous. I wanted to scramble up the steep bank, to add my voice to the still-rising throng, but twisting, thorny briars and nettles taller than me blocked the way. Then, the crashing of wings against leaf canopy, and a kestrel broke cover. I watched it casually wing-beat, dropping over the field below. With only its back visible, there was no line of vision to the talons or the bill, no way of knowing if it held a fledgling, struggling for just a few seconds more.

The uproar from the nests fell away as quickly as it sprang into being.

◉ ◉ ◉

The blackbird fledglings had become increasingly insistent. For the first time, when one of the youngsters embarked on the usual food-demanding chirrup, the sound changed pitch, rising halfway into the staccato fluting of the adult call. The cock sat on the corner of a low roof four gardens away. He looked down, knowing exactly where each one of his brood were.

Spires of *Ligularia* freighted with bursting buds nodded their tips. They bended and bended again, gifted with the sensuous curves of a seahorse. From the window, I watched a goldfinch swaying along with the breeze, clinging like a small boat tossed on a roughening sea on the flower-head of a lilac scabious. There was but a mere moment to take in the bright red-and-black head markings – like a masked Mexican wrestler – the goldfinch and I at eye level, before it zapped away, following another goldfinch, leaving behind an afterimage flash of yellow.

It is never necessary to be outside in order to know that there are goldfinches about. Their repeated two-note up-down, up-down phrase and the rising flourish that follows is high-pitched and clear. They sweep down from the fell over the road, or come in over the gardens to see what food might be on offer. They bounce along on the air in ascending and dropping flight, as if on unseen trampolines, launching themselves along in per-petual motion. Voracious, tenacious feeders, goldfinches have all but taken the place of some of the more usual garden suspects. Nowadays, we're far more likely to hear that sparkling song than the chaffinch's mundane *pink, pink pink*.

This year, for the first time, a dunnock made its nest some-where close by, though I never did find exactly where. I did, though, find shards of their brilliant blue eggs, like pieces of fallen Mediterranean sky.

June 19

One of the fledgling blackbirds ran across the flagstones outside the kitchen, stopping momentarily beside the bird bath – a broad, shallow dish set on the ground and surrounded by plant pots filled to bursting with bedding plants: pansies, all white-and-lilac faces and deep-purple centres; white geraniums and blue-trailing lobelia that has, as yet, to trail. The fledgling eyed me, and I saw that one of its wings was held awkwardly, too low down from the body. It hopped down the three steps and ran, staccato, across the lawn. I followed. The bird knew I was there – of course it did.

The fledgling crept over the ground between the base of the birch tree and the dry stone wall and hopped up onto a narrow, blackbird-sized stone-ledge. It remained for several minutes, pinning the not-right wing against the wall, its good wing to the outside. From a crouching position, I noticed the developing plumage, the almost thrush-like chest feathers speckled with chocolate brown and fawn, and each upper wing feather tipped with the same lighter tones, each longer, lower primary feather edged with a fine line of silver. The tail feathers were fanned, darker in tone, with one edge flicked up against the wall, the other down, as if for balance. They had become the tail feathers of a true blackbird. The eye that watched every move I made was the brown of Rembrandt's painted shadows, but the ring around it was yet to become that daffodil yellow. I wanted to scoop the youngster up into my hands, to whisper to it that all will be well, to stroke those beguiling feathers, and keep it forever.

I saw it again later, the wing still held in a worrying fashion; it was up in the birch tree, the cock bird higher still, uttering softly, *cuck cuck cuck.*

June 20

Ben Osborne, the Shropshire-based wildlife photographer, once said to me that a clear blue sky is problematic: a sheet of uniform colour lacks action or drama. But me, I'm not averse to a lack of cloud – and who wouldn't be, living this far north? But a busy sky offers endless possibilities of light, shadow and mood. With a wind too, everything shifts continually.

Ignoring the washing, the washing up and all the other never-ending chores, I set off to the fell. Cumulus clouds sailed riotously and bright overhead. An intermittent breeze pegged the temperature to perfect.

Much, though not all, of Kendal's wild fell was appropriated in 1897, and a golf course laid across its back and flanks. The course designer described the location as 'admirably adapted for golfing purposes and in such an admirable situation.' Here, however, the usual golf course politics don't apply. With access rights enshrined in history, the whole of the fell remains common land. Anyone can wander at will, and dog walkers, runners and golfers rub along in an 'admirable' state of co-existence. The prospect from the summit is a daily reminder of the remarkable nature of the landscape that is home – from the Coniston hills in the west to the central Langdale Pikes, Red Pike above Kirkstone Pass, the fells of the Kentmere Horseshoe, swinging round to the Howgills in the east, and to the south, Farleton Fell. From the southerly aspect, the edge of Morecambe Bay swings into view. Though named 'The Heights' on the OS map, this formal nomenclature is rarely used.

That morning, the groundskeeper, up in his tractor, was smoothing a swathe of fairway into broad stripes that illustrated his journey around a windbreak plantation of native trees – ash, birch, sycamore, oak and hawthorn, this last like a Chinese ancient hunched over bent legs. Maybe one day that stunted tree will develop into a more fully rounded version of itself.

Stopping at the edge of the small, broad, oval pond on the far side of the summit, I found a stick and began throwing it into the water, the dog almost disappearing inside bursts of droplets that refracted light as she jumped. The pond is a semi-urban thing; set on the golf course, that's almost inevitable – even more so because of the red lifebelt suspended from a stake at one side (though God alone knows how anyone capable of walking here on their own two legs might drown in such shallow water). Around the circumference of the pond are intermittent, yellow-painted wooden posts a couple of feet high, mirrored by sheaves of wild iris: yellow flag, one of my favourites, in full bloom, rimming the pond with its sun-catcher flowers.

Something moved over the water surface. Something electric blue, darting from one place to another, onto lily pads or over the scimitar-shaped iris spears: damselflies. I counted twenty, then saw that the entire pond was colonised by hundreds of these iridescent shapeshifters. One moment the fine filaments of their wings were visible against the brown, weedy bottom of the pond; the next, as sunlight burst out from behind clouds again, lighting up the water surface, they became mere floating bodies, as if devoid of their oscillating flight membranes. The damselflies nipped from plant to plant like tiny zeppelins threading zinging currents of blue.

A memory: of swimming at Nibthwaite Cove, on Coniston Water. Of irises by the boggy field path, of walking through jumbled oak woods, and then above the shingle beach, an arc of yellow flag brightening the cove, their luminous yellow flowers a magnet for scores of electric-blue damselflies, and more damselflies skimming the water around me as I swam. Another memory: of sitting on the shore of the Cove with friends, wearing bathing costumes, our hands covering glasses of chilled white wine as a thunder storm rumbled distantly, drew closer, and the gang of us laughing through it all, mildly hysterical, as fat wet droplets splashed onto our heads and bodies. Later: swimming in rain.

Something altogether larger zoomed over the water. Brilliant in its bright summer regalia, abdomen an intense lapis blue, the thorax and head sage green: a male emperor dragonfly. Another flickered into view, this one brown-bodied, bulkier, the abdomen broadening out, cigar-shaped. It was, I thought, the kind of creature you wouldn't want to mess with. I have a healthy respect for dragonflies; years ago, a friend, out cycling, noticed a dragonfly mid-road, and stopped to move it out of harm's way. The thanks? A stinging bite.

I sat by the pond for ages, watching the purposeful occupations of the dragonflies and damselflies, the dog fetching sticks from the water as clouds moved overhead and an easterly breeze pushed the water, little pulsing waves breaking, twinkling. As the clouds shifted, revealing and hiding the sun, so the light danced on the surface. The damselflies jigged their darting dances and the dragonflies, all bluster and vim, articulated their wings through all six planes of movement, as only a dragonfly can. I resolved to begin our much-talked-about garden pond.

Later, in identification mode, I read that the male emperor is one of the larger species of hawker dragonfly that is highly territorial and 'difficult to approach.'

June 21

An early morning walk up the fell. In the new hedge (in hedge years – it was planted for the millennium), a young thrush practised its song, all spindly legs and stubby tail. Droplets of dew clung to the long grasses of the big sloping field, so the rising ground was layered with an oblique mist. The sheep had been sheared and were suddenly more goat than ewe, all stomach, head and legs. When the grown lambs attempted to suckle, the ewes stamped them impatiently away.

When first or last rays of sunlight break over the ground, the ancient field systems that extend over the whole fell are easy to see. They are evidence of early co-operative and collective working, visible as broad, slightly rising mounds, striping the land. Walking over the same ground, though, brings no impression of undulation. They are fixed, subtle remnants of another way of life.

It was warm, and a soft breeze pushed in from the west. There had been early morning rain and the land was washed clear, recalibrating the distances between me and the mountains. Every wood, hedgerow, tree, building, and road, each moving vehicle travelling silently towards the Lakes, was suffused with the same vivid clarity. Clouds cast deep blue shadows that moved almost imperceptibly over the earth.

A couple of newly shorn sheep and two lambs burst out from a small copse of trees and careered onto the golf course. They ran headlong towards the mower that was at that moment gunning back up towards the top of the fell, leaving another perfectly parallel stripe of soft green in its wake. The sheep slowed to a dawdle, and the driver cut a sharp turn and began chasing them down the hillside towards their rightful place in the fields below, hitting the horn as the tractor flew along, the sheep turning and racing ahead of him.

Some time later, returning along the path through the fields, a farmer appeared, leaning over the wall and aiming small stones at the rear ends of the absconders. They sauntered nonchalantly down the steep ground. The farmer and I met at the stile in the wall.

'I see your sheep are partial to a round of golf,' I said.

'Oh aye. The buggers. Did your dog chase them down off the top?'

'No,' I said. 'She's terrified of sheep.'

'Well, if she had've done, she'd've done a good job!'

I told the dog to lie down and moved in to help corner the sheep. After a bit of predictably sheep-like vacillation, the offenders headed to the crumbled wall and, by pressing themselves through the low gap between barbed wire and stones, jumped down, returning to the fold. Whilst this vignette played out, a woman I presumed to be the farmer's wife – dwarfed in the corner where two walls met at right angles – lifted great stone cobbles from where they had fallen, her head disappearing and reappearing as she repaired the wall. There were dozens of gaps through which bolshie teenage sheep could escape into the wider world.

June 22

I'd been thinking about meadows. Traditional meadows that are rich in wildflowers and grasses have declined to just three per cent of the overall number since the 1930s. These days, fields are generally a mix of specific grasses and buttercups and, lovely as they might seem, they're part of a relatively homogenous mix. Daily, the nearby fields turned yellow and bright green. Up on the wild, uncut areas of the fell, buttercups were knee-high, and the grasses were, too. Sewn in amongst the mundane was an understory of rich, purple orchids. The dog lost herself inside it all. At home, the boys sneezed and sneezed.

I was out on my bike, pedalling the back road from Kendal to Staveley. Beyond the village of Bowston, the road climbs steeply, and on one side, a high-banked hedgerow was full to bursting, shouting with colour: pink campions, lesser stitchwort needling through dandelions, pale-blue giant bellflowers, white phlox and steeples of cow parsley. Spires of rosebay willowherb were yet to burst into flower, but lower on the bank, the little suns of common hawkweed infiltrated the grass underneath dog daisies, all white petals and canary-yellow buttons. More hidden, the violet pagodas of bugle. Amongst it all, hoverflies hovered and honey bees thrummed. In the field beyond the great hedge, cows ruminated, dreaming whatever cows dream.

I cycled on through Staveley, then over the weir where once I saw a kingfisher: all confidently statuesque and stiletto beak, poised on an overhanging branch, then wings opening as it dived down and buzzed in a blue gyroscope across the falls before winding itself upriver to disappear amongst reeds.

Down the winding lane and pushing hard up the short sharp hill below Craggy House (wishing I were more fit). Up there, under the dome of Craggy Woods, dark, ancient yew groves compete with oak, beech and birch for their place on the cliff-faced escarpment. Every now and then, another splinter of rock falls away from the high buttresses which give the wood its name. The most recent fell away in the night, thank God, toppling like a caber towards the bottom path; it would take twenty or more men to lift it. More recently, its surface has been colonised by mosses and the beginnings of lichen. At the top of the woods, or 'Craggy,' as it is affectionately known, there's an eye-level perspective into and through the crowns of vast trees whose trunks plummet to the ground far below. The sky above is the hangout of buzzards. On summer days, parents take the youngsters gliding. They rise and hover on thermals above the vault of foliage. Take a seat on the wooden bench at the highest point and look out: the ring of the Kentmere hills, Brunt Knott, the bridleway to Longsleddale, the tall cairn on Williamson Knott, and the understated but delightful summit of diminutive Black Fell.

My tyres fizzed along the lane, and intermittently, the gentle conversations of the River Kent passed into hearing. I carried on south, cycling between shadowed pastures and ancient coppice woods. On and on, into and out of shade where bird's foot trefoil and buttercups lined the roadside along with more foxgloves and more campion, nature arranging itself in co-ordinated partnerships of colour. Other memories: of summer bike rides through these lanes when our boys were little, such rides beginning with chatter or singing. They might shout in excitement, frightening away the roe deer from the middle of the meadow, and we'd stop and watch together as the red creatures looked up and sprang away over the mossy field walls and melted away into the woodland.

But the voices would invariably diminish as the small people were lulled by the motion of the bike and the drift and dream of the woods and the river and the fields. And a moment would come when I'd feel a slight shift in the weight of the bike, and I would know that sleep had arrived.

Turning onto the Potter Fell road, and another, much longer climb, meadows were glimpsed through gateways, all gold buttercups, and beneath, grass the colour of a fox's pelt.

I stopped beside a small wood where the oaks and beeches were widely spaced, and on the grass beneath them, a single male blackbird ferreted. He stopped work and eyed me before resuming the business of picking up last year's leaf scraps and old grass stalks, tossing them away, *cuck, cuck, cuck-cuck,* hunting for grubs and worms.

At the top of the climb I took a breather, drank water, soaked up the view. From my vantage point, the land slipped away, rolling down over fields and farms, over the town and beyond towards the lowlands and Morecambe Bay. The Pennines defined the eastern horizon; west, the Furness hills, the Coniston hills and then the central mountains. Cloud streets formed themselves into orderly rows and drifted slowly away towards the Irish Sea. The south Cumbrian landscape is all folds and dips and hills; being here feels like pulling the duvet up and snuggling down.

◎ ◎ ◎

Late evening, a dish-faced, gibbous, fairy-tale moon rode a sky half gunmetal, half aquamarine, luminous against the tattered edges of deepest night.

June 24

The colour of the young blackbirds was changing, darkening, by the day. And they were gaining in confidence, too. They could be seen out in the middle of the lawn looking for food – and finding it. The cock kept watch and occasionally gifted them luscious morsels of worms and caterpillars. Miraculously, the youngster's injured wing appeared right again.

Late afternoon, a sparrowhawk glittered across the sky, circling against high white cumuli. Swifts took turns, dropping out of their high arcs, haranguing the unwelcome interloper that had come to patrol their airspace. As a swift cut close, the hawk dropped height – by the merest margin. It remained there, indifferent, hovering, fluttering, hovering. The swifts moved on.

June 25

The young blackbirds have gone, melted away into the world beyond the five gardens. I miss them. Was the cock travelling with them, offering final words of advice? Sometimes, there came the rising cadence of his warning call, and worse, sometimes the hard *tac, tac* of alarm.

The end of June approached, and as yet the summer still tantalised and occasionally charmed. Tomorrow I would be heading north to the Isle of Mull, and so spent the day organising the washing and deciding which books to take, which to leave. Before heading into town, I asked Cal to hang the washing out. When I returned, he had not, so we went out to hang it up together.

Then the cock blackbird materialised from the garden next door. He dipped towards us, and as he passed low over my head, I felt a ruffling in the air. He disappeared inside the clematis. A minute later he was back, repeating his party trick, but this time I swear the tip of his wing touched the top of my head. He fluttered inside the twiny growth. No rest for the wicked; one brood gone, and a day later, another on the way. It was all kicking off again.

A phone call from Mull: 'Do you know about the ferry strike?' I didn't. My friend on the island told me about a wedding, about people needing to get to the island and a man named Cameron who was taking them across the water in his small boat. 'You could try phoning him, see if he can take you.'

June 26

The journey from Kendal to Glasgow and on towards the north was full of rain and grey. Two and a half hours from Glasgow, the train pulled into Connel Ferry station, and soon after rounded towards the coast. Sheets of cloud began to drift apart, and suddenly, that heavenly pale, high blue materialised – the particular blue of sky at the edge of land. In Oban, the sun shone, the sea sparkled and that ethereal, pale cerulean grew and grew as the cloud cover disintegrated. I pulled my suitcase along the harbour front and soon, there was Cameron and his boat, with eight of us on board. The big CalMac ferries were berthed, immobile. The rib made the crossing in thirty minutes flat.

◎ ◎ ◎

Catching up with Hylda and John after a year, the talk was of the Northern Lights visible last week from Skye, though here in Tobermory the clouds had refused to budge. Oh, how I would love to see the full-blown coloured lights. Once, from Torridon, on a still, black velvet night, I'd seen white lights beaming into the dark from behind the rising bulk of Ben Alligan. At first, we had mistaken them for search lights, and it wasn't until ghostly white shimmerings began rippling across the space between the beams that we understood we were seeing the Northern Lights. We'd stood and watched with our necks aching, on and on, until we felt the pull of malt whisky and relinquished the night.

After a mug of tea and unpacking my bags, I set off down the hill into Tobermory, the slightest sense of moisture on the skin and the in-breath. The island air softens distances, obscures nothing. Swallows click-sang, like high-pitched whale song as they swam through the sky. On the silver water, sail boats beguiled. It was good to be back.

◎ ◎ ◎

Each time I come, I realise I've forgotten how different the length of the days is here – and we think *we* live in the north. Late in the evening, I looked out from the window towards the Sound of Mull. On that beguiling sheet of water, nothing moved. I sat and looked – adjusting to the transition from home to here, and in particular to the lack of noise. The memory of this remains with me all year. It's what I long for when I'm not here.

By 9.30pm the birds had fallen quiet. Low sunlight illuminated the gable end of the white cottage across the road, beyond the garden and the great copper beech tree, and there was not the slightest intimation of night. I took a walk up the path behind the house, the surface created from broken cockle shells, the white of them an eerie glow ahead of me. Birds: still on the wing.

The vacant sky gathered itself around the sculpted layers of Ben Hiant across the Sound, bordering Ardnamurchan. Light from the slowly westering sun melted over the land and the sky lost substance, becoming pale and yet more pale, so that it was silver and blue and white, underscored by the merest pale pink glow.

Then: two red deer hinds, exposed, in the middle of a field, grazing. As my footsteps crunched on the shell path, the deer raised their heads. They regarded me, then lowered their heads to the grass again. There was a hooped Victorian stile leading over a dry stone wall to climb into a rough field, and the roar of a red deer stag came bellowing over the hillside.

The profiles of a couple of standing stones appeared above a ridge in the field, one monolithic, the other only slightly less so: the Baliscate standing stones. Between the two, I found a third, lying slantwise in the grass. At some point in the past, it had deliberately been toppled, doubtless to transform the site from its pagan origins into the rough shape of a cross. A fourth stone was found during more recent investigations, smashed into pieces that had become sunk deep into the peat.

Precisely positioned by the people who lived here, and no doubt after decades or even centuries of making painstaking calculations, the stones align exactly to the North Star in midwinter, and at midsummer, to the sun's equinoctial zenith. The people who made this astrological timepiece were not only closely attuned to the natural world, but also to the laws of physics and mathematics. And then some bunch of religious zealots comes along and tries to smash away the meaning. I know where my sympathies lie.

Oh, but the view! Over the tops of the few houses across the Sound of Mull to Ben Hiant and all its dusky layers, and further, to the wild bounds of Ardnamurchan and Morvern, then further again to where distant mountain peaks float across the iris like dreams.

I dragged myself away, set off again towards the dark of a conifer plantation, the pathway bordered by occasional hawthorns still deep in heady blossom. A sudden roar emanated from scrub willow below me. I was lost in thoughts of the stones and the view, and the sound made me jump out of my shoes. Then it came again: a stag, I thought, confident that his call had nothing to do with me.

The path dived uncompromisingly inside the plantation, into a web of dark spires and broken lateral branches. It was a bad dream of a wood. Nailed every few yards to the trunks of the trees, way markers in the design of a Celtic cross pointing onwards until, eventually, the path emerged into the soft light of a small clearing. On another tree: the sign of an historic monument, though what or where it was, I couldn't determine.

Scanning the soft-lit space, shapes began to clarify – a low, elliptical mound overrun with long grass and bracken. Further in, offset to one side of the clearing, a rectangular platform made of raised stone blocks, foxgloves growing from crevices in between, pushing up towards the light. There in the wild woods was something that seemed an altar to the wild, with a small wild offering of foxgloves. There were other structures too, indecipherable, all overgrown.

Walking further, the path dropped towards a small lochan, and beyond it, a movement in the trees. Immaterial at first, then becoming corporeal, two hinds materialised from the darkness, one following the other, appearing and disappearing again and again, like the red ghosts of deer. They were captivating, the way they moved – unaware of me and making their stately progress between the trees. It was like watching a film of deer moving through a forest. In there, all was darker still.

I turned for home. Out of the wood again, the sudden light of dusk was surprising; checking my watch, it was after 10.30pm, the light perhaps of 8pm back home. On the apex of the hooped stile, a male blackbird, poised in characteristic pose, tail upright and flicking. Further down the lane, three blackbirds crossed the glowing shell path ahead of me, their bodies moving through the air in a horizontal line from the tip of their beaks to the end of their tail feathers, wings hinging downwards from, and never rising higher than, the mid-line of their bodies. They came down into the late glimmer of a hawthorn. Then three more appeared, accompanied by another male: there was no mistaking that keen, sun-ringed eye. A moment later, and all the blackbird families evaporated into the growing shadows.

June 27

Woken by light and bird talk. Down in the twittersphere of the garden, all seemed well. The cordial, light-hearted deliberations of sparrows drew me to the window. One of them landed on the edge of the roof below my window and began to hunt out insects from the undersides of slates, then a small, flustering flock of them criss-crossed the garden path in perpetual motion. A family of blackbirds arrived, the young ones running onto the lawn and stopping, running and stopping again, poised at each interval – ballet dancers on a stage, the cock observing every move. Above the sparrows' constant chatter: goldcrests, unseen, their songs were tiny high-pitched trills. Underneath it all, a woodpigeon, spreading gossip.

A still-life in front of the window: a table and a small cream jug, dog-daisies picked from the roadside, a map, walking guide, notebook and pen, binoculars to soak up the distance. The Sound of Mull glimmered, and beyond it, the hills of Morvern. I like this arrangement of things, the familiar nearby and the land-scape further away, as if in a painting by Winifred Nicholson. At Auliston Point, the land moved down effortlessly into the sea, and at Drimmin, the road end, becoming a track that carries on to places now unpeopled. Ardslignish, Glenmore, Glenbeg: the view is more than one momentary thing, is many layered. And so many colours of green and grey.

The entrance to Loch Sunart, and beyond that, Ardnamur-chan, where the rocky tiers of Ben Hiant caught the light. A CalMac ferry ploughed the Sound, travelling out from Oban to Coll – or Tiree, or Castlebay on Barra, or Lochboisdale on Harris. Like someone flicking a switch, the light changed and the sea turned blue-green, then cobalt and silver. A sea–path of aquamarine glowed for a moment, and faded. The switch flicked again, and everything turned grey. The single white sail of a yacht slipped into the mouth of Loch Sunart, then changed direction and was gone: a snowflake melted.

I can sit there for hours, looking, nothing more, and never be anything other than lost – and found.

June 28

For perhaps an hour or more I sat in the evening light sheltered by the walls of Dun Ara. Built into the top of a rock stack on a volcanic plug beside the sea, and perhaps only forty feet high, this small medieval fort is reached by a track that begins passing through rhododendron woods. At a wooden gate, the sea comes into view along with all the glittering prizes that are the Hebrides. Between the path and the Sound of Mull lies a headland where winter's brazen wind has pushed Scots pines into a rolling sea of branches. In sloping meadows below the fairy-tale pile of Glengorm Castle, Highland cattle grazed.

I reached the stack, climbed the cut-rock steps and sat above the fidgeting sea, looking out to the low-lying islands of Coll and Tiree, berthed in the Sea of the Hebrides. The light shimmered and sparkled and, to the north, the mountain peaks of Rum were almost translucent against the pale silver-blue sky. Further out, five hours from Oban by ferry, outlined in all its undulating topography along the horizon: the dark island of Barra. The highest point of the island is the small mountain of Heaval, which I once climbed with my boys, and considered then the notion of looking back towards the land instead of always out to sea.

There was a slight wind. The remnants of ancient walls were perfect for resting my arms and steadying my hands as I looked through the binoculars. From this private lookout, I observed all the things that didn't happen.

Below the fort, on black rocks lapped by the sea, cormorants held their wings out to dry, or torpedoed past on a mission to somewhere over the waves. Gulls watched the restless water. At some point in the evening, along the Hebridean horizon an exotic pink glow grew from beneath bands of moody cloud. The sun was there, somewhere, hidden. It threw down sea-roads of light across the water, trackways that evolved and disappeared.

The people who built this place had no need of physical paths and trackways. For them, communication was by sea and by boat, and it would not be too fanciful, perhaps, to think of the old adage: that they would have known their local routes like the backs of their hands.

The fort's lower wall sections are older again, and scattered around the base of the plug, the remnants of eight low, rectangular buildings have been reduced to turf-grown footings, a rough harbour, cultivation strips and field clearance heaps: a small township, where no doubt life offered little opportunity to merely sit and look.

Alone and with time on my hands, I could in some small way become absorbed into the landscape, become part of the scene and lost from life's seemingly never-ending demands. There was a frisson of letting go, of being utterly alone – and of no one knowing where I was. I like this, the sense of being lost whilst at the same time knowing exactly where I am.

Later, much later, I tore myself away from the sea, walked the track back to the car, past the wind-battered trees, past the castle, through the gate and underneath the rhododendrons, and set off back to Tobermory. At the bend in the road, the place where, depending upon your direction of travel, either the castle comes into view or there's a final glimpse of the castle and the sea and the islands, I pulled over for one last lingering look back towards the silvered water and was struck by a sudden, unlooked-for thought about home, about my family, my boys: suddenly, I missed them all.

Then the phone on the car seat next to me burbled. A text from Callum – my eyes and ears on the clematis had delivered: 'There are *loads* of new chicks in the nest!'

Eight

THE WORLD AGLOW

July 1

Waiting by the slipway in Tobermory. Dr Conor Ryan of the Hebridean Whale and Dolphin Trust had offered a lift to Ulva Ferry on Mull's west coast; we were catching an evening sailing to Staffa.

It was late afternoon. The fish-and-chip queue at the van on the pier was long and growing longer. The smell of frying fish was good, and suddenly the sandwiches I'd packed seemed boring. Something black and tattered fluttered onto the slipway. There were feathers poking up at strange angles, interspersed with bald patches. New feathers sprouted like a double-layered Mohican along the bird's back, though in far less orderly fashion. The tail feathers were ragged, and the wingtips were scrag ends ready to fall away. A male blackbird in full moult: this is what bringing up babies does to you.

Conor arrived and we set off. He told me he's from Cobh Harbour, near Cork in Ireland. I'd been there once, I told him, and I remembered the sculpture of a man in what was half bath, half boat, holding another tiny paper boat in his hands, as if about to set it down, all flimsy and insubstantial. Cobh – the place from where the Titanic set sail.

At the top of the hill, Conor's girlfriend Vivvi jumped in, and the three of us fell into conversation.

After a while I asked Vivvi, 'Are you from Cork, too?' She spoke perfect English with a definite Irish burr.

'No,' she said, 'I'm from Finland.'

We stopped again to pick up Gemma – the director of the Whale and Dolphin Trust, then zipped down the island road to Salen, crossing Mull at its narrowest point and following the winding road around the coast of Loch na Keal. Mull's highest mountain, Ben More, loomed into view. Gribbun's sea cliffs carved themselves out of the sea. The Ross of Mull and Iona floated distantly to the south, and the wide sea was set with the jewels of small islands. This: my idea of paradise.

The boat set out, silky water reflecting the evening light and the land-shadows as we slipped past Ulva's layer-cake geology and rounded into the Sea of the Hebrides. Then the remote and unlikely big house and cottages of smaller Gometra swung into view, only visible from the seaward side – there's remote for you. The boat pushed on. A layer of light cloud had developed, and the sea began to swell into broad troughs and smooth hills. Seabirds rafting on the water dropped from view, reappearing moments later as the boat rode the next mounded wave. Clouds thickened, the sun tantalised, brightening the water and vanishing again.

We motored towards the Treshnish Isles, each with its own distinctive silhouette. Bac Mòr – the Dutchman's Cap – humpbacked, brimmed with a rim of low rock: Lunga, named from the Norse for 'Longship Island'. Fladda, and coming closer, the ruins of buildings became clearer – notched crenulations, a gable wall in the shape of an upturned hull.

'That's the ruins of a chapel,' the skipper said, pointing. 'They reckon it was built around the time of Columba, and the other building was a barracks – built by the English at the time of Bonnie Prince Charlie. Crazy, eh?'

Conor shouted, 'Porpoise!', and looking east we caught the rising forms of a female, a calf close to her side. They rolled symmetrically through the water. The skipper cut the engine and, with the sea quietly sloshing against the sides of the boat, we saw the porpoise surface again, then once more. Lacking the brio of dolphins, porpoises invariably take to the water's underworld once encountered close to. Guillemots and occasional puffins floated past us, unperturbed.

We rounded Staffa on the seaward side, then Conor and Emily – who perhaps has the best job in the world: she is the National Trust for Scotland warden for Staffa – began to count the sea birds nesting on the island's ledges: black guillemots, all smooth and dark, a snow-patch of white on the wing, and northern fulmar, once almost extinct, found only on St Kilda, and now doing well on Staffa, Mingulay, Fair Isle and Unst.

The swell roughened. The sea slapped against the cliffs and roared and boomed into MacKinnon's Cave. On skirts of rock underneath Staffa's basalt columns, cormorants watched the waves. Wings held out to dry, they stood: wraith-like sentinels at the exact place where the waves divided and washed back down into the sea, the birds' black webbed feet unwetted. Waves ran up the rocky foreland, smashing against vertical cliffs, milky and boiling white. The place took on a troubling atmosphere. Fingal's Cave was unrecognisable from the times I'd been there before. My previous visit, on a day of heat, of flat calm and Aegean blue, I'd taken my turn to walk the basalt pathway into Fingal's interior, and someone offered to take my photo. In that picture, I was standing just there, where the sea was now crashing in.

A scratchy recording of *Fingal's Cave* began to play over the tannoy. 'You can't come here and not play the music,' the skipper said, and laughed; Mendelssohn would have been turning… A minute later, the skipper's face turned serious, focusing. The boat came around to the small jetty.

'I don't think we can get in just now – the tide's too high. Maybe come back in an hour, eh? We'll go further out and see if we can catch sight of your whales and dolphins,' he said to Conor, then turned the boat away, and she nosed out into white waves. We continued out beyond Staffa, and further into the Sea of the Hebrides. Just the boat and us, the seabirds, and another distant glimpse of porpoises, rotating through the water toward the horizon. The boat engine, deep and running.

Something shifted. The clouds began to break, becoming all smoke and mirrors as the sun burst through. We turned back towards the small piston of the island, a plug of rock rising and lowering as the boat rode the rolling waves on the great machine of the sea.

By now the tide had lowered and the jetty was almost free of the wash, and the boat pulled alongside and was tied in. The engine cut, there was just the sound of the sea sloshing over the bottom of the jetty, sometimes further in. Having dodged the waves, we scrambled up steep, rock-cut steps and carried on over island turf.

I walked between remnants of rig and furrow. Puffins whirred in and out, over the island and the water, like little animatronic toys. At the edge of their burrows, chests pushed outwards and backs straight like nineteenth-century naval officers, they regarded us with their bright eyes, and we crouched close by, enrapt by puffin magic. Out on the water, the puffins were silent, but on land they uttered a series of soft, guttural growls, like the distant revving of a racing-car.

Emma said, 'They feel more secure when there are people about. The lesser black-backed gulls and the bonxies won't try to take them with us here.' A single pair of 'bonxies', the piratical great skua, had bred on Staffa for the first time that year.

Most of the puffins were out on the water surface, rafting in groups. Emma asked if anyone wanted to join in the counting.

'I wouldn't know how to begin,' I said, but the man next to me had already raised his binoculars. 'Break them down into smaller groups,' he said, beginning to count.

'If you see puffins standing on the water beating their wings, that's a sign they're getting ready to come back in. They signal to others like this and wait for group action before setting off – safety in numbers,' Emma said.

We saw it then, individual birds amongst the three hundred or so the man had counted standing on the water, beating their wings and, eventually, lifting off. The puffins made repeated sorties, flying past their nest sites, coming in close, and swerving away around the rim of Staffa's cliffs and out to sea again. One of them landed close to my feet and hurried into a burrow. I peered in after him, through the grass-framed entrance, and there he was peering back at me, two eyes straddling his white face and the characteristic striped beak.

'Might well be two of them in there,' Emma said. 'The hen's likely sitting on eggs just now.'

I walked on. At the highest point of the island, Conor and Vivvi had set up a telescope looking out over the sea. Clouds had formed again, sealing the sun in. The sea and sky became silky grey. Towards Mull, a thin line of vapour formed, obscuring the joining of land and sea. To the south, the outline of the abbey marked the island of Iona. We talked in low voices, telling each other how beautiful it all was. We didn't see whales or dolphins, but the sun broke through again, opening a seam of gold in the clouds. The light cast a spell on little Bac Mòr and poured an island of light onto the horizon.

◎ ◎ ◎

At 11pm we came back to the land. It was night, and yet it was not. We set off, and at the highest point where the twisting road crosses the shoulder of the hill before dropping down away again towards Loch na Keal, there above the summit of Ben More: the risen moon. And what a moon! Swollen, wearing a cloth of deep orange that glowed against the phthalo sky, it was so close to the land, and so vast, that all our notions of what the moon should look like were confounded. A faint, glowing copper pathway lit the sky above it, as if the moon were travelling along a road of its own making – a path above to light the way, a path below to leave a trace of evidence behind.

All talk of the sea and the cetaceans we'd seen and might have seen fell away. We were held in awe in the moon's lucent grasp. There was talk of how we could climb to the mountain summit in this extraordinary moon's light. We traced every crag and corrie, every shadowed gully and each quietly glittering bank of scree. That full moon, the closest to that summer's longest day, rode the sky in silent brilliance.

'Imagine,' someone said, 'being up there, now.'

July 2

Early morning, and the Baliscate blackbird family was in the garden, the youngsters continually demanding food with their fruity, squeaky calls. I noticed them, of course I did, though these were not the familiar blackbirds of home, and I watched them more dispassionately. A gingerbread-coloured chicken followed in the wake of the blackbird family as they fed. She fanned her tail and strutted inside a bush as the blackbirds came out from it. Flag irises pushed up from the edges of the pond, and a wooden bench was slowly being consumed by nature beneath the spreading branches of the copper beach.

◉ ◉ ◉

Seen from the road to Grass Point: the outline of a deer. I stopped the car. Another deer appeared, and another. The hind I'd noticed first lay in the long grass in full, late morning sun. She was just a field away from me, her fawn at her side. The deer seemed content out in the open, under the rising intensity of the heat. Then, in wobbly fashion, the fawn pushed itself up onto its legs, shook itself and walked just a few faltering steps before flopping down again into the grass. The fawn repeated this again and again, as if getting used to the idea of propulsion, gathering its spindle legs together before navigating small circles around the island of its mother. All the time the hind's head was erect, her ears alert above a sea of wind-blown grass.

At the top of the hill, the land terminates in a grassy cliff above the sea. Below, black rocks descend into deep aquamarine water. Two yachts passed close enough for me to hear the snap and ruffle of shifting wind on sail. Where the Grass Point road ends, the former ferry house overlooks the wide blue stretch of water. It was from this place – called Auchnacraig at the time – that from the 1600s until the 1860s, cattle were ferried to the nearest island across the Forth of Lorne to Kerrera and on to Oban and the mainland markets.

To the north, the rough bounds of Morvern and the elongated wedge of the Isle of Lismore were visible. On the tiny island that lies tantalisingly close to Lismore's southern tip is Lismore Lighthouse – that most photographed of lighthouses, passed so many times each day by the CalMac boats. The mountains of Lochaber rose in the distance. Ben Cruachan's bulk reduced into a bent pyramid, its summit piercing high cloud. From Grass Point, the sea feeds into a creek that then widens into the Abhainn Lirein. The inlet was bursting full with the high tide, the river travelling sinuously towards the interior of Mull.

A handsome stonechat crossed the path as I walked back down the hill. It landed in the topmost spines of a gorse bush. The size of a robin and similarly orange-breasted, this attractive bird wears an even finer regalia: a hood and cloak of dark feathers with white epaulets and a small flash of white on the wing.

Driving over the small hump-backed bridge further upriver, a large bird appeared, rising from the drying mud banks – the tide had already turned. It unfurled its wings, revealing black wing tips and bright white underneath. There is no mistaking the aerial agility of a male hen-harrier. He dropped beneath the parapets of the bridge and was gone, like an illusionist, the air holding the dramatic afterimage of its passing.

◉ ◉ ◉

It was 10 o'clock at night and tomorrow I was heading home. I gave in to the light and went out again to walk to the standing stones. John was in the garden, his head inside a rhododendron bush.

'Have you lost something?' I asked.

'No,' he said, pulling his head out again. 'It's these stupid hens. For some unknown reason, they've taken to laying their eggs in here.'

Hylda came over. I told them about finding the raised platform in the forest several days earlier, and she told me that the platform is indeed an altar. Not only that, but she had discovered it, and because of her research and tenacity, the site was investigated and subsequently became the subject of, first, a Time Team archaeology programme, and then a full-blown, fully documented community archaeology project. Thanks entirely to Hylda, Baliscate Chapel was placed firmly back on the historical map after being lost for centuries. Archaeologists believe it to be one of a chain of small chapels dating back to the time when the Celtic Christian message was being carried outwards from Iona. A burial had been found at the site during the excavations, radiocarbon dated to 610-690 AD – placing it within the lifetime of Saint Columba's biographer, Saint Adomnán, the ninth Abbot of Iona.

We talked about the chapel, and then I told them of hearing the stag on my first evening.

'That wasn't a stag,' John said, 'wrong time of year. That would have been the hinds. They were barking a warning to you to keep away – if you ever get between a hind and her fawn, you'll know about it.'

◉ ◉ ◉

I walked up the shell lane to the standing stones. A small bird landed on the top of a fence post up ahead, something dangling from its beak. Through the binoculars, I saw an orange chest and the tell-tale white strip above the eye: a whinchat. Whatever was in the bird's beak was in the process of being dispatched; the whinchat bashed it again and again on the top of the wooden post. It was the body of a dragonfly, perhaps five inches long, and the creature's banded body was still moving, still fighting. Then I noticed the lack of wings…

Late hawthorn blossom seemed to intensify the evening light, saturated with afterglow from the sun. A group of Friesian heifers turned their heads to watch as I climbed the stile into the field. I walked to the stones. The moon, still huge, had risen above the forest. Flotillas of flamed orange clouds sailed north; oh, to be on the island's western coast tonight.

A pair of crows flew lethargically over the fields and the forest, over the site of the chapel. They moved as a pair but at a distance to each other, uttering medieval proclamations as they winged towards the interior of the island: *craw, caaw! craw, caaw!*

One last time, the sun flared from behind the clouds and the world hinged between fading day and falling night. This far north, at this time of year, true night never really arrives. Chattering swallows escorted me out of the field and home.

July 3

Back in Kendal, and the foxgloves were suddenly as tall as Fergus. The cream *Scabiosa* 'Miss Wilmott' was in full dazzling flower at the bottom of the garden. Sweet peas no longer loitered around the base of their frames; they were up and reaching higher. The dark sanctuary of the *Clematis montana* still bore occasional flowers, like night and her train of stars.

⊚ ⊚ ⊚

We've been weeding on our allotment over the road. The familiar if unexpected *cronk, cronk* of a raven drifted down from the higher ground of the fell. In the next allotment, Peter saw me looking up.

'Aye, there've been ravens about. Dead lamb up there,' and removing the habitual cigar stub from his mouth, he indicated with it the fields above the allotments. There was a spread of dirty white across the ground, the carcass of the lamb, and stalking the ground around it and in between the scatterings were two ravens and a gang of crows and rooks. Ravens rarely come this close to the urban world. How far, I wondered, does the stench of rotting carcass travel, to reach these birds of the higher realms?

July 6

There was an air of worry about the female blackbird. She patrolled the roof of the neighbour's shed, *cuck, cuck*. The male winged into the garden, carrying a beak full of offerings. He didn't fly into the nest through the usual portal in the clematis but chose instead a side entrance, and then he was off. From somewhere close, unseen, he fretted and worried, uttering that eloquent single syllable: *spink spink, spink spink.*

Earlier in the morning I'd heard a youngster call. Had a chick already fledged? Was it, perhaps, biding its time on the ground, deep in the shelter of the foliage?

Weeding, rooting out the ground elder. In places, it had produced flowers. Next thing I know, Steve says, *it's really pretty.* I said, if he says that again I'm filing for divorce.

The stuff had annexed every corner of the garden and even made forays into the grass of our supposed lawn. Every time I weed, I curse it, remembering too late there may be people passing on the lane above.

By evening, rain. All was quiet. Nothing moved but the swifts.

July 7

The dreaming spires and creamy flowers of *Scabiosa* 'Miss Willmott' were at their tallest, flounciest best. Bees worked amongst them all day and far into the evening; I took photographs so that I could identify them later. The bees didn't seem to mind having the camera pushed up to their workplace. Through the close-up lens, I watched them walking over the pin-cushion flower heads, each foot lifting carefully from out of the frilly tubular petals, as if wading through something so delicate that at any moment, it might fall apart.

Another bee worked the foxgloves. Thrumming into the narrowest part of the flower's tube, the buzz was amplified by the tightening dimensions.

A walk down the garden was now met by the heady fragrance of vanilla from my favourite peony, the pale yellow 'Lemon Chiffon,' the 'star turn' of the early July border. Its long stems and gorgeously decadent flower heads are held in place by a homemade kit of bamboo poles and garden twine. Undoubtedly, the elegant peony deserves better than this, but any plant in our garden needs strong survival instincts; my inadequate attempts are led by instinct and last-minute management rather than pre-planning or individual responses to each plant's unique needs.

When the flower heads first open, the creamy white outer petals cluster around an elaborate central posy of lemon-coloured petals. Surrounding these, another layer, each one serrated and resembling, upon close inspection, exotic bird feathers. Then the inner flower of a deeper, more concentrated yellow. Over the brief weeks of its flowering, the external petals fall outwards, and the stamens are revealed. Gradually, the intense lemon colouring begins to bleach, and the peony becomes a ragged bundle, like remnants of an ancient bridal gown. Were I a bee, the transient beauty of this flower would be mine.

July 8

Forget everything you think you know about Lancashire. Now reinvent it as a Cotswold village with narrow lanes between honey-coloured terraced houses and occasional loftier properties with walled gardens – and a pub, the White Bull, with a naïve wooden bull atop the portico entrance. Throw in a village post office for good measure. All of this falls against a backdrop of rolling green hills and closer in, across the river, fields in which the grass is risen, almost ready for the cut. The lane passes the school and the village hall and swings right, following the river's curve into the shade of weeping beech trees where swallows loop and dive. Labradors and spaniels swim for sticks and climb out dripping. There are home-printed signs pinned to the riverside railings: 'This way to the Dig'. This is the small town of Ribchester, celebrated for its rich Roman history.

Following the lane past the rose garden of the vicarage, I saw the tower of the ancient church rising above it all.

There was time to pass. I wandered through the churchyard, and some locals stopped to talk – asked if I was visiting, mentioned the weather, the colours of the flower borders, the history and explaining: 'Just go behind the church – you'll see the

Roman granary buildings – and if you follow the signs, there's the new dig going on. There's a wonderful amount of history for such a small place.'

Swifts circled the crenellated top of the tower. I looked for evidence of nest sites, but failed to see any of these aerial acrobats swooping up into cracks in the render or disappearing like a trick of the light. On each face of the tower was a Norman window, arched and stone-mullioned, set with slate louvres below.

A car pulled in to the carpark. I walked towards it and met Hugh, the bird-ringer I'd come to meet. Then a man walked through the lychgate beyond the tower, and Hugh introduced me to Glynn.

'We don't have long,' Hugh said, 'the bell-ringers arrive at 6.30.' We entered the church through heavy oak doors, then passed through a miniature door and began to climb the narrowest and steepest of stairs, corkscrewing up and up.

'You need to be fit for this job then,' I said, and Hugh answered, 'Try carrying a ringing box up.'

Managing to keep my breath under control, I followed the men into the room at the top of the tower. There was little light. A complicated wooden structure of great spoked wheels dominated the space: the bell-ringing mechanism. The tops of greened bronze bells were bolted into place, each one hanging in its own void. We stood on a small platform off to one side.

Hugh placed the ringing box down on the floor and took out a kit of pliers and plastic bags with numbered rings inside, then passed a piece of hessian to Glynn. Glynn lifted a long black sheet attached to the wall, revealing a set of plywood boxes constructed on the inside of the louvres. On two of the doors was a tick marked in pencil. If I hadn't known what was happening, I might have thought that I'd stumbled into some ancient dark practice – though in a way, I suppose I had.

Glynn began to open an unticked hatch and, holding it slightly open, peered inside. 'One in. She's sitting on two.' I caught the merest glimpse inside the box where the torpid figure of a swift lay, immobile, her back towards us, apparently unruffled by the intrusion. Glynn closed the hatch door. A second door was opened: empty, revealing signs of recent use. There was a swift-sized entrance hole, and on the opposite side of the box, a cut plywood ring as a permanent base for a nest.

'This has probably been made by an immature bird, one that's not ready to lay. She's practising nest building though.' On first sight, there was little to see but something shiny, and something else that was dusty and dull, like an abandoned fairy ring. I asked Glynn what the nest was made of.

'Looks like cobwebs to me, or spider webs. I think that other stuff is plywood dust.'

The next box was opened, the same careful peer inside. This time, a better attempt at making a nest; I was learning that swifts are hardly the great architects of the bird world. I thought of the woven blackbirds' cup at home in the clematis, the opportunism of interwoven found objects: nylon string, shreds of plastic wrappings and last year's dead grasses, even the cut-off ends of garden twine all supplementing the basic framework of clematis off-cuts – the stuff of the near, and the further away. But there in the box in the tower was the merest loose accumulation of down and straw and feathers, of swift feathers and found feathers; to say the nest was woven would involve a leap of imagination. It was more a conceptual nest – Tracey Emin's unmade bed.

In the next few unticked boxes – nothing, and then another putative attempt at nest building, this time with two marble-white abandoned swift eggs that had rolled across the box interior.

'Right,' said Glynn, 'now we're onto the ones we know had birds sitting on eggs.' He opened a hatch. 'Two,' he said, then stuffed the piece of hessian into the entrance. For a couple of minutes, the adult birds would be unable to come back inside.

'Have a look,' he said.

But what I saw looked nothing like a pair of chicks. The contents of the nest resembled nothing so much as a pile of ashes, as if someone had set fire to a sheaf of papers inside the box and left the heaped fragments behind. Then something in the small mound began to stir. Glynn took gentle hold of a chick and placed it inside a hessian bag. He took the remaining chick in his hand, and he and Hugh conferred. Hugh noted down the number on the ring before placing it, with infinite care, onto the chick's leg, and Glynn checked that the ring could move up and down around the leg.

'Won't it pinch as the chick grows?' I asked.

'Their legs are fully formed now – this one already has a mighty grip,' and, holding the chick so that I could place a finger underneath its claw, I felt it too, the ability to grasp on, tightly, at only two weeks of age.

It could not be said that swift chicks, or pulli, are creatures of beauty, though for me they hold an allure I've felt since childhood, encountering these urban-dwelling avian madcaps screaming over our home. They are otherworldly creatures, and looking at the strange clothing of emergent feathers (or pins) I saw the line of long lashes above the eye, protection from the intense glare of the African sun.

The second pulli was ringed, and this time I saw the mechanism that turns these enigmatic birds into the second-fastest animal on earth – only the sparrowhawk is faster. Hugh carefully extended the wing. Each white, bone-like pin was barred with more emergent pins.

'They fledge before each pin is fully grown in. Then it's straight off to Africa.'

With legs that are clearly not made for walking, swifts are dependent upon high places, ledges or crevices to nest in, places from which they can launch forwards into space. Once inside their nests, they merely shuffle along, unable to walk in any real sense. And like blackbirds, swifts function through unihemispheric slow-wave sleep: at any time, half of their brain functions, whilst the other is asleep. This facilitates not only their phenomenal migratory flights, but also the fact that for some three years after fledging, young swifts remain almost perpetually on the wing.

The pulli were placed carefully back into the nest-boxes, and the ringing box and its paraphernalia were packed away.

'Job done,' said Hugh.

We returned to ground level. The bell-ringers were gathering, apparently unfazed by three people and a large box stumbling out from the tiny door.

'Been ringing again, Hugh?' someone asked.

'Yes – all done for this year.'

July 10

I walked down to where the River Kent comes closest to our house. Ducking beneath overhanging branches and through a hole in the hedge, I scrambled down rough-cut steps onto the footpath below a terrace of Georgian houses. Coming out of the scrub on the riverbank, I spied a goosander, *Mergus merganser*, standing on the prow of an exposed boulder. The goosander grunted and crapped, sending out a splash of whitish paint, as if spilt from a tin, down the face of the rock, on the bird's face an expression of cartoonish indignation at my intrusion into her peaceful morning. I observed her red dagger bill, red-brown button eyes set in the red-brown face, and those ostentatious, cartoon feathers fanning from the back of her head. She took to the water, running upstream, wings outstretched for balance with her puritan grey-and-white chest pushed forwards. Under the surface she went, and I saw the water-slicked body torpedoing against the grain of weed streamers and the rocks of the river bed.

I crossed the river by the Victorian suspension bridge, then followed the path between trees. Swallows and swifts hunted over the corridor of water, and the dog made wide eddies across the path ahead, nose down in scent trails. Giant hogweed skulked in dense undergrowth at the river's edge. A heron took to the air from under the bank and wafted upriver.

Further on, where the path passes through open meadow, an alarm call rose from the river. The dog ran towards the sound through a trail worn in the long grass. I called her to heel, and followed. From the riverbank I saw a bird in high dudgeon, flitting from stone to stone, and a second one, tail flicking like clockwork, further upstream. They were small wading birds, but moved too fast; ringed plovers maybe, I thought. The first swung upstream, returned, then swung upstream again, calling with a high-pitched, rising alarm. Whatever it was that disturbed them was no longer in evidence, though I doubted it was us – neither I nor the dog could have been visible to them. Somewhere close by there must have been a nest, though I didn't linger. The first repeated the swerve up and downstream between rocks on the water margins, white bib flashing, and there, the dark neck ring and characteristic Mexican-bandit eye mask.

I sat awhile at Sandy Bottoms – which is anything but – and threw stones into the shallows for the dog to charge after; she has still to release her inner swimmer…

◉ ◉ ◉

An evening walk on the fell. The fields and hills of the valley of the Kent glowed under low sunlight, everything suffused with warmth and golden tones. A deep drone came in, travelling distantly. Two Hercules transport planes appeared from the south, heading towards the Lakes. They travelled below the level of Potter Fell, tilting in unison, following contours. As they passed, I felt the vibrations they made travel up from the ground, into my feet and body.

The jackdaw colony lifted from its roost in the trees below the road, vocalising grievously – *chack, chack, chack* – and travelling in unsettled groups, dispersing over the rooftops and chimneys. The planes disappeared, passing into the gap in the hills and on towards Lake Windermere, progressing at what always appears to me to be an unfathomably slow speed. With them gone, the jackdaws settled back again into the tops of the trees. Everything fell quiet.

July 11

Alchemilla Mollis and all her limey skirts, flouncing over the edges of the border all the way along the garden path. She's all show and no substance, but we can't bear to trim, so instead we walk on the grass and leave her be. After rain, she bestows pearls of water onto the bottom of jeans and over our shoes.

A commotion in one of the gardens. An unhappy blackbird, *tac, tac, tac*, but there was nothing to be seen. I considered trespassing, but thought better of it.

Later, a blackbird up on the weeping birch offered the morning her soft, staccato coo. Then her tone changed to one of alarm and she swooped away down the length of the neighbour's garden. I caught sight of her a few feet away on a piece of trellis. Looking through the binoculars, there beside her under the plants: a fledgling. It watched me watching it. New feather tips were beginning to form on the head, each wing feather adorned by a sleek silvered line, a patina of bronze, of umber and chestnut across the young bird's chest. It changed posture, sinking down on its legs and pushing its feathers out like a robin in winter. For all the world, it had the demeanour of an abandoned child.

◉ ◉ ◉

A curious and unfamiliar *seep, seep, seep* travelled in through the open kitchen window. Monotonous, something I'd not heard before. I abandoned the cooking, fetched the binoculars and headed into the garden. The sound came from the Scots pine, though there was nothing to be seen. The timbre was that of a squeaking wheelbarrow or a rusted door hinge being repeatedly opened and closed. Was it even a bird? The call was as curious as that of a corncrake, and like the hidden corncrake calling to its mate through long grass, it seemed that whatever made the sound was travelling unseen inside the dense needle foliage of the pine. One moment the *seep, seep* travelled towards me, the next it travelled away. I gave up. Back in the kitchen, the sound continued, on and on and on.

◎ ◎ ◎

Late evening, and I was half lying on the floor in the sitting room, propped up on cushions reading, the curtains wide. The half-moon had risen above the fell and floated on a Persian-tile-blue sky. Looking up from the page occasionally, I charted the moon's trajectory around this small quadrant of the earth. It disappeared behind the bay window frame, reappearing in the right-hand pane, glowing and radiant. Stars began to come out. Gulls travelled in loose affiliations over the house and the fell, wing-beating lazily across the deepening blue, south towards the distant bay. The sun, about to set, gilded the undersides of their wings, the upper wings nothing more than travelling shadows.

July 12

Walking home from the green, that sound again: *Seep, seep, seep. Seep, seep, seep.*

I turned into the narrow lane at the bottom of the gardens and there, on the garage roof next door were two small birds calling to each other. One was slightly stockier, brown of back, a little paler of chest, and unremarkable. The other was prettier, mottled with four beads of white patterning on the upper wing coverts and on the head. The chest was soft grey, scallop-patterned and downy. Spotted flycatchers. Although they've nested in Brenda and Cliff's garden down the lane, I had never been aware of them here. The youngster called out the squeaky hinge call, *seep, seep, seep*, its eyes never leaving the parent. I watched them, and though there was little distance between us, they took their time, eventually flitting into the dense growth of a lilac where, once again, I traced their movements by the constant sound of their contact calling.

◎ ◎ ◎

Walking at Silverdale, over the fields of Heald Brow and down to the saltmarsh where the salt tang of the receding tide flavoured every in-breath. Rounding the coast at Jenny Brown's Point, we arrived as the tide ebbed. Battalions of oystercatchers gathered in formation on newly exposed sandbanks close to the shore. Facing out to sea, they were like an army waiting for the enemy to show itself over the horizon.

On the journey home, we stopped in to buy bird seed at Leighton Moss RSPB reserve, and how it happened, I'm not exactly sure, but I found myself leaving with a brand new pair of binoculars – the real deal.

This is how to choose new binoculars: test them by looking over the reed beds and find a marsh harrier floating into your vision. Like a foppish lapwing, it tilts this way and that at the edge of the water. Binoculars sold; unless I become unexpectedly and fabulously wealthy, these will be the ones I use for the rest of my life.

In the wildlife garden behind the cafe, a couple of real birdwatchers began chatting, the conversation turning to blackbirds.

'They become very secretive in moult,' one of them said.

I didn't tell them about the one working the fish and chip van queue in Tobermory.

Back home, I took the new 'bins' out into the garden and scanned the sky for swifts, but the sky was empty. Just an odd jackdaw atop a chimney and a single gull loping home. Minutes later I spied a solitary swift and followed as it arced above the garden, uttering the occasional high frequency *chit...chit*.

The swift spun away, and where it passed above the lane I spied something moving, floating into the lens: a feather. It floated and fell and shifted on eddies of air. As I followed it, I saw the fine shaft and each individuated downy hair. I saw the curve of the quill, the denseness of the vane and the place where it splits open along one edge. I saw the soft open afterfeather at the base. Like a snowflake, I wanted to catch it in my hand.

July 13

A fledgling on the weeping birch and, a short distance away, one of this year's jackdaws. The young blackbird was jumpy: *spink, spink – spink, spink*! The jackdaw moved stealthily towards the blackbird, and the blackbird hopped to a lower branch. Once the jackdaw had flown away, the fledgling moved back to the top branch, where it was joined by a collared dove. The dove began to preen, and was, I noticed, closely observed by the blackbird. A couple of minutes later, the youngster began to preen itself.

July 16

A fledgling feeding party, 7am. The cock and the three offspring were close to the back door, the three youngsters demanding food with their fruity call, only stopping momentarily when dad turned up a morsel. I watched as he flew up to our other clematis, which sprawls over the dividing wall between the gardens. He had, of late, taken on a slightly demented air. He apple-bobbed his head into the clematis over and over, tail to the sky, emerging triumphant every thirty seconds as he found another small yellow snail for the youngsters.

One fledgling on the top of the garden step and the other huddled under the table; the cock needed to be two places at once.

I grabbed the camera and pressed the shutter as the family gathered on the garden bench, and as they hopped towards the steps, I slipped outside and hid behind a climbing rose beside the wall. The cock continued fetching snails from the clematis, the youngsters feeding – as if me being this close taking photographs was just a normal part of family life.

July 18

Back to Mull for the family summer holiday. We arrived, unpacked, and by the time we'd eaten it was 10pm but the light said it was 8. Steve and I drove the short distance to Loch na Keal to watch the sunset. Getting out of the car and wondering if we'd catch a glimpse of any white-tailed sea eagles this holiday, a large raptor passed fifty feet away over the shore, taking a late evening inspection of the wide head of the loch. There was no mistaking that huge hooked beak and white tail. It passed close enough for us to hear the creak of wings. And what wings! I remembered when Steve's stepdaughter had seen her first sea eagle from the back of a boat sailing for the Isle of Rum. The bird had loomed out of nowhere and flown over the stern of the vessel; Anna later described it to us as looking 'like an eagle with barn doors attached'.

The sea eagle looped around the head of the loch, over low water where gulls stood, immobile, on exposed sandbanks. It made a wide, slow curve through the air, each wingbeat taking forever, and began to travel back towards the west. Following its line of flight through the binoculars, I saw the place where it disappeared into the tallest tree in a plantation above the shore, only a couple of miles distant.

July 19

My brother Andy, Fergus and I cycled the road along Loch na Keal, climbing far above the water and eventually, at the summit, the adults stopped to take in the view. Fergus, meanwhile, did not stop even to draw breath, but accelerating at break-neck speed, flew down the other side at such velocity I hardly dared look. Our destination: the Isle of Ulva. Towards the south, the great carved cliffs of the Gribbun and further, the Berg. Inch Kenneth Island dominated the foreground and beyond, the undulating Ross of Mull. Then, pale and distant, blue Iona.

At Ulva Ferry, Steve, Fergus, and our nieces Freya and Eva were waiting. We caught the small ferry across the narrow sound, and after the necessary coffee and cakes at the Boathouse Café, we followed the footpath towards the island's southern coast. We passed through wildflower-rich meadows, and down at the edge of the shore, chocolate-brown Hebridean sheep nibbled at the salt marsh. A wooden signpost pointed the way: 'The Sea, The Sea', it says. I love this, the reference to Iris Murdoch's novel, one of my most memorable reads. We followed the path between a dry stone wall and a bank of wind-contorted hawthorns, the outer reaches of Loch na Keal coming into sight. The teenagers were ahead, marching along with their arms around each other's shoulders. And beyond them, out on the loch, something black – two of them, no, three spheres rolling through the water. I shouted for the kids to use the binoculars, pointing to where the dolphins spun and leapt and were momentarily lost again.

A pod of perhaps ten or twelve dolphins moved towards open

water, rising up and revolving downward again, dispersing across the water, so that we had to keep watch for where they might surface next. Hastening past the sandstone rocks, brushing past brambles and bracken and banks of cow parsley, we ran to the shore. The dolphins, meanwhile, wanted more of the inland waters. They turned, corkscrewing back into the loch.

'There!…There!' the teenagers shouted as the dolphins surfaced, occasionally leaping, clearing the water and ploughing onwards. They stayed around long enough for us to unpack our lunch, sit and – almost – become indifferent. Then the sun came out. The sea flickered with tiny lights, and long white clouds formed above the cliffs on the Mull mainland. The dolphins gone, we walked on to a low headland and into a meadow full of hay rattle, pignut, buttercups, hawkweed, hawkbits and orchids. Cloud shadows moved across the sward, and the path led us up a short, steep bank of rock and into the cool of oak woods. Birch gave way to beech, the path moving onwards past ancient, deeply-mossed walls. And then? What else? More tea, more cake.

July 22

Iona, heavenly Iona. From Dun I, the island's highest point, battered by the wind to the point of madness, we looked out over the Sea of the Hebrides, and together Eva and I looked down the steep slope into the fields near the island's northern tip. Through binoculars, we watched the gathering of sheep. A collie ran low to the ground. The sheep seemed to know what it was they had to do, bunching together into the pens, though some, as usual, separated themselves from the rest of the flock and ran, chaotically.

The farmer sent the dog away, and the recalcitrant sheep were corralled and penned. Then the task of dipping began: the sheep were turned one by one into a narrow pass of fences, the only way out to swim through the dip tank, unceremoniously dowsed as the farmer pushed with his stick until each one was completely submerged.

Later, sheltering from the mad wind in the lee of the big rocks on Traigh Ban beach, we contemplated swimming, and soon thought better of it. Eventually, tearing ourselves away, we set off back to the ferry, passing the fields where the farmers were still hard at work. The sheep were still being hauled up and squeezed through the gate into the dipping tank whilst the collie worked the line of them, up and down, missing nothing, keeping a weather eye on his flock.

◎ ◎ ◎

At Torlochan, more farmers. Some of the kids took turns riding a Highland pony while an older girl led it by the hand. A boy of maybe ten pushed a sleeping toddler up and down the path in front of the house. The sleeper's bottom lip was pushed out, his head to one side. The older boy multitasked, pushing the buggy with one hand and texting with the other. The lambs were separated from the ewes, and the ewes were moved into the field below the houses, apparently wholly unconcerned. As they orientated themselves to their new pasture, swallows dipped and dived over their heads, following the flies that followed the sheep.

◎ ◎ ◎

In the late evening, I went down to the shore close to the sea eagles' nests. I scanned the sky and the tree: nothing. I scanned the water, the rocks and the kelp for the possibility of an otter: nothing. A young lad came out of a farm gate, striding over the foreshore in wellies, fishing rod in hand, singing to himself.

I turned back to the sea eagle tree and there, as if by sleight of hand, appeared an eagle, immobile, its back to me, facing the clear blue sky and improbably tall towers of cumulus clouds. It was so immobile that I had to ask myself if it was really there – surely it was just a conglomeration of branchlets and pine needles. Then came the unmistakeable yap of an eagle, and the bird turned its head to profile. There was no mistake. I scanned the nearby trees for others, and there, spotlit as if by stage lighting, another. The white head and pale chest, the enormous yellow hooked bill and even – yes, even at that distance – the eye, catching and throwing back a glint from the sun.

The second bird was more mobile, rotating its head from side to side, surveying – surveying me, for all I knew. Then a rise of wings, a shake, and the great bird settled again. I shifted the binoculars and, again in profile, further along the same branch: a third eagle, this one subsumed by shadows.

The birds called to each other, *yap, yap*, the sound reaching me by the shore. Above their statuesque heads, travelling like dust motes on the air, tiny birds dipped and rose in small surges of flight against the bright clouds.

The boy cast his line out into the filling tide, and I turned for home.

On the drive up the track to the farm, in the gathering dusk: a white stag and two roe bucks, like an apparition. I stopped the car and took hold of the binoculars. They had been feeding, but now the stag raised its head, his reaction mirrored immediately by the youngsters. They watched me watching them, then turned and jumped effortlessly over the fence, spirited away back into the woods. A sickle moon hung its bright crescent against the coming night.

July 24

The cousins and Andy set off home a day early, leaving the three of us heading up the northern coast of Mull. The previous year, I'd walked to Croig and beyond, alone. I'd stopped to look out over a glassy sea, its texture like spun steel, dissected by thin pathways

of dark and light, and scanned the water surface through binoculars as far out as the island of Coll and further, past the grey,
cloud-gathering silhouette of Rum. On the distant horizon, the
Isle of Barra appeared like the faint roll of a whaleback. Then: a
crack like gunshot, a second later a retort like a muffled echo, and
I'd wondered why anyone would be shooting here, disturbing
the utter peace.

◎ ◎ ◎

The day before, I'd paid my fifty quid and sailed into the Sea of
the Hebrides on a whale-watching boat. There was a small group
of punters on board, some of the new breed of whale hunters
out for the day. We stopped on the way up the Sound to spy on a
white-tailed eagle in her headland nest whilst the water slopped
quietly against the sides of the boat.

The skipper said, 'On the headland, follow the green band,
above the third small tree. Now look up into the branches of
the highest pine.' And there she was: a female, pale-chested, yel-
low-beaked, immobile. The young eagles had fledged a week or
two back; what a place to bring up the kids.

We motored on past Ardnamurchan's lighthouse and out into
the open sea. Inky shearwaters rafted on the water surface, and as
we passed by, they lifted and turned into wave-riders, their wing-
beats passing through holes where the sea collapsed momentarily
before rising again, wingtip to wave-tip.

In the particular intimacy of northern light, cloud shadows
brought the small isles of Muck, Eigg and Rum up close, as if
they were a mere stone's throw away, or a few beats of a gull's
wings. The sea was blue and grey, the water bouncy, waves picked
up and dropped again by a wind that pushed in from the west.
Gannets passed feet away from the boat. They travelled in chains,
following one behind the other as if on a mission, or solitarily, eyes
all a-gimble, weighing up the catch and diving with their wings

articulated behind them, entering the water like white spears, sur-
facing again with a fish, then lifting off and banking away. There
were razorbills and guillemots, too. Every time I see them I think
I've worked out which is which, then I have to stop and think
again. Every so often a puffin passed in front of the boat on a
burr of quick wings. It was one of those days where you couldn't
decide where to look next – so much to do, just looking.

Every so often the skipper left the engine to idle and took
up his binoculars to scan the sea for a whale or dolphin, or for
anything worth reporting. A German couple looked like a photograph in a brochure for a whale-watching trip, him with a leg
raised onto the seating, eyes scanning the sea, and her leaning
back, elbows wedging her into place on the gunwales. He had
on black leather and she white. They were optimistic, expectant
even. The wind messed about with our hair, hands sweeping it
back behind an ear over and over.

We came amongst the Cairns of Coll, a group of rocky outcrops to the north of the Isle of Coll. Doe-eyed seals watched
us with an air of bored interest. The skipper pointed out a pup,
recently born.

'Maybe just an hour old,' he said. 'We won't linger.' The mother
seal fretted, putting herself between the boat and the pup, keeping watch until we'd slid away.

I'd been here the year before, too. On the journey out, we'd
seen singleton minke whales cruising the eastern coast of Coll,
but always distantly, just tantalising glimpses. We landed for our
picnic on an islet with a small white beach. The higher ground
was covered in tall, knotty plants so that it seemed as though
we'd been abandoned in some other hemisphere. One of the
crew snorkelled through jade-coloured water with seals following in his wake, checking out his flippers. He emerged laughing,
and frozen. Then the sea fret came down, and we motored along
the coast of Coll. With the engine cut and the sound of water

slapping the boat sides, we'd heard whales blowing, just metres away between us and the shore. Like Ahab, one of the crew stood with a leg raised on the seating and a hand to his ear.

'Did you get that?' he'd ask, time and again.

And we had. The outflow of breath like a gunshot and the in-breath like an echo.

◎ ◎ ◎

The morning after the trip on the whale boat when no whales had been seen, I walked the track to Croig with the call of great northern divers for company, that haunting sound of the far north. I wanted to go to a small beach I knew, a place we'd been with the kids when they were small. But when I got there, an oystercatcher had other ideas; it began to beat a path through the air, low to the ground, skimming the rocky headland over the white sand, enraged by my presence. So I walked further to a jutting headland of black rocks stained cadmium by blooms of lichen.

Sitting at the very edge of the land above clear citrine-coloured water, I took out my binoculars and began to scan the sea. With the water surface so utterly still, surely there'd be a good chance of a whale, though most likely far away.

I'd seen minkes from land a number of times, most memorably one midsummer as Cal and I returned from a late-evening bike ride along the Sound of Ulva. Simultaneously, we saw the dark forms of whale backs rolling through the sea; there were four of them.

Telling Cal to go down to the shore, I ran to the cottage, grabbed Fergus and the cousins from their beds, then raised Steve and my brother. We carried the kids out into the glowing evening: 'There are whales! Come and see them!' The little ones stood in the field next to the sea in their pyjamas and nighties, rubbed sleep from their eyes and said yes, they could see them, a couple of minutes before they did.

We watched the minkes for ages – feeding and blowing – until the kids asked to go back to bed. Ah, well, only whales, after all.

❂ ❂ ❂

The sound was coming closer, much closer. Then, with a sudden retort, five long black backs rose simultaneously from the water, dorsal fins last to disappear. They were only a matter of fifty metres away, and heading straight towards my place on the rocks. As the whales dived again and their blowholes closed, this stoppering up generating the sudden explosive sound. The whales were following the coast, crossing an inlet between headlands, and were heading straight towards me. Picking up the camera, I ran to the edge just as they disappeared, then pressed the shutter as they rose again and thought, 'Why isn't anyone else here to see?'

The water was aquamarine, clear as a bell. As the whales rolled beneath, I could see them in their entirety – long, black backs, white sides, the beaked snout and smaller tail flukes. A mother and youngster travelled side by side, three more in their wake. The matriarch led the group, rising and falling with her calf through the pellucid sea, and I the only witness to their passing.

The whales breathed and rolled. The light fell on the sea. I put the camera down to savour the moment. They pushed on, that steady, controlled rise and fall.

Fifteen minutes went by, but it might have been hours. The whales travelled, splitting the water surface, disturbing the darker bands that crisscrossed the sea. Each time they went beneath, the water returned to its untroubled state, as if nothing had passed. I began to predict where they would surface next, and sometimes they rose up into my vision through the binoculars. Each time they did, I caught my breath. On they travelled, until I could no longer see them, no matter how hard I looked. I stood to go. Then an otter swam into view in the sea below.

❂ ❂ ❂

Now two years on, and Steve, Fergus and I walked the track from Croig, looking out over a sea that was all sloppy waves jostling against the shoreline rocks. We walked beyond the small beach with perhaps the same oystercatcher I'd encountered the last time I was here, winging admonishingly over the white sand. Eventually we came to the same rocks from where I'd seen the whales.

'It was here,' I said, as if recounting the story might bring them back again. We sat down, ate our sandwiches, talked and looked out over the sea, but nothing happened, just the waves, rolling in, and sea birds, passing offshore. The menfolk moved on but I stayed a while longer. Then, as I stood up, I heard the distinctive slosh of something disturbing the water. Turning around, I saw a long and gleaming fish, a sinuous, energised plume of silver, plunging from its audacious vertical leap back down into the sea. Then the water surface settled again, and I walked away.

July 30

The garden was beginning to win. Bright red wands of *Crocosmia* 'Lucifer' and their elongated, spear-shaped leaves lay in wait, leaning at angles of forty-five degrees across the garden path, ready to snare us into a drenching after rain; it was time for action. I cut the *Crocosmia* and trimmed the stems into a bunch for a birthday bouquet. High cumulus clouds, spaced with the regularity of a painting by Magritte, cruised the paintbox-blue sky.

I turned my attention to the plant pots on the wall: deadheading pink geraniums and Wedgwood-coloured pansies. I noticed a movement on the path over the wall. A blackbird, fluffed out, no tail; I presumed it was a youngster, perhaps from that second brood? The blackbird paused, a long grey worm dangling from her beak, and hopped into the undergrowth. In no time, though, she was back on the path without the worm. Settling on soil spilled onto the edge of the path, she fanned out one beautiful brown wing. Caught by sunlight, it was bronzed. She dustbathed in soil. I could have sworn she looked at me, to see if I'd noticed how lovely she was.

Cal came into the garden and together, camouflaged by the plant pots and geraniums, we watched. Then Cal said, 'She's not a fledgling – look – she's feeding a young one – in there.' Deeper in the undergrowth, all fluffed out, gape open, receiving another insect morsel from the hen's beak. Open wide.

I fetched my binoculars and a bag of raisins from the kitchen, then pinged raisins one at a time onto the path. The hen emerged from the shadows and took the bait. Each time I fired another raisin, she ran towards it, and delivered it to the fledgling. After eight or nine raisins, she'd had enough, and scuttled off in search of real food. Watching the fledgling in turns through the binoculars, we saw sunlight catching its eye, and whether or not it understood that we were there, that eye seemed tuned to where we were.

So, there *had* been a second brood. Or maybe even a third?

We drifted back to the gardening, Cal cleaning out the birdbath. Within minutes of it being refilled, the female entered the garden with a burr of wings and alighted on the edge, drank, and began to wash. A little while later: the high-pitched contact call of an adult blackbird.

'Evening, and the widower blackbird sings his evening song.' Aged fourteen I wrote a poem about blackbirds. I won a competition with it too – perhaps almost no one had entered. But it is this evening song of blackbirds that is so moving, and so poignant, linking me back to that time in a house on an estate at the edge of town. It was after rain, and I had been possessed.

July 31

Out late watching swifts. Battalions of them screaming over the rooftops, travelling at such speed that they were impossible to count. I'd taken to wandering down to the allotments at the bottom of the green lane, close by. I leaned against the gate of an orchard where traditional English apples had been trained and espaliered in perfect formation along wire frames. When I go there, I feel nothing but guilt at the poor unfortunate fruit trees left to get on with it on our allotment – survival of the fittest.

The swifts passed so low overhead that I could feel the air moving above me, and sometimes there was a particular sound – almost like sonar – as they beat the air with their wings. They zoomed through the gap between the eaves of two neighbouring houses. Swifts scream as they pass close to a nest, so somewhere nearby there will be cracks or crevices in stone-built houses. Watching them each evening, I felt that inevitable twist of sadness; any day now they would be gone, beating a wild path all the way to Africa.

But before then, they must feed by following insects and farming them from the skies. As insects spiral higher and higher in turbulent weather, up to a height of a thousand feet or more, the swifts will follow. They have even been known to fly south to France just to get out of the way of storm fronts, the young left torpid in the nest until the parents return.

Opening the gate, walking down the steps into the back garden, the hen without a tail *prinked* quietly from the shade of the Japanese maple, a worm dangling from her beak. She turned her head to one side as I told her that she was beautiful – even without a tail. She flitted across the lane, disappearing behind the tall beech hedge of the garden over the road. New neighbours had moved in; a baby's cry came from an open upstairs window – the first in our patch since Fergus was born.

Nine

SWIFTS IN THE
BATHROOM

August 1

'Any chance you can come over this afternoon? The last few fledglings will be leaving any day now.'

I'd been waiting for a visit to Tanya and Edmund Hoare's house and their colony of swifts. The Hoares are national experts, advising local communities and authorities on swift nesting sites and speaking at the British Trust for Ornithology Conference. I set off for Lowgill.

The Grayrigg road rises out of Kendal, winding and twisting, passing the eastern end of the Whinfell Ridge where a panoramic view of the western mountains opens up. Through Grayrigg itself and on, along the narrow lane leading past meadows bounded by dry stone walls, down the steep hill passing under the M6 and the West Coast Main Line, then taking the turnoff to a row of sandstone ex-railway-workers' cottages.

⊚ ⊚ ⊚

On the TV in the sitting room, four sets of images – all from nest cameras. Two of the nests were empty, the young already flown, but the third had a single pulli cupped by the shallow circular nest, and it was performing swift press-ups. The fourth camera showed two youngsters, one occupying the nest itself and also doing press-ups. Up and down the swifts went, pressing down on their outstretched wings to build muscle and strength for that maiden flight. The second swift had manoeuvred itself to the edge of the nest and was perching on the lip, beneath the eaves of the house.

'They stay like that for days,' Tanya said, 'then off they go and we've no way of knowing if they ever come back.'

Edmund said, 'Come outside – you never know – you may see that one leaving.'

Down a flight of stone steps into the garden, the Howgill Fells were close in, just across the woodland and the River Lune gorge below the houses. These are the smoother, more rounded hills of Lakeland's far eastern terrain. There were garden sheds, washing lines, painted garden furniture, trees, flowerbeds and lawns.

Edmund brought me back to the job at hand. 'If you look up there,' he said, pointing to the black-painted eaves, 'count three stanchions along and you'll see a gap – that's the nest with the two young ones in.'

There was no movement, no adult birds winging in and out – they had already set out for Africa, leaving the young to make that momentous flight alone.

'We have twenty-two potential swift nest sites – in the eaves, nest boxes or swift bricks. Fourteen have been occupied this year, and we expect more will be over time,' Edmund said.

'There's been a forty per cent decline in UK swifts over the last twenty years,' Tanya said. 'The problem is mainly people doing up old houses. They fill in all the gaps, all the crevices where swifts make their nests. These birds are faithful to their nest sites, and they're not adaptable to change, so if they return to find their entrance blocked up, that's probably one more season without breeding. You can see them trying to get in, flying up to the entrance and coming away again. It's so unnecessary. Swifts are very clean too – they don't make a mess like swallows or martins.'

I looked up at the eaves, imagining the youngsters inside, the impetus to leave pulsing through their bloodstream.

I told them of the big old house on Kendal Green that had been put on the market after twenty years or more of standing empty and quietly crumbling, the garden increasingly impenetrable. Inevitably, the new owners had the builders in, and I'd seen screaming parties of swifts zooming between the chimney stacks and the narrow passage between that house and the next.

'That's exactly the kind of place they could be using, and if they were, it's highly likely they've been displaced,' she said.

I thought of the scaffolding, the roofers, the constant jab and bang of nail guns, the drilling out of crumbling mortar and the systematic, hermetic re-sealing, of the chimney stacks being re-pointed, of the swifts, night after night careering around the chimneys once the builders had left for the day. Next year, our house will have swift nest boxes.

◎ ◎ ◎

My closest encounter with a swift came early one morning years back, when I rented a studio space in an ailing Georgian building on the main street in town. In winter, gaps in the roof and the ceilings rendered the place as cold – colder, I think – than Siberia. But in the summer, it was a cool place to work, and I favoured getting there early. I went into the small kitchen to put the kettle on. Lifting the washing-up bowl, something – a treacle-brown creature – struggled uselessly in the bottom of the sink. I am ashamed to admit it: I shrieked.

Instantly, I felt an idiot. I'd behaved stupidly, though to be fair, I had not previously encountered a brown, shuffling creature underneath a washing-up bowl. The poor thing must already have been scared half to death, even before I came along. The swift attempted to manoeuvre itself hopelessly around the sink. After what could have been hours of being stuck there, it was clearly exhausted. My friend Lara arrived. Gently, she wrapped the swift in a tea towel and together we took it down into the yard at the back of the building where, with great good fortune, the local RSPCA office was located.

'I don't hold out much hope,' the man said. 'Birds in acute shock rarely survive.'

Later, we called in, but of course the swift had died. It must have found its way through cavities in the stonework and somehow into the kitchen, where a high window offered the enticement of daylight. What an ignominious end for one of an avian tribe that, in a lifetime, will clock up an average of over two million kilometres.

◎ ◎ ◎

'Come and see the bathroom,' Tanya said, and we went back inside, climbed the stairs and turned into the bathroom at the back of the house. Set into the white-painted wall were six neat, white-painted cupboard doors, each about twenty square centimetres, finished with a small brass handle.

Edmund opened one of the doors. Inside, protected by a double-glazed panel, was a nest box, complete with a circular wooden nest cup lined with white feathers. More white feathers were strewn across the plywood floor.

'They seem to be attracted to white feathers,' Tanya said.

More doors were opened, revealing similar deserted nests and more white down. This would, for me, be heaven – soaking in a bath with that view of the Howgill Fells and occasionally looking across to watch swifts winging in and out. Suddenly, I had a severe case of swift-nest-box-cupboard envy.

'We put all the infrastructure in whilst we were being re-roofed. It was all ready to go when the swifts came back in the spring.'

We went into a bedroom at the front of the house. Two more cupboards were set into the outside wall. Edmund opened a door, and inside was the single chick from 'Swift TV'. We peered in, talked in whispers.

'Sometimes the young need to lose weight to be able to fly. The bodyweight-to-wing ratio is critical. If this were a human, the wingspan would be eighteen feet.'

The youngster began its press-ups, and again I saw those crumpled feet and legs, the pale edges to the primary wing feathers.

'They'll leave here,' Tanya said, 'and head down to the Congo where they'll stay maybe until Christmas time, then some go on even further south to Malawi. We think that the further north they breed, the further south they fly in winter. In April, they begin to move to West Africa, and then north to Europe. One tagged bird took only six days to travel from Liberia to Cambridge.'

'That's some speed of travel,' I said.

'They're too small to carry satellite tags, but geolocators are beginning to be used. The BTO have asked if we could tag some of our swifts with them.'

Downstairs again, Edmund asked if I'd ever seen a swift parasite. I wasn't sure that I wanted to, but he disappeared into the room next door, returning with a plastic jar, the lid mercifully fixed tightly in place.

'*Crataerina pallida* – the flat fly,' Edmund announced, handing the jar to me. 'Collected from the nests after the swifts have gone.' With the slightest movement, the dead parasites rattled together like voodoo charms. I held the jar, at once repelled and horribly enthralled. The parasites were black with three pairs of legs that looked specifically designed to grab on – and not let go. Seeing them, it was impossible not to think about scale: were swifts the size of humans, *Crataerina pallida* would be like a medium-sized crab. Thanking the heavens for small mercies, I handed the jar back.

◉ ◉ ◉

On the television screen, the swift on the lip of the nest peered out from beneath the eaves. I wondered about the magnetic allure of the outside, about how exactly the bird might sense the world, or the idea of scything through the sky for four years, over a continent as different and distant as Africa, when its current experience is little more than the view of a flight of steps, a grassy path, a shed – not that the swift knows them as such, of course.

The fledgling shuffled around on its hopeless feet and came to rest facing the camera. Close to, the face is surprisingly pale compared to the rest of its peat-brown feathers. The eyes are large, bright, very round and very dark, rimmed with the same pale colouration that spreads around the face and down to the throat. Face on, the beak is a cupid's bow, almost cartoon-like, sweet and perfect. It is hard to reconcile this with the sky-farming machine that is a swift, collecting several hundred tiny insects at a time, compressing them into a ball, or bolus, and storing them in their crop ready for disgorging at the nest.

The sweet face turned away, the feet shuffled and the swift perched again on the very edge of its knowledge and experience. The bow-shaped body rocked slightly, its scythe-like wings crossed at their tips. What must that be like, to be on the edge of such a momentous journey?

We talked some more, drank mugs of tea and watched 'Swift TV'. I found that I was simultaneously willing the young swift to leave – and to stay. I wanted to bear witness to the moment of departure, but I wanted it to stay, too. For when would I be in such intimate proximity to a swift again? This was television like none I'd seen before.

August 3

We gather in small groups and loiter on corners, watching the skies. We meet mid-evening and stay out late – or until darkness falls. Oh yes, we know how to live. God alone knows, though, what people make of us.

Wednesday night is swift night. Our group, one of a growing network across the country, gathers to record the places where swifts nest. Once you've got your eye in, it's an addictive pastime. Kendal is great swift territory, given the number of old stone buildings replete with cracks and cavities, though our sub-Saharan visitors also take well to swift bricks and boxes installed on newer houses. The trick is to plan ahead, install the infrastructure ahead of their arrival back from Africa in May, and even play recordings of swifts screaming from tiny speakers set next to or inside the boxes. Then stand well back and wait for young breeders to investigate. With a bit of luck, they'll turn it into a home.

◎ ◎ ◎

We were a glum lot as we met up on Queen's Road. Any day, the swifts would be gone, our skies emptier, less exhilarating. This was the last meet of the summer. The season had been a good one, and several new colonies had been mapped on our data sheets. That night though, the sky was quiet; perhaps they'd already gone.

Last week we'd loitered in our usual menacing fashion at the back of a terrace of houses behind the corner shop. Three times we'd seen swifts reeling overhead, the characteristic swoop down and rise up, disappearing like a conjuring trick into a tiny gap in the stonework. In one of the houses, a bathroom light was on, and the sound of singing came through the open window.

A young man came out of a gate. Speaking in precise English, he said, 'Good evening. Is there something I can help you with?'

'We're watching swifts,' one of us said, and I took a leaflet out to show him – a picture of swifts in flight with that scythed wing shape. Then a swift obligingly swooped in and magicked itself inside its nest, close to a drainpipe.

'So, this is why we have problem with leaking,' the man said.

'Oh no, they don't do any harm at all. They don't even make any mess. They just nest in small cavities between the stones.'

'I report to landlord. He can fix holes.'

'It's not a problem – they really don't do anything. Most people don't even know they're there.'

'Okay. I let landlord know about leak,' he said, and took his leave.

We looked at each other, did that '*he just doesn't get it*' thing with our arms, and despaired; that some folk are so removed from any sense of relationship with wild things, their knee-jerk reaction is attack. Give me strength.

◎ ◎ ◎

Cliff said, 'Look!' – and there they were: dark, fast-moving pin-pricks at altitude. The clouds they moved across were high, filmy and white. Gradually the swifts began to beat a lower circuit, moving in wild, swirling patterns, a gang of perhaps forty, or more.

Following the swifts, we too moved, down the steep cobbled lane to Serpentine Road. The top houses have flights of access steps and, sitting at the vantage point of their doorstep, were a man and a woman, also taking in this transitory aerial spectacle. The evening was still. The sound of vehicles moving through town below reached up to us, but there was a kind of Mediterranean stillness, and against this the swifts swirled in mad, careering pathways, lower, ever lower, until they seemed almost, though never quite, amongst us.

The terraced houses fit together in an organised jumble of layers. Cliff had the address of a woman who had told him she had swifts nesting in the back of her house. We called by. The woman answered the door and said, 'Follow me.'

Round the back of a short terrace, we entered a series of small inter-connected yards. Next door to the woman's, an empty house had been scaffolded from the ground to the roof. We ducked underneath it and found ourselves in a small yard dominated by a single apple tree, its branches extending out over a steep drop to the backyards of the street below. Swifts whizzed overhead.

'There's a nest there,' the woman said, pointing to a crack between the limestone blocks high up in the wall, 'and there's another' – she changed the angle of her arm – 'though they've fledged now.'

The house with the scaffolding was being renovated for sale, but the builders hadn't been seen for months. That house, too, was home to swifts. Would they return next year to find themselves out of a home? Imagine travelling four thousand miles from the Congo back to Kendal, recognising not only the airspace, but the town, the exact rooftop and chimney, the exact sliver of a hole that was yours a year before. And not being able to get in.

Back on Serpentine Road, one of our group, Ros, was talking to a man. People often ask what we're up to. They're interested, though rarely do they know the difference between a swift and a swallow.

Alone, on a hunch, I walked to the access path behind the backs of a terrace of tall houses, and as the sky drained of light and evening brought down her sombre cloud, swifts began their mad arcs of flight, cleaving a path downward and rising up into tiny dark spaces underneath the eaves. I stayed until darkness had gathered in and the sky had emptied of its bewitching cargo.

August 5

On Cunswick Scar a kestrel hovered and fluttered over the rising ground, dipping and climbing as it hunted. I gained the skyline only to see it drop into a hawthorn. I took up the binoculars, watched the kestrel drop to the ground, lift effortlessly into the hawthorn, and then down to the ground again. I took in the details, the white face, chin and wing bar, before it took to the air again, veering far away over the edge of the Scar, colours shifting as it swivelled in flight.

August 10
Swift countdown. This morning one lone swift reeled through the sky above the house.

In the evening: five swifts, hunting in silence.

August 11
At the top of the fell, early, a vignette of grey wagtails walking and feeding on tractor tracks imprinted in the grass. I'd heard the tractor from our allotment, recognising the frantic to-ing and fro-ing as it razored the turf into golf sward. By some unknown process, dew had formed on the grass but not on the tyre tracks, and the wagtails were keeping their feet dry. A jackdaw floated past, swivelling artfully. Swallows skimmed the ground, low enough to drink the dew.

◉ ◉ ◉

An evening walk up School Knott and a grandstand view over Windermere towards the blue hills: Coniston Old Man, Wetherlam, Greyfriar in the gap, Crinkle Crags, Bowfell, Scafell and Scafell Pike, the twin peaks of the Langdales – Harrison Stickle and Pike o' Stickle – Pavey Ark, Sergeant Man, the Fairfield Horseshoe, the Kentmere hills. Drinking in the panorama under billowy light spun between clouds of pale grey, a single, late swift appeared. It circumnavigated the hilltop, and me, twice, then cut a scythe-like dash, dissecting north from south, cool England from equatorial Africa. I like to think it was the swift's farewell.

August 18

A morning walk beginning on the shadowy path underneath the Helm with my friend Wendy and our dogs. The rosebay willow-herb was beginning to form its characteristic seed capsules, each capsule bearing up to four hundred seeds, each plant carrying as many as eighty thousand. As summer segues into autumn and on into November, willowherb, or fireweed, converts into spires of candy floss – interwoven, curlicue seedheads with silky hairs that aid dispersal by the wind. Lest anyone should fear that eighty thousand seeds are a paltry sum to send off into the world, willowherb, once established, also spreads by a burgeoning network of underground roots. For now, though, the seeds are forming on the lower stages of the plant, whilst the flowers towards the top are yet to burst open – a veritable Mexican Wave of flowering, seed formation and floating away.

We climbed the southern crest to the summit of the hill and the trig point above the remains of an Iron Age fort. Just south of Kendal, the Helm stands in isolation and offers a three-hundred-and-sixty-degree view. Across the fields and folds of small valleys, traffic on the M6 hurtled silently towards its future.

We walked and talked, the dogs ignoring each other though meeting on the common ground of scent trails. We headed downhill to the small tarn in a sheltered hollow. The Helm's resident Fell ponies were there, mid-tarn, paddling, cooling off, their long black tails trailing in the water. The ponies pulled up pond-weed from beneath the surface, nodding their heads, water pouring out from the weed back into the tarn, the sound of it carrying.

There were seven black ponies and a grey. One of them sauntered over, indifferent to the dogs, who just wanted to chase sticks in the tarn. I was talking to the pony, rubbing its forehead, when Wendy said, 'My phone's gone completely dead. I was taking photos and it just went.' I tried to press the shutter on mine and nothing happened. 'Weird,' I said. 'Mine's dead, too.'

There was a pause whilst we both phone-fiddled.

Wendy said, 'Huh, maybe we're in some kind of freaky dead zone.'

Then we got lost – twice, ridiculously failing to find the path back to the car, ending up dead-ended by gorse bushes. And the dogs, though we urged them to find the way, were spectacularly useless.

Three hours later, my phone mysteriously came back to life.

August 22

Driving along Queen's Road, a twiggy branch fell onto the tarmac, mid-road, dead in front of the car. In the arching branches above, a grey squirrel was hanging over the middle of the road by its two front paws: James Bond in squirrel-land. The driver of the car coming towards me stopped too. The squirrel eventually swung itself back up onto the branch, shook itself and headed off back into the cover of the canopy. The other driver and I smiled and waved as we passed.

◎ ◎ ◎

I know a place where the rock drops away from the edge of Scout Scar. I go there sometimes to sit down, to drink in the liquid evening light that pours over the Coniston hills. It was 8.30pm. Clambering carefully down, I disturbed a colony of rooks. They had been dozing on the sun-warmed ledges and shelves of limestone. Crossly, they peeled away into the wide air, *chack-chak, chak*. But one slept on, its eyes still closed. For a moment or two more, the rook was blissfully unaware of being left behind. But the airborne chorus of disapproval continued, and finally the rook awoke and scarpered off to join the gang. I swear he looked aghast. The collective noun for rooks is a 'parliament'; it seemed I had caught one member napping.

August 23

August is the month of scabious on the fell, the soft lilac haze of them spreading across the sloping, unmown meadows. Evening sunlight slides in sideways from the north-west. It illuminates all, turning the mown fields beyond the town lime green, the bracken-covered slopes of Potter Fell auburn-blushed. The small fells interwoven between here and the mountains are patchworked by hedge and hedge-shadow. Cumulus clouds sail mountain-ward, streets of blue between. I climbed up into the last of the light. Looking down from the fell, it seemed the town was at the centre of all things. It is the pivot point from which the landscape unravels, the place that keeps me grounded.

Much of the cow parsley had already gifted its white lace to seed – dull-gold, like doll-house coins. Some retained their glowing, creamy umbels. Bees and hoverflies worked the late shift. Swallows looped and twisted through the air; I missed their sibling swifts.

August 27

Dark sky, 11pm. The light had fallen below the western rim of the hills. There were no clouds, only stars, and I couldn't settle.

'Helsington?' I suggested to Fergus. Any excuse for a late night. We got in the car, and though the Perseid meteor showers had been and gone, I wondered if we might still see something.

We drove the lanes and, a handful of miles out of town, turned down the narrow road to the small country church. There was one other car, and a man stood by the viewpoint. The capacious darkness of the Lyth Valley was punctuated by tiny points of light from scattered farms and hamlets. Morecambe Bay shimmered with a linear, crepuscular orange radiance.

Overhead, the Milky Way scattered its silvery light. I picked out the Plough, Orion, Castor and Pollux, Gemini.

'Hello,' the man said. 'Come to see anything in particular?'

I wasn't sure, but offered, 'I think we're too late for the Perseids, but we fancied a look anyway.'

'They're long gone – I'm taking pictures – have a look.'

He had a camera on a tripod and a giant telephoto lens. Placed on the top of the viewpoint illustrator was an iPad.

He showed us the night sky reinterpreted through the screen, and began to zoom in. We watched as the black depths of space began to fall away, and stars, more than I'd thought possible, filled the screen. The more the man zoomed in, the more the white starlight took over and the dark space was utterly reduced, turning all my knowledge and experience on its head.

He told us about a star that died aeons ago, yet its light was only reaching us now, and in less than a week, it would fade and never be seen again – though the process of fading would in reality take a cool few billion years or so. He was here to take its portrait, to catch it and keep it. He showed us the extinct star on the screen. And I had been hoping for a mere shooting star…

The electric light at the corner of the church, meanwhile, had been flashing off and on, and large moths frazzled into and out of its glow. I watched them quivering in and out, and then I saw the bat. The clever bat. It had worked out that by flying past the corner of the church, the light comes on, and stays on long enough to bring moths. The bat beat its nocturnal hunting path through the glow, twisting and returning, hoovering moths from out of the night.

August 30

I left the house mid-evening in melancholy mood. Summer's end. As if anticipating the season's shift, a robin sang his small waterfall of song from the brambles in an abandoned allotment.

The sun had shifted place, setting further to the south over the

Coniston fells. The lowering rays slid down towards me through the shivering dry grasses, the harebells, the pale-blue disks of field scabious. It was as if the earth itself emitted light. In the north-west, clouds, like waves about to break, were brightened at their prows. In the ethereal blue of the southern sky, clouds formed like ripples in a pool. The first field-mists rose above the River Kent near Burneside. A blackbird *prinked* constantly, somewhere in the smir of darkness amongst the leaves of a garden maple. Buried deep in cloud, an aeroplane rumbled away towards the east.

Ten

ON WOLVES AND EAGLES
AND EMPTY FELLS

Early Autumn

Years ago, someone told me about a cave on Kendal Fell where the bones of long-extinct animals had been found. The story stayed with me and, frequently, as I walked the path through the trees and came into the old limestone quarry, I would linger, investigating dark recesses underneath great bulwarks of limestone, wondering if this might be the place. None, though, revealed anything other than the earth and rock peeling away from each other, scatters of stones, wild flowers and the odd abandoned drink can.

Recently, the local newspaper ran the story of a wolf skeleton that had been excavated from the same cave, discovered in the late 1800s by amateur Victorian archaeologist, Kendal resident and master chair-maker, John Beecham. At the age of sixty-five, Beecham had discovered the entrance on a scrub-covered, little-visited part of the fell, and over a handful of summers, he spent his evenings digging.

Beecham was one of a band of amateur archaeologists who had been inspired by Sir William Boyd Dawkins, a Manchester-based archaeologist whose book *Cave Hunting* was published in 1874. The book not only gave details of the new and exciting archaeological finds being used to determine the age of early human life, but also offered advice to the amateur explorer on how to set about cave excavation. In the second half of the nineteenth century, popular science and journalism keenly followed burgeoning research into early human existence, and the most significant human finds were being found in caves.

In the photograph in the newspaper, the wolf skeleton seemed small and hunched – more greyhound than lupine. Beecham had found the almost-intact remains at the very back of the cave and only after resorting to blasting the last recess open with dynamite, having 'worked on with dogged pluck for five continuous summers'.[12] It's a miracle, then, that anything much survived. I can picture Beecham now – lowering himself inside and working away in the narrow cleft, sending shovelfuls of earth out of the entrance until he came to the last aperture in the sediment. Then, lying flat on his stomach, head twisted sideways on the cave floor, catching the tantalising glimpse of a further space, brief shadows from his candle dancing.

Beecham is recorded as having said, 'The poor brute, feeling, no doubt, that its end was approaching, had retired behind a large rock, and there had died in self-imposed solitude.'[13] It's not inconceivable that the wolf walked over the ground where my house now stands on its routine journeys in search of food.

Enthusiastic if inexperienced Victorian museum staff articulated the wolf skeleton incorrectly, lending it a cowering, dog-like demeanour. The name 'Helsfell wolf', as it has come to be called, is derived from a little-used name for Kendal Fell: Helsfell Heights. And what better name for a wolf, and a wolf hideout? A cave, a wolf and a plethora of evidence of the fauna that once lived here, of how our landscape once was, all no more than ten minutes' walk from my back door.

Along with the wolf, Beecham discovered the bones of a

hedgehog, bear, fox, wildcat, polecat, otter, pine marten and sheep. There were also red deer, roe deer, goats, house mice, short-tailed field mice, *Bos longifrons* (Iron Age ox) and rabbits.

At some point, Beecham sold his collection to Kendal's Literary and Scientific Institution where they were put on display. A few years later, the Reverend Macpherson, author of *A Vertebrate Fauna of the Lakeland*, published in 1892, recorded the eighteen mammals that Beecham also found in the cave.

◉ ◉ ◉

At Kendal Museum, curator Carol Davies led me up the grand staircase, through an upper floor past natural history dioramas, mineral collections and a case of vibrant yellow moths. In the storeroom were avenues of steel shelving and walls lined with more shelves, all stacked with glass cases containing birds of all shades and sizes. Hanging over the glass face of one was a white label, handwritten in thick ink: 'White Thrush – Damaged – Awaiting Conservation.' There were hoopoes, Arctic skuas, Brünnich's guillemots, a golden eagle. Fifty different species of hummingbird in a Victorian glass dome, frozen mid-hum. Carol peeled back a layer of protective film, and I found them to be iridescent, compelling, though ultimately flawed because of what they represented: the paradigm shift in attitudes to conservation since the time they were caught and now. High up on the wall at the end of the room was a set of giant antlers – Irish elk. Under grey plastic wraps, other giant creatures, awaiting the conservator's touch.

'We're a small museum,' Carol said, leading me over to her desk, 'but our natural history collection rates second only to the Natural History Museum.'

On a computer, she opened a picture of the Helsfell wolf, an image of such forensic quality that zooming in close brought the bones into ever-sharper detail. In that intimate view, made more potent against a simple black background, I saw that the wolf's skull was minutely fissured by the cranial sutures, that the teeth were white, undamaged, and that the jaw had been bound at some point in the past with fine wire. There was, though, nothing to suggest that the specimen was ancient; although the bones were pitted with stains from having lain in cave sediment for goodness knows how long, they seemed, to my amateur eye, well preserved.

'Isn't it wonderful?' Carol said.

Then there were photographs of the Helsfell Cave's interior. It seemed nothing to write home about – just a narrow fissure in the limestone, perhaps a mini-adventure to explore if you happened to stumble upon (or into) it. But it's well hidden, in an off-route piece of scrubland, accessed through a mere hole in the ground. In the next picture, there's a hand extending out of the earth attached to a blue rope: someone in the act of being lowered down inside.

'That's me going in,' Carol said. 'It's not easy – as you can see. You have to be lowered down, then the passage goes back underneath the hillside for some twenty-three feet.'

The wolf skeleton was currently elsewhere, awaiting restoration and re-articulation at the Lancashire Conservation Studios in Preston – an urban residence for a wolf if ever there was one. But in a matter of months, the Helsfell wolf will once again be wolf-like – and *Canis lupus* will be coming home to Cumbria.

◉ ◉ ◉

Later, I went for a walk. Following more instinct than reason, I went off-track on the fell into an area of scrub and woodland, then clambered up steep ground over shale and long grass. Brambles and self-seeded ash trees blocked the way, forcing me to continually change direction. Eventually though, I found it – a small person-sized hole in the ground. Crouching at the edge, I peered down into nothing. I dropped in a small stone, heard a chink as it hit rock some undiscernible distance below.

Having been there and seen it for myself, I can confirm that it is testament to Beecham's capacity to search such inaccessible ground that the cave was ever found. But what of the rest of his finds? Some were sent to the Natural History Museum in London by Macpherson, and after Beecham's death, his personal collection was dispersed. In the 1950s, most of it, though not the wolf, was sold to Liverpool Museum, where it remains to this day. And whilst Beecham himself had taken good care of the finds, late nineteenth- and early twentieth-century professionals caused nothing short of archaeological chaos. Bones from other dig sites became mixed with the Helsfell material, and thus dispersed, the scientific importance of the collection was utterly diminished.

But oh, give me bears and wild boars, give me wildcats and wolves. Give me a wolf called the Helsfell wolf. Though it was named after a place, that very name lends it a sense of the wolf archetype – the slavering beast, red-eyed, roaming and terrify-ing settlements, killing livestock, and, justifiably (on those terms), hunted into oblivion. But today the world view has shifted exponentially.

'Bring back the wolf!' cry the rewilders. Bring back the wolf that it may restore the balance. Wolf: now a symbol of land reform, the bringer of reason to a skewed world. Over hundreds of years, our Lakeland fells have been reduced to nothing more than 'sheep-wrecked deserts'.[14] Sheep – and deer for that matter – eat everything, they strip the land bare. You've only to look at the difference between an area grazed by conservation grazers, native Fell ponies, or Galloway cattle to see the difference. Both sheep and deer move slowly, grazing everything right down to the ground. They target flowering plants, and over time those plant species die away, reducing diversity. Conservation grazers, though, leave areas uneaten, allowing plants to thrive and regenerate.

Meanwhile, local and county councils, the National Park Authority and others, including hill farmers backed by central government, have put the Lake District forward in a bid for inscription as a UNESCO World Heritage Site. What the hill farming community argue is that it is essential to preserve the historic, 'cultural' landscape that the farming of sheep across the fells has created. Non-indigenous, the Roman-nosed Herdwick sheep are descended from livestock introduced by the Vikings. But what, I wondered, is there to celebrate when the uplands are a mere fleeting shadow of their former selves? Far too many of our valleys and fells are denuded, ruined by overgrazing. Where is the tree cover and scrub with all its attendant wildlife? Where are the sustained corridors of woodland that would make it possible for species to travel, to re-establish their presence in our landscape? Where is the reason, even, in *not* re-establishing them in our uplands? Ours is now the only country in Europe whose uplands are almost wholly devoid of forest cover. If wildlife corridors *were* reinstated, that would indeed be something to celebrate. I've walked the fells for years, and on most days in the mountains it's typical to see, at best, a couple of crows, perhaps a buzzard and occasional summer migrants, wheatear, the odd raven and pipits.

In the Middle Ages, when the Helsfell wolf and its grey cohort roamed across the territory, the land between the cave and the mountains would have been a collage of grassland, woodland, wood pasture and glades kept open by grazing mammals. The closed canopy woodlands would, in time, thin out and become pasture woodlands. There may, too, have been small areas of strip farming. The gradient of the fell would have continued downwards towards the valley, and no doubt the river was an important source of food. I like – no, *relish* – knowing for certain that wolves once roamed the land on my doorstep – that in all probability, they passed through what is now the garden, following scent trails, nosing the air, implicitly wary.

⊙ ⊙ ⊙

In 2015, the Royal Geographic Society held a debate at the Rheged Visitor Centre called 'Whose Broad, Sunlit Uplands?' The auditorium was packed. Most of the audience appeared to be from the farming community. We listened to the panel members: sheep farmers, a member of the UNESCO bid team, a representative of Friends of the Lake District, Cumbria Tourism and conservationists Ian Convery and Steve Carver, professors both, who talked about how the planting of trees brings with it the natural consequence of an expansion of species, how trees take up vast amounts of water and stabilise mountainsides – things that will become pivotal in our changing climate and times of intense rainfall.

Then there was talk of reintroducing the Eurasian lynx – an original native species of the UK. Naturally secretive animals, lynx rarely kill livestock, preferring to predate on roe deer, red deer and agricultural pests such as rabbits and foxes. They also feed on game birds. Reintroducing a top predator would allow more vulnerable species to regenerate. It would protect forests damaged by over-large deer populations. Add to the mix eco-tourism, now a major worldwide industry, and the financial gains to the local economy could be significant. (I thought of the huge draw of Mull's white-tailed sea-eagles, and compensation schemes for farmers, if and when the eagles take lambs). To me, it was all compelling stuff. But Phillip Walling, the barrister-turned-sheep-farmer-turned-writer-on-sheep, accused the conservationists of being terrorists – *terrorists,* dear God. And he would not let them speak.

Even amongst the chaos of climate change – something we in the north understand only too well – we appear to be no nearer to understanding what the land is telling us. Deeply-entrenched positions rooted in the idea of preservation, rather than conservation, serve no purpose.

Sometimes the Lake District feels like a battleground. When the RSPB took over the running of three farms in the Haweswater and Swindale valleys, on land in major water catchments owned by United Utilities, they began to remove excess numbers of sheep from the fells and to plant trees. These tree plantings were essential, their farm manager told me over coffee in the kitchen at Naddle Farm, necessary to improve all kinds of things – water quality at source being one. The new trees will help to hold the soil in place, preventing it from being washed away into the rivers. It's a powerful and convincing argument, but the tree planting had begun without a dialogue with the farming community – in a community where talking to your neighbours is key.

Cumbria contains thirty-five per cent of all the common land in England. It is used by farmers whose sheep are traditionally hefted to a particular area of the fells, and most of the neighbouring farmers in the Haweswater area wanted their traditional system of sheep farming to remain. To them, the new trees created a challenge, some seeing it as an attack on their traditional way of life. There was talk of enclosure by stealth, that the planting of trees is radical, its benefits unproven.

But things are no longer as they once were. The need for change is upon us. In fact, it is being demanded of us by the greater test of climate change and the negative effects on towns and communities downriver.

I wanted to see this changing landscape for myself. I walked into the Swindale valley, passing remnants of ancient Atlantic oak woods bounded by old dry stone walls. Both walls and trees were dressed in refulgent mosses, the woodland peppered with the bright white stars of wood anemones, bluebells made cobalt under shade and the first, fresh-green uncurlings of bracken. Atlantic oak woods are an internationally important habitat for many species. Improve the wild infrastructure, and here will be barn owls, tawny owls, little owls, pied flycatchers, redstart, great spotted woodpeckers, ring ouzels, merlins, peregrines, red grouse, ravens, skylarks, meadow pipits, whinchats and wheatears that dart up the fellsides with that flash of white rump. On the open ground, mountain ringlet butterflies, the biplane whirrings of golden-ringed dragonflies, keeled skimmer dragonflies, numerous moth species, and plants that include bird's-eye primrose, rock lady's mantle, bog rosemary, northern spleenwort, Alpine Enchanter's nightshade, Snowdon eyebright, petty whin, bog orchid, spring sandwort, pale forget-me-not, wood fescue. By carrying out those tree plantings, the RSPB and United Utilities are contributing to the ingress and expansion of those species and more. Some that are not present will arrive, others that once were – the native plants and brambles, remain in the earth, waiting for the opportunity to come back – once the dominance of sheep is reduced. Now think of those species expanding over an incipient wildscape. Think of how many birds would fill the sky.

◎ ◎ ◎

It was April. I walked along the road past three farms, the last of which, tucked under a dip of land at the road end, had been sold off and was in the process of being renovated. In the lush springtime, the riverside meadows were full of sheep and new lambs, and the hillsides were aflame with gorse. New tree plantings rimmed the valley-sides. Somewhere up on the fellside, a cuckoo spread joy and alarm in equal measure. Further into the valley, I scrambled over mounds of old glacial moraines. They were covered in the blue haze of bluebells – genetic markers, the remnants of ancient forest cover, as if that in itself isn't reason enough to re-colonise the landscape with trees. I walked past the vertical plume of Hobgrumble Gill, then climbed beside the enticing pools and water-shoots of Swindale Beck Forces Falls. Infant trees had been planted in their thousands, all the way up onto the fellsides. The landscape was in the process of change;

time will be its illustrator.

On another day, I returned to walk the old way towards the drowned village of Mardale Green on the north shore of Haweswater, its sheet of dark water restless, made uneasy by a blustery wind. Pencil-thin rivulets of white spume drifted across the surface, wavelets lifting. Above and below me, spanning the fellsides, were the plantings – native trees being brought back, though their future impact on the landscape could only be imagined through the lens of thousands of plastic sapling tubes. Change was imminent. What would happen to the view down towards the water? Would it be lost? Would we walkers eventually become hemmed in, our field of vision narrowed, framed by trees? I had come to see the plantings, to rethink the fellsides: the true impact would not be felt for decades. This was landscape management on the grand scale – being reimagined for the future.

I'd come here to think about trees and fells, about sheep and farmers and the waking up of dormant life, but I left with a completely other and unanticipated image seared into my memory.

Long views lead down the length and breadth of the lake to Harter Fell and the steeply rising crags of the Riggindale Ridge, the profile drawn by the spine of a broken-backed dry stone wall. It draws the eye, the eternal marker of the place where the village of Mardale Green had been, before the valley was drowned. I marked out its craggy knolls moving down from the summit – Caspell Gate, Rough Crag, Heron Pike, Eagle Crag.

In the preceding days, there had been much rain, and before long I heard the sound of Measand Beck coming in on gusts of wind. I stopped on the wooden footbridge crossing the falls and watched the roiling black water foaming as it poured over boulders aged by acid-yellow lichen. Rowan, ash, birch and gorse crowded in towards the torrent, lining the path of the beck before it broke again onto the open fellside below.

The mewing of a buzzard overhead – following the sound, I looked up the fell and saw what I thought at first was a pair of buzzards interacting with one another. One of them banked away towards the fell-top, the other contoured across the open fellside with lazy wing-beats, some one hundred feet above me. But this second bird was larger, much larger than the buzzard. I saw that the undersides of the wings had pale patches. As it skimmed a stand of gorse, the buzzard moved in close again; the two were neither of the same size nor species. The buzzard made a second pass and the eagle – for that is what it was – swivelled upside down, talons almost making contact with its aggressor.

The buzzard climbed the sky and disappeared beyond the fell. The eagle moved across the complication of bushes and trees, then broke against the background of the sky. Its appearance there provoked a gathering of rooks to scatter from the tops of a plantation of forestry pines. They began to mob and harass the eagle. It manoeuvred, folding its wings and falling, before resurrecting its flight and resuming its climb into the grey sky. Next, two tiny birds, too small to identify but the size of sparrows, joined the rooks. The eagle's wings folded again. Its body swivelled artfully to one side, then to the other, so that it dropped out of the fracas purely by the weight distribution of its body. The rooks, like loitering teenagers, seemed undecided what to do next. They lingered close by, filling a space of sky with their scattered forms. Then, regrouping, they moved in again to drive their point home. The eagle dropped away into the far side of the skyline, but I stayed on, waiting and watching. A few times more it reappeared, always trailing a small number of rooks, moving higher. A group of gulls came into focus, passing high above the action, as if the matter was of no concern to them – which undoubtedly, it wasn't.

◉ ◉ ◉

Another week further into April, and I headed back to the valley, walking around the marshy, beck-spangled head of the reservoir, and rounding the base of the Riggindale Ridge. I dropped down into the 'valley of the eagles' (or, as it was from 2004 to 2016, 'eagle', in the singular). It was late afternoon. The bright sun was dowsed by high clouds moving in from the west. But still, at last, the evenings were drawing out.

In the middle distance, a man was walking back down the valley. As we passed each other, he said, 'Good luck – no sign of the eagle today, I'm afraid.'

Up at the eagle observation point: a wooden shed, now closed; sheltered in the lee of a dry stone wall, I settled in. Ravens floated over the ridge of Riggindale and disappeared again. They were high, but very dark and very 'raveny'. I leaned over the wall, binoculars ready, occasionally lifting them to scan the rocky crags or to follow another raven pair rocking and rolling over the distant ridge and, minutes later, following as they came careering back into the valley. Clouds shifted from white and bright to brooding and grey. Bright patches of colour were extinguished from the steep brackeny ground of the valley sides. The temperature dropped, and I took out my hat and gloves. If places had moods…

When it came, the sighting was brief. The last eagle in England broke above the ragged outline of the ridge – high up where Long Stile ends and the final pull to the summit of High Street begins. Its wings beat the air slowly and steadily, palmate at the broad tips, before it moved off into the next valley, and that was that.

◎ ◎ ◎

There was a time when I'd journey to Haweswater several times a year in the hope of an eagle sighting. I would either climb the ridge or walk to the hide in Riggindale, where telescopes would be focussed on the female on her cragged bridal nest, brooding, or on the male, elsewhere, remaining perfectly stationary after

feeding, apart from that swivelling head and those keenly observant eyes. One memorable, drought-ridden summer, prior to the
death of either the male or the female, the lake level had fallen
dramatically, leaving a deep rim of water-scorched gravel around
the reservoir's rim, rendering the lake-scape bleak and industrial.
I'd climbed the Riggindale Ridge, and high up on Long Pike, I'd
lain on my back on warm grass, eyes shielded against the sun, and
watched the male and female together, soaring upwards on thermals, their silhouettes etched on high cumulus clouds. They circled above the confines of the valley, silhouetted against the great
white clouds, and I watched them continuing their stratospheric
climb, moving ever higher on thermals with barely a wing-beat,
until they were so high, they simply disappeared.

With the female found dead in 2004, the valley was left with
a lone male. The poignancy of his display flight every spring,
signalling to a mate that never came, was difficult to see, to say
the least. When I had met the eagle warden at Naddle Farm, I'd
asked what, if anything, might be done to maintain the presence
of eagles here in the valley.

'If you brought another adult bird in, it would have to be five
years old, old enough to breed. And there are massive problems
around capturing a mature eagle – they're a protected species.' He
went on, 'The landscape here isn't big enough to support more
than one eagle territory. Unlike sea eagles, goldies are really sus-
ceptible to disturbance by people. Riggindale works as an eagle
territory because it's one of very few valleys in Cumbria without
access. There are no footpaths beyond the hide and no way off
the fells – the terrain is too steep, but it's still too busy in eagle
terms. The Lake District is just too small.'

But these birds *should* be widespread. A former RSPB warden
and ornithologist, Dave Walker, studied the Lake District eagles
for over twenty-six years. He made the most comprehensive
study of them, and believes that more, *much* more, could have

been done to support their existence in our landscape.

One of the most compelling parts of Dave's testimony was that of the lack of food. Eagles will take small, live prey – Dave had once witnessed a squirrel being snatched from the top of a tree. But they take carrion too, and there was simply not enough carrion or small mammals around to keep a pair of eagles fed. But rather than do nothing, to accept the line of non-intervention, as the RSPB had, Dave's answer was to provide food for them himself. He brought in the carcases of sheep and culled red deer. It was Dave who found the last female's lifeless form on the hillside in 2004.

In February 2016, the RSPB announced the death of England's last golden eagle. No corpse has ever been found, and sightings of the eagle continue to be reported. But why stick around an empty Lakeland valley, when you're hungry, and alone?

So England's last golden eagle 'sky-danced' over eleven consecutive years as spring arrived, in a vain attempt to attract a mate. Launching himself from a high crag, the eagle would flow upwards to a great height above the valley. As the ascending trajectory neared its completion, and with the speed of ascent slowly contracting, he would fold his wings tight against his body, which continued to rise, then, at the zenith of his arc, he would tilt forwards, ready for the dive back towards the earth, gradually releasing his wings to fall in a shallow parabola of flight, over and over again.

There was always the hope that a young female, forging her own path out from the Dumfries and Galloway hills, might travel south across the Solway and find herself here in the last eagle's territory, but what, I wondered, were the chances of that? I'm no statistician, but I guess the odds were always slim, especially with the sheer numbers of people out on the hills around the valley. Writing of that futile spring display, an RSPB comment in the press read, 'We should be pretty proud; it's fantastic.'

❂ ❂ ❂

But I digress. Back to the wolf. Recently, the Helsfell wolf has been graced by modern conservation and re-articulated into the correct bone structure. The head is erect, the limbs are tensile – wired, one could almost say. We know now that we are in the presence of a wolf. Though records believed that the wolf dated from the sixteenth century, Carbon-14 dating now places it much earlier – as having lived between 1139 and 1197. The new museum literature cites the skeleton as unique in its Cumbrian context, and that archaeological sites for *Canis lupus* in the north-west of England are rare. The next bit I love – that 'the density of place-name distribution reveals the shadowy presence of wolves in the region.'[14]

It further states that 'the Helsfell Wolf provides important evidence of the region's historical biodiversity; it enhances our understanding of Britain's zoology and ecosystems and contributes to current debates about "rewilding" which link local and global concerns.'

It says, too, that people are very much a part of the wolf's story, and that on display, the museum will situate the skeleton 'in a history of human perceptions of and responses to wolves in and beyond Cumbria.' That it will 'nudge us towards a reconsideration of our relationship with buried natural histories and ideas of the wild.' For one, I'm happy to be nudged. Bring it on.

Eleven

MOON WALKING

September 4
A late brood – up on the chimney pots of the house beyond
the garden, a family of jackdaws. Two youngsters fluttered their
wings furiously, anticipating food. The parents obliged, and the
juveniles hopped one at a time inside the jackdaw-proof chimney cowls, then *plop*, dropped out of sight, like kids jumping into
a cylindrical water-slide.

September 8
Clustered on red stems, the ripening berries of our elder tree
were jewels of green, red and black, depending on their degree of
ripeness. Like ornate beading on an Elizabethan gown, they were
all dressed up, ready for autumn.

September 14
A quarrelsome, persistent rolling chatter from halfway up the silver
birch – a small flock of siskins feeding on clusters of red-brown
birch catkins. Seed dispersal by the wind and its avian accomplices.

The birch leaves were modulating into the acidic yellows and
browns of autumn. The seeds, meanwhile, had begun to infil-
trate every part of the garden. The doormat to my study seemed

perpetually embedded with them, and each new trip inside resulted in more golden accretions, more layers of tiny spheres making their way indoors. The seeds dot the lawn, accumulate on windowsills, on the fence-tops, on the soil of the borders and planters. They are caught on spider webs and are trodden inside the house. In their proliferation, they are the substance of a fairy tale, a golden, tidal rain which grows and grows by the day.

I picked up a small handful of seeds and placed them on a piece of white paper. Scrutinising them under the hand lens, I saw they possessed a startling resemblance to butterflies, with delicate, buff-coloured, papery wings, a copper-coloured thorax and even antennae-like protuberances. In our garden, a monsoon of butterfly seeds, ready and waiting for dispersal by the wind.

September 16

Washing up the supper dishes, I looked out over the garden to where two pale orange shreds of cloud were adrift, side by side, in a sea of yellow sky above the mountains. As summer began to fade, so the quality of light shifts and changes. Beyond Potter Fell, the western-facing slopes of the Bannisdale hills caught and reflected the late sun, painting the rough ground and crags the colour of unfired earthenware and deep, blood red. I pictured the bracken up there on the fells, fast becoming that other version of itself – the brittle stems of autumn and winter.

Someone flicked a dimmer switch: the light shifted again. Jackdaw emissaries from the sycamore spirited themselves away out over the chimneys and rooftops.

September 17

At 8.30pm it was almost, though not quite, dark. I pulled on my trainers and headed up the fell. It seemed an eternity since my last walks in dusky evenings. The dog followed. The moon rose in a fattened crescent above the treeline horizon ahead of us, and sheep scattered, spooked by our intrusion into their increasingly sepulchral field. I sat on the big boulder, a glacial erratic conveniently deposited beside the path, and looked over the valley of the Kent and the surrounding fells. Electric lights began to flicker into existence, like stars coming out one by one – at Benson Hall, High Jenkin Crag, Oak Bank and Red Bank, at Tenement Farm, Braban House and Larch Bank on the high road over Potter Fell, at High House and Gilpin Bank. In the east, a star appeared, another to the north-west.

We walked on into the quarry wood where what little light remained was soon obscured. Right on cue, an owl cast its rising *keewick* spell into the darkness: a female tawny. I scrutinised the branches, trying in vain to catch a glimpse, to make out the Russian-doll-shaped figure in the tangle of branches and the midnight blue beyond. The penetrating call came again, close to, but the owl remained unseen. We passed out from underneath the trees into the amphitheatre of the old quarry, its limestone walls gifting the arena a faint grey luminescence. A bat materialised out of the night. I scrambled down a slippery, stony bank and crossed the low stile in the wall to follow the path down to the lower fields, the bat continuing to circle above, as if it was attempting to interpret *us*. Then it lost what little sense of propriety it may have had, and began to move in, dipping repeatedly, soundlessly, towards the top of my head. The effect this induced in me, witnessed mercifully by only the dog and possibly the tawny owl, was that I began to duck and dive while at the same time running like an idiot down the fell (think Manuel dodging Basil Fawlty's right-handed slap). Fortunately – for me and every other sentient witness to the occasion – reason eventually prevailed. I got a grip and walked sensibly again. The dog, though, had had enough. She set off alone down the now-dark fell, wanting the familiarity of the house and the rooms full of warm light.

September 18

Steve and the car disappeared along the road back to Kendal. There was an instantaneous sense of quiet, and a moment's pause. A breath to take in the shift from town to open land. I like this – the immediate transformational power of the countryside. Leave all the everyday stuff behind. Declutter your head. For a few moments, I did nothing more than look out from the high vantage point of Helsington over the flat farmland of the Lyth Valley, then south towards the bay, and north towards mountain-obscuring clouds. The valley is some seven miles long and over a mile wide, bordered by the limestone escarpments of Scout Scar in the east, Whitbarrow to the west, and the undulating foothills of the mountains to the north.

The name Helsington has obscure origins, but by digging just a little into local history, I found the word *helsingas*, 'a farmstead of those dwelling on the hals,' with the word *hals* signifying a 'neck of land or pass' – in this case, and in this landscape, clearly a reference to the long ridge of Underbarrow Scar. The Old English word *haesling* means 'hazel copse', and hazel, locally abundant, has for centuries been associated across these valleys with early industries like charcoal burning. The origin of the name 'Lyth', meanwhile, comes from our Norse forebears, the settlers whose word *hlith* referred to a sloping hillside. Stitched throughout the Lyth Valley are extensive peat beds, known locally as the mosses, created after the glaciers retreated in the last ice age.

A whole raft of peat mosses fans outwards from the valley towards Morecambe Bay and has given rise to a host of place names: Stakes Moss, referring to the stakes and 'corduroy roads' found underneath the peat, Levens Moss in the centre of the valley, Rawson's Moss below Rawson's settlement, Helsington Moss in the north of the valley, and Meathop, Nichols and Catcrag Mosses to the west. The granddaddy of them all, Foulshaw Moss, lies between the rocky bluff of Whitbarrow and the great, shifting sands of Morecambe Bay.

◎ ◎ ◎

A murky haze obscured the rising ground beyond the valley, the kind that will burn away as the morning begins to warm. At the edge of the Scar, a northerly airstream pushed at vague vestiges of white vapour. In rising, they also dissolved. The bay shone distantly.

The world knew that it had already swung into another season. Every few minutes I passed through invisible barriers dividing the territories of robins. I dropped into a small, wooded defile, and continued up the short and steeply rising ground to the plateau.

In this topsy-turvy year, when everything has been late, the heather was only now beginning to flower. Pricked out in low-growing mounds, the heathers indicated linear cracks and gullies in the limestone – into which sand had blown and settled aeons ago. The heathers blushed the ground soft purple, drawing the eye along the escarpment towards the mountains.

A woodpecker spread raucous mirth from the larches on higher ground. Below, the songs of woodland birds rose from the oaky greens of Honeybee Wood. A crowd of rooks blustered off the crags beneath the edge, peeling away, the fields and hedges and drainage channels of the valley passing below them. Occasional swallows flittered over the heath, no doubt sensing the shifting nature of the seasons, and of the temperature of the air beneath their wings.

I remembered walking the Scar one autumn day of bright beginnings several years ago. I had made the fatal mistake of leaving my jacket at home. The inevitable, thunderously heavy showers came bowling in from the south, blown in on a head-wind and given an extra push by the incoming tide down in the bay. When the rain came, it beat onto the leaf-canopy of Brig-steer Woods below, and was the sound of rain dashing across an ocean. For a moment only, I stayed to listen, then ran like hell.

September 19

The River Bela flows out from Dallam Tower parkland, then passes beneath the arch of the road bridge and dashes on through the fields beyond, dropping over a low weir, and making a lazy left-hand turn before widening briefly and pouring out into Morecambe Bay. I wanted to see if the pink-footed and grey-lag geese had begun to return from their breeding grounds in Iceland and Svalbard. The geese set out from the far north in early September, making landfall on the rich coastal margins of Scotland, a refuelling stop before setting out again, their next landfall here on the bay, or further south on the estuaries of the Wyre and Lune.

I meandered along the river's edge, its liminal sand and mud-flats exposed by the low tide, and in that brackish place I found them: assembled in small groups, a flock of maybe two or three hundred geese. Only yards away across the slinky, slow-moving water, perambulating in the shallows and along the bank, they prattled contentedly, or dozed, as if at the end of a long journey – which they undoubtedly were – their eyes half closing, bod-ies shifting. Up on the saltmarsh, more geese were semi-camou-flaged, pale chests and white rumps marking them out from the ochre-coloured sedge. Whilst they drowsed the warm afternoon away, one or two of them maintained watch, standing with heads and necks erect.

Difficult perhaps, to tell apart, pink-footed and greylag geese both have a pale grey-brown and buff colouring, but the trick is to look at the feet and the bill; the pinkfoot has indeed been blessed with pink feet, along with a narrow band of pink embellishment midway along the neat bill. The greylag, meanwhile, is a larger goose with a white-tipped orange bill and paler legs.

I took off my shoes and paddled at the edge of the river, my feet imprinting amongst the webbed symbols of the geese and the smaller arrowheads of oystercatchers. Bubbles of air erupted from worm casts, forming concentric moving rings in the water. A strand line of white feathers had been gathered and deposited by the outgoing tide, the line of it running at an angle to the water, emerging again on the opposite bank as a curving line that connected back to the geese.

The sky was pale and white with high cloud. Above the bay, flotillas of smaller clouds sailed languidly eastwards on the slight westerly wind. To the south and west, the light and land faded into a pallid equivalence. The northern aspect, meanwhile, was all sunshine and shadows.

A helicopter buzzed low overhead, then veered off towards the mountains, though the geese were ambivalent. I took photographs from the river's edge, and as I focused on the birds closest to me, others began to peel away from the ground, rising and joggling into a roughly formed skein, flying low over the marsh. They grouped, journeyed upriver, then passed in front of the cliffs of Whitbarrow Scar. The geese that remained on the ground looked up to watch their companions, to measure the mood, to gauge the imperative for departure, their heads swivelling like periscopes. Then the airborne birds began to whiffle – rolling sideways, holding their wings vertically and swinging back again, losing height. They dropped rapidly and came back to the ground with their wings outstretched. They settled.

Over winter months, the geese gather along the coasts of the north-west in vast flocks, roosting out on the marshes or sandbanks to be as safe from predators as possible. As dawn comes, they begin to peel away from their roosts, flying off in whatever direction their instincts tell them, to where the food is. Wildfowlers call this unpredictable directional journeying 'flighting.' It is virtually impossible to determine the direction they will travel; after a number of days heading off in a certain direction, the next day their journey may take them somewhere else entirely: the origin of the term 'wild goose chase.'

The Lune and Wyre estuaries are staked out by wildfowlers. Arriving in the very early mornings, they hide out in the ditches and channels of the edgelands, sometimes lying in wait for hours as dawn comes in. They may wait in vain, never having good enough sight of the geese or never being close enough to flying birds to take a shot. They say that the numbers of geese across the region have increased exponentially because of the creation of the Wyre and Lune Sanctuary – by wildfowlers themselves. In 1963, there were thought to be only around five hundred geese, though these days the figure is more like forty thousand. I'm all for increases in bird numbers, but I don't think I'll ever understand the camouflage of conservation when the ultimate aim is to kill.

September 27

I'd left it late to set out. It had been one of those days when, despite the warmth and sunshine calling me out, life kept getting in the way. By the time I parked the car down by the bay, just a seam of orange light remained in the western sky. Below it, the scattered lights of Grange-over-Sands interrupted an increasingly monotone landscape.

The wooden gate swung closed, and I followed the well-worn path through the fields beside the River Bela. In the growing dark, I searched for, and failed to find, the head torch I was sure I'd put in my pocket before I'd set off from home. Then something disturbed the river, and a tawny owl hooted into the almost-dark.

Right on cue, September's full moon rose above a stand of pines in Dallam Park. I continued by the steady glow of that fortune-teller's orb, its light reflected in the slow-flowing Bela, guiding me onwards towards the edge of the bay. On the lip of the weir, the rounded form of an otter, curled on the ledge, morphed into the hollow end of a traffic cone. 'Get a grip,' I told myself.

Following the river's brushed-steel sheen to its outfall, there was an absence; the geese so recently returned from Iceland were gone. No doubt they were out there in the middle of all that darkness, disappeared into the tidal absence, roosting on sandbanks. There was nothing to find but the hummocks of the saltmarsh and the almost imperceptible sound of water sliding away towards the bay. I stood on the lip of the land, taking in the lack of familiar, orientating landmarks, the sensations of being alone, the way the night plays tricks, fooling us into thinking we should not be out alone, and creating the imperative to remain attached to street lights and the warm interior glow of a home.

The night pressed on, gathering itself around me.

The distant blether of sheep pulsed in from low-lying fields. Then the rolling gossip of lapwings travelled out from the empty sands. It was low tide. The lapwings were moving closer. They morphed out of the darkness, flying inland, navigating along the seam of the river. A moment later, they oared themselves across the face of the extravagant moon. They circled, reorienting themselves to the sands; it was as if the act of passing across that circle of light had woken them from a dream. They flew overhead and vanished into the blank night. As I turned for home, the jumbled, anxiety-ridden calls of geese issued out from the darkness. A small gaggle of them came winging over from adjacent farmland. Five, maybe six geese, heading out towards the empty sands, the creak of their wings signalling their passage overhead.

By moonlight I saw their shape-shifting figures, the singular line of them, travelling purposefully into the night.

◉ ◉ ◉

Back home I still couldn't settle. That full moon was riding high, its lucid force over the town. Finding the head torch where I'd left it on the kitchen worktop, I set off up the fell, the light radiating from the full moon eclipsing the street lights, and wandered up the path between the allotments. A roosting bird took off softly from a gate post, and immediately afterwards the familiar call of a tawny owl came from the big sycamores on the edge of first field. I looked into the not-dark, listening to the owl. From inside chicken sheds, nothing. Giant moon-shadows were cast from the sycamores in broad bands onto the fields, like sledge-tracks in snow. Cars droned up and down the road into town. It seemed I was the only one there, soaking up the moon, its gleaming presence countering the notion of sleep. By its light, this is a cooler, less-knowable world. It felt as if the planet underneath me hummed softly in attendance to the glorious night.

By the time I reached home again, a dusky halo had formed around the moon. That night was to be a so-called 'supermoon', when our most familiar celestial neighbour passes closest to the Earth or, as astronomers say, *reaches its perigee*. And as if this were not a sufficient astrological experience, there was also to be an eclipse as the Earth passed between the moon and the sun. And more still – it was to be a blood moon: as the Earth's shadow falls across the face of the moon, its surface would be coloured an unnatural, dusky red as sunlight was scattered through the Earth's atmosphere, all other colours removed. But would I sleep through it all?

Sometime after 3am I woke and peered out from the bedroom window. There, suspended above the fell like a gothic lantern, was the moon, its face in the later stages of eclipse, emitting a rusty glow, as if hot metals were cooling unevenly across the surface, and pitted by craters. Just the slightest crescent of light remained, then the eclipse was complete, and the moon burned.

September 28

Out early on Scout Scar. Light scattered over the fells like mercury, and the white vapour of ground mist rose above the fields of the Lyth Valley. At the beginning of the ridge, there was an intruder: a tent, the occupant apparently still sleeping, boots outside the flap. I wouldn't like to put my feet inside them, I thought, given that heavy dew. I remembered last night's astronomical event and put two and two together: the tent must belong to a dedicated moon-watcher.

Further along the Scar, two men walked towards me, rucksacks carried in front and rolled sleeping mats and tents on their backs.

'Were you out for the moon?' I asked them.

'We were,' one said. 'What a great view it was from here. Didn't get much sleep though – it was too bright.' And the other man said, 'Not too far to go – home to Kendal for bacon butties and dry the gear out.'

'That'll be the dew then,' I said. They nodded and told me they'd be out in the hills again that night – Angle Tarn for more moon-watching, and just for being amongst the hills.

Swallows – still here at the end of September. I wondered if they'd left it this late to set out in previous years, or were simply in tune with the way the year had gone. Looking down into the valley, in the fields of Barrowfield Farm, the cows were already out from the milking, their slow walk back to the fields marked by a series of intertwining doodles, hoof-drawn in the grass. In Brigsteer Woods, autumn was a memory resurfacing amongst the trees.

◉ ◉ ◉

Driving home, two robins fell from the trees at the edge of Serpentine Woods. Fighting beak and claw they fluttered and fell, fluttered up and fell again, at last reaching the relative sanctuary of the double yellow lines by the kerb, claws locked together. I wanted to stop the car and tell them to pack it in, not to be so aggressive. The delightful doyen of the Christmas card is, in reality, an aggressive beast – a purveyor of nature, raw and untrammelled.

September 30
In the big tent at Wigtown Book Festival in Scotland's far southwest, listening to Liz Lochhead. It is as if she were at home in her kitchen, talking with a few good friends after a meal and a glass or two of wine rather than two hundred or more folk in a marquee on the town square. She recited her poems almost entirely from memory, and was captivating. But something drifted in from the world outside, the sound of geese calling overhead. They were flying out from the land towards the high tide that at that moment was filling Wigtown Bay. On the move again, 'on passage' as birders say – maybe travelling in from Iceland or Svalbard, dropping in to overwinter on the Solway marshes, or heading further south. Liz Lochhead *and* geese – I was doubly transported.

In wondrous Scots, Lochhead recited the opening lines from her play *Mary Queen of Scots Got her Head Chopped Off*. In the play, the chorus is illustrated by the Scots' national bird, the crow: '*Ragbag o' a burd in ma black duds, a' angles and elbows and broken oxter feathers, black beady een in ma executioner's hood,*' adding that Le Corbie (the crow) feels she is possessed of a kind of 'black glamour'. [15]

Twelve

CHANGE IN THE AIR

October 1

On the fell, the irritable rattle of a jay. I'd not heard jays in this particular place, where the fields meet the path that leads up from the road, and I turned to see it launch out of an ash tree, then forge its interloper's trail uphill. Above the line of its flight, something moved against the sky. I looked up to see a skein of geese, travelling in from the north, flying at low altitude just above the treeline on the top of the fell. The image of an aeroplane on its descent to a runway came to mind. They were heading towards the bay, and I wondered about their silent flight; were it not for the unfamiliar presence of the jay, they would have passed without notice.

October 2

The temperature on the first of the month had risen to over 20°C. People were wearing shorts, and I resorted to a hat to keep the heat off. But it was short-lived. The morning dawned misty and cold. Very cold. I felt hemmed in. I wanted views. Meeting the other few early morning dog walkers who appeared, looming out of the clammy mist on the fell, we commiserated.

Our resident sparrow family was in excellent voice, and no

wonder: they were costing me a small fortune in sunflower seeds. For the past couple of weeks, the dog had been eyeing the ground under the bird feeders below the clematis, and I could have sworn that, as I walked down the garden to peg out the washing, something small and grey had disappeared under the low-growing plant foliage.

Washing the dishes at lunchtime, I looked out to see a wee grey mousie running out from the foliage and disporting himself amongst the dropped sunflower seeds. He sat down, and with great efficiency – although a little too fast for good table manners – pushed the seeds into his mouth, then scuttled off into the foliage again.

The marigolds had not failed me. Their bright orange and yellow faces made a welcome burst of colour at the end of the garden. I picked a handful for the spotted green jug on my desk. The nasturtium seeds I'd planted in May had only just grown tall, entwining their climbing tendrils amongst mid-summer's prolific, white rambling rose that clambers in unruly fashion up the trellis beside the study door. The nasturtium flowers grew towards the sun, adorned with pale, broad yellow trumpets and deep orange stars to guide the bees. And the bees worked constantly, visiting the marigolds, nasturtiums, and the purple flowery clusters at the apex of tall, slender wands of *Verbena bonariensis*. The sweet peas had grown leggy, twining lazily around the metal frame, the flowers lasting for days in the dry weather, and more of them each day. A bee drifted aimlessly inside the study, visiting the jug of marigolds next to me as I typed.

At 4.30pm, the sun was high over the rooftops, and in the half-sun, half-shade of the gardens, galaxies of small flies swirled and drifted, lured by the warmth and the light.

By 5.30pm, the sun had disappeared behind the rooftops. It was as if someone had turned the central heating off; the temperature dropped and, reluctantly, I closed the door.

October 4

The view from the flood bank looks out over low-lying fields bordered by hawthorn and wire fences. Here the final meanderings of the River Kent cut jigsaw pieces out of the land at the northern perimeter of Morecambe Bay. The flood bank extends from Crag Wood in the west to the outfall of the River Bela near Dallam Park in the east. It is a monolithic endeavour, built around the turn of the twentieth century and designed to protect the fields from Morecambe Bay's highest tides. It measures some twelve metres from front to back and two and a half metres in height.

With my friend Fiona, who has spent years watching, photographing and painting the wildlife of the bay and its edgelands, I walked the top of the flood bank, gaining an elevated view. Walking upon it alerts anything wild to human presence, however, and the first to lift was a little egret, soon followed by a second, their white forms ghosting across the river towards Sampool, where a third egret stood immobile on exposed sandflats. Fifteen years ago, an egret on the bay would have had birdwatchers' pulses racing and no doubt produced a 'twitchathon' of camo-clad birders with banks of telephoto lenses. These days, egrets are always here, standing beside the channel like unlikely marble sculptures, and they've been around just about long enough to be considered local.

Sleek grey clouds defined the early morning distances, from the great limestone prow of Whitbarrow, to the steeple of Levens' church, to the last of the Forestry shelterbelt trees on Foulshaw Moss and a handful of farm buildings closer in.

Fiona and I watched a singleton curlew rise from the fields and make looping patrols wide of the river before landing further away. The next to rise were some eighty lapwings, rowing through the air from Hallforth farmland to Levens Moss, calling their joyous rolling gossip. It was affirming to see so many of them; they are one of many wading birds whose habitats have been under sustained attack since the radical intensification of farmland began in the 1960s. These days, along with the curlew and others, their numbers are feared to be in potentially terminal decline. I miss their massed presence in the landscape. In my horse-riding days, travelling from the stable through the lanes and onto the open heath of Birkrigg Common, lapwings were always there, lifting from the fields with their peculiar rusty, rising call.

Beside the outpouring River Kent, a smattering of starlings flew in the lapwings' midst, travelling to the fields across the water. These starlings, those great northern European settlers, would soon be joined by thousands more as vast overwintering flocks arrived. We stopped by Marsh Farm in the relative cover of sedge and wild cabbage gone to seed. On the sandy riverbank immediately below us: the tracks of a single otter. Deposited in the grass above them were the intestinal remnants of a recent kill – if only we'd arrived earlier.

Black-headed gulls, in their winter plumage of a dark dot behind the eye, rafted out on the river. Others wandered through the shallows uttering occasional remonstrations. A flight of mergansers winged upriver, the art-deco white of their wing-bars leaving an afterimage of their passing. In the water, the sun's reflection materialised briefly from the clouds before becoming lost once more. Then something else intruded into the clouded surface: the reflection of a red hot-air balloon, gaining height and moving up in a straight vertical line.

We lingered, watching the early morning life of the river unfold, the air so still that the balloon seemed to remain immobile, hanging in space.

We walked past the final meandering curves of the river and through a gate onto the hawthorned prow of Fishcarling Head where the Kent broadens into the bay. We ambled out onto the marsh where a recent high tide had washed away the colours, an opaque rinsing of bay mud covering the whole marsh, ending in an undecided line below the flood bank. Fi said, 'Last week the whole marsh was white – like snow – covered in flowering scurvy grass. It'll recover again – until the frosts begin.'

We returned to the quiet road, passing low-lying fields, each with an open gate, the cattle having been moved inside to the shippons for winter. In the middle of a tractor-rutted field of stubble, a rook colony foraged for beetles and worms. In their midst was a leucistic, or white, rook. We had both seen it before, but could we get closer? We turned in to the next gateway and, using the dividing hawthorn hedge as shelter, moved quietly along. We found a lifeless rook under the hedge at the halfway point, its breast and legs turned to the sky and its eyes glazed with the milky membrane of death. Hawthorn berries lay spilled on the ground around it, like grave goods. We passed a gap in the hedge, and the rooks were instantly spooked by our silhouettes. They lifted from the earth, and spirited themselves away.

October 30
The clocks had been put back. It was 4pm, and I was looking through my binoculars from the bedroom windows to see what the changed afternoon light had brought.

Sunlight caught the undersides of jackdaw wings as they glimmered over the rooftops and the gardens. Over the ring of hills that printed themselves against the autumnal sky, the birds transformed into a flock of rare creatures. Small birds had gone to bed early, and the maple tree across the road was the colour of plums past their prime. Seven layabout juvenile rooks landed together, bending one of the upper branches of our elegant silver birch into a springy whip. Then, as they peeled away one by one, the branch rebounded to point at the clouds again. Over the hill towards Longsleddale, a telegraph pole caught the sun. Blackbirds were about on the fell, fretting amongst fallen oak leaves. A Japanese maple simmered burnt and orange. The bracken on Potter Fell was the colour of a bruise. Rooks fell upwards. Sunlight located a single boulder on the Whinfell Ridge, and craggy little Whiteless Pike wanted to be noticed amongst a backdrop of bigger hills. The town was in shadows, the last of the light belonged to the land. A late flurry of goldfinches burst over the fell like airborne embers. The light was moving further away, was letting go.

October 31

Our neighbour put the blackened remains of a sunflower head on the garden wall. Blue tits and great tits arrived to feed, then retreated into the cover of the clematis. A robin flurried in. As the robin took his small share, a mouse emerged from the clematis, sprinted along the wall and began to take seeds from the sunflower head, too. The robin regarded the mouse with curiosity, as if it were a thing he had not seen before. But instinct soon took over; the robin flew up and began to harass the mouse, dropping close to its small grey back again and again. The mouse did not linger.

Later, looking out from the back-bedroom windows, I saw three blackbirds, close to each other on the grass in the garden at the end of the row of houses. A male and two females, investigating worms. One by one they flitted up to a brick wall backed by a wooden trellis, beyond which was a small greenhouse. Were they, I wondered, one of the families of blackbirds raised in our garden this summer? The male led off in his distinctive run and pause, run and pause, the females following, run and pause, run and pause: the blackbird's courtly dance.

A bathing party. The male blackbird was in the birdbath, his wing and body feathers held open, beads of water clinging to his dark feathers. Sunlight caught on the droplets of water, making tiny rainbows all around him. A sparrow family arrived, dipping and diving, fluttering and twittering. The blackbird tolerated the invasion; then, having finished his ablutions, he lifted and dropped out of sight into the garden next door. A moment later the sparrows were gone too; only the ripples remained.

Fresh rain on sweet peas. They continued to push out new flowers every day. I wondered when they will slow and inevitably stop, when the weather would turn.

Thirteen

THE LAND REMADE

November 1

A late afternoon round from Helsington Church to Scout Scar and back through the Barrows, the land locked in low-lying cloud. The branches of the dark green yew trees were twisted and crabbed with age. In the mist ahead of us, Fergus and the cousins seemed to be walking into nothingness, as if they were merely on the edge of our perception.

Later, our neighbours recounted their walk up Grey Friar from the Three Shire Stone, above Little Langdale. Setting out in the early morning, they had walked up through thick clag, eventually coming out onto the Coniston ridge and finding an ocean of cloud below them – a temperature inversion covering the whole of the Lake District, mountain peaks pushing through like new lands. And they had seen a Brocken spectre: their peculiarly haloed and much magnified shadows were cast upon the clouds below, keeping pace with them as they progressed along the mountain ridges.

November 2

The country was divided in two. The radio told of fogbound airports in the south, transport chaos and long delays, but in Cumbria, all was light, and very bright. Walking up the fell in the morning, the haws and hips were rosy in the sunshine, and syca-more leaves had turned the pale-straw yellow of stubble fields. At the bottom of the garden, the yellow nasturtiums were clinging on, grown almost to the top of the rose trellis.

Working through the afternoon, the study door open to let in the unseasonal warmth, there arrived the unmistakeable sound of geese. This was a rare event; geese migrating north or south, to their feeding grounds on the bay or further down the coast of north-west England, more usually pass much further west. I ran into the garden and looked up to see a skein of pinkfoots passing high over the rooftops, calling and shape-shifting. As they flew south, the leading wave of their formation vacillated, so that instead of an arrow shape, they moved through the sky in something more like a 'W'. I watched until they disappeared, and reluctantly, went back to work.

I love the high-pitched, rolling sonic prattle of pinkfoots. It's as if they want us all to know they're here, passing through.

Somewhere in the five gardens, a blackbird *spinked*, petulantly.

Sunset came in like gauze – pink, and low to the horizon, drifting to orange and yellow, making the mountains appear transparent. The first hint of frost snagged on the evening air.

November 16

Two weeks of rain. Two weeks of Cumbrian downpours, which are nothing like mere rain. On the radio the talk was of floods, and my friend along the road in Burneside phoned to say the road between the village and Kendal was impassable. For the sec-ond time in fifteen years, the Kent was rising, and people in low-lying properties were evacuated. You could feel the collec-tive sense of apprehension in the air.

The next day dawned brighter, and I took off early to Hever-sham. I'd been ill, unusually ill, with a cold that had taken a grip and wouldn't let go, and I'd been feeling that dry, incapacitating sense of not having enough air. As soon as I was able, I had to get out.

By the farm at College Green, between Heversham and the bay, I walked along the flood bank, but birds were unusually absent. Just one mute swan investigated the ochre reed beds on the small island upstream. The river had burst its banks and run over the grass below the flood bank, mirrors of flood water casting impressions of the grey sky back up again. The sheep were staying put on what higher ground they could find.

I didn't want to walk alongside the troubling river, so I backtracked. I passed the farm again, and a young man in grey overalls came out of a barn, hefting a sack of feed on his shoulders.

'Not much weather for farming,' I said.

'I still don't get a day off,' he answered.

I walked the die-straight narrow lanes across Heversham Marsh. In the first field, the ground had mostly escaped the effects of the rain. Pheasants wandered the edges of woodland and explored further into the open. Two of them searched for food beneath a hedge and seven more, earth-red in colour, ranged in a line across the edge of the flood water, investigating the ground underneath. The water lapped the base of the flat-topped hedge and continued as far as it was possible to see. Further away, across the parallel field boundaries, a gathering of black-headed gulls flittered white in the air, the transformation of their feeding grounds no doubt of little import to such great colonists.

At the crossroads, I turned left. The fields on either side of the lane were no longer fields but rather vast lakes stalked by telegraph poles. A sheep-fodder station was up to its metal knees in water. Four mute swans were a flotilla sailing across a new world.

In this landscape, hedges divide the fields, and there are trees interspaced along their lengths. Some had grown to full height. They punctuated the landscape, providing food and shelter for birds. Low sunlight shone from the east, emanating from below the line of the hill where squat Dallam Tower reaches at the sky. The sun sent beams of light out across the floods and made the trees seem black, denied of light, as if they hadn't been rendered black enough with the rain slicking their skins day after unyielding day. Up in the branches of an ancient hawthorn was a male blackbird, silhouetted. I watched him take a single red berry, one of very few that were left. He moved further up into the tree to take another and then another. Soon, all of them would be gone.

On either side of the lane, the drainage channels, imperative in these low-lying lands, were filled to bursting, and in places the water had already breached the top: linear puddles of water washed across the metalled surface of the road. Tufts of grass illustrated the divide between field and drain, or between what was now lake and canal. Drowned grasses had been scoured and deposited on the verge, evidence of even higher waters, and at the next crossroads, the water flowed up to the rim of the arch beneath the small bridge. Then at last, a field containing only sloshes of water, and there a flock of lapwings probed the grass in mid-field. Beyond them, sheep.

I came to Sandside and looked out and down from the old railway track onto the place where the rivers Bela and Kent meet. The volume of water washing out into the bay seemed unprecedented. Gone were the two distinct channels, replaced by one troubled sheet of moving water. Such was the force of the water spiralling up into the small bay below, that it seemed as if the tide was moving in. Just offshore, the edges of an exposed sandbank were eaten at by the water. A huge branch had become beached upon it, and beside it stood a single cormorant, wings outstretched. Then it lifted and flapped purposefully out toward the middle of the bay, like a dark omen. I looked back and saw that the tide was not moving in, but out. The force and volume of water washing down from the valleys and out into the bay was such that the two rivers had created their own backwash, swirling below me. What I'd taken for the breadth of the incoming tide was river.

November 23

The first frosts arrived towards the end of the month. I set out early with Fiona for the new hide overlooking Brigsteer Wetlands. Driving along the lane from Levens toward Brigsteer, passing Cinderbarrow Farm, Fi told me of her concerns about a new tenant farmer, how the retiring farmer had been a friend to the hedgerows, encouraging birdlife. Nothing in this landscape is constant, nor can it be taken for granted.

We parked the car and walked the narrow road through Brigsteer Woods. Fi pointed out two whinberry bushes in amongst the winter trees. The pendulous, star-anise-shaped berries were bright pink, the last of the blackberry foliage intertwined amongst the thin stems. We walked the field path towards the cedar-clad hide as a buzzard lifted from beyond the sheltering line of sedge. It lifted on lazy wingbeats into the freezing air.

At this edge of the Lyth Valley, former peat-cutting areas had been purposefully flooded, creating a new wildlife haven. We looked out at a vast flock of teals, numerous mallards, coots, wigeons and a pair of mute swans with two juveniles. Written up on the notice board inside were recent sightings that included (excitingly) a bittern, marsh harriers, peregrines, little egrets and kingfishers. In the spring, the waders come in to take advantage of the easy feeding the wet ground provides – curlews, lapwings, snipe.

We settled in to watch. The surface was frozen in patches of ice and interspersed with open water. A coot broke cover and ran delicately across the icy skin before disappearing into sedge. A buzzard mewed, unseen. Then, rounding from behind the dark trees of Colley Green Wood, a group of mute swans came into sight, travelling low against the green flanks of Whitbarrow and passing across the darker ground of the Crosthwaite hills. We counted ten, their white forms evanescing in the cold air, and they spooked a flock of black-headed gulls that rose as one into the sky and dispersed like shreds of paper blown by the wind. Then the waterscape settled, just the ongoing cackle of the mallards underscoring all the other quiet comings and goings of birds.

Focusing on the wood behind which the swans had appeared, there were birch and oak, ash and sycamore, and just a tinge of copper gilding the domes of the taller trees – the very last of the season's leaves. Smaller birches crowded in amongst their neighbours, and in the subdued light, the distinct purple mass of next year's buds appeared velvety, like an animal pelt covering the trees.

It was cold inside the hide, freezing cold. We should have brought a flask. Fi sketched, commenting in her inimitable way on the colours, the light, the life of the place. Ducks upended, pointing their white rumps, like cartoons of duck bottoms, towards the sky. Swan families floated past like small, elegant galleons, occasionally upending, or dabbling in the water. Later, leaving the hide, a red-brown kestrel glided over the water, coming to rest high up in a hawthorn, the last of the berries bright below.

November 27

Returning from Grasmere with my photographer friend Florence. The road runs dipping, rising and curving beside Rydal Water for a glorious watercolour mile, and above it, on steeply rising ground, a flock of two hundred or more Canada geese. They walked forwards across the turf, as if collectively fixed on a particular place.

'Look, it's like the ground's moving with one all-seeing eye,' Florence said.

I told her, 'I wish I'd said that.'

November 28

Finally, the rain stopped. I packed my wellies, put the dog in the car and headed down to the marshes by the Kent and the bay. I walked the flood bank. The air was still and the last shreds of rain-bearing clouds moved towards the east. A blackbird *jink jinked* from a hedgerow, and a hidden rook called *craa* from an ash tree beside the road. The River Bela slid off the weir and boiled back up against itself – such was the measure of rainfall in those gloomy, year-end days. Just downstream from the weir, a heron, a mere foot away from the roiling edge of water, eyed the flow as if mesmerised. A wagtail flitted across the bank ahead of me and flew up into the heights of a sycamore. Close to it, there was a large, bedraggled form: a bird of prey, that was for sure, but what it was exactly I couldn't tell.

I took out the binoculars, but even then, I couldn't fathom distinguishing features, just a brown-grey bird with puffed-out feathers. It was hunched, the head and bill tucked into the chest, with what could reasonably be described as a miserable countenance. After weeks of rain, I could easily empathise. The kestrel, for that is what it was, lifted and flew further along in front of me, coming to land on the broad bank top, as if it was too rain-laden to fly. Inevitably, as we came closer, the kestrel flew back towards the trees, coming to rest in the higher branches of an ash. There: the black-edged, gunmetal-grey tail feathers, the grey stippled chest and face with yellow bill, and that lovely warm-toned russet back. The head feathers were scruffy, almost crested with the perpetual rain. It bobbed its head down and forwards twice and settled again. One dark wing drooped slightly, and at the wing tip, the feathers were ragged. The kestrel peered in my direction, as if watching me watching it.

Between the bay, the river and the fields is an interplay of worlds. I thought of the topsy-turvy happenings of recent weeks: swans living on fields, sheep flood-bound on slight inclines, trapped between the familiar hedgerow and unfamiliar water. If a farmer had felt the urge, he or she could have crossed their fields by canoe. Birds moved constantly in and out: in towards the rede-fined water-land, or out into the heave and flow of the bay. Out there, the sands were the colour of pale red earth. Rooks flowed overhead, crossing and re-crossing the liminal spaces.

Beached against the flood bank were the remains of a mas-sive tree. Broken-crowned, it was a leviathan – a megalithic beast whose heart had cracked open with fissures radiating from the flat, saw-severed base. I tried to imagine the power of the water that had fetched it here. It had been scoured either from the place it was cut down or from the place of a previous stranding, and carried downriver to wash up here against the flood bank, aided no doubt, by the combination of last week's full-moon high tide and those heavy rains.

The tideline was hardly that, more a jumble of grasses and sedge and great quantities of wood. Rarely had I seen such a volume of wood fetched up. And then, innumerable fence posts and branches, inspiring all the necessary comparisons to broken limbs: some long, others shattered, whole planks and everything in between. Below the flood defence, one high tide's worth of wrack, a forest of possibilities rendered sodden, without prospect. If you had the wherewithal, though, there was enough here to keep a wood-burner going over the coming winter, and probably the one after that, too.

Across the marsh, the sea pools had been tide-filled, remain-ing like shattered mirrors fallen to earth. On the field below Fishcarling Headland – a low, hawthorn-edged bluff of farmland

– were geese. Were it not for the single alarm call emanating from their midst, I might not have seen them, so well were they camouflaged against the water-streaked land. They were Canadas, a small group of them, perhaps sixteen, cropping at the marsh grass. As the dog and I moved against their horizon, they became unsettled, lifting and landing again a distance away. A small flock of goldfinches fizzed out from the midst of the wrack-line, flying on ahead of us, sewing a zigzag line across the bank and back again.

I crossed the headland accompanied by the burble and bubble of curlews. A little egret wafted inland. I ran down the bank and walked next to the river. There, where the space opened out and the bay and the river joined forces, I felt the rise of wind accompanying the change of tide. The water surface was restless, brackish, pulsing with the incoming water ahead of the tide. Suddenly, it was bitter cold, and I pulled up my hood, fastening it tight against the wind. Under Whitbarrow's prow, traffic flowed soundlessly towards Barrow. But the wind had taken the traffic's voice, and for that I was grateful.

A flock of birds lifted from the fields, passing in front of a wood, and for a moment they were lost against the dark silhouette of the trees. They appeared again, moving against the sky, streaming through it, rising, falling like lazy waves at the edge of the sea. Lapwings – and what a flock! Flickering against the grey, their black and white forms coalesced, a murmuration! I counted a small section of them and multiplied that number by the area of the whole flock, calculating some five hundred birds. Maybe this was a sign they were increasing in numbers: more likely, a network of overwintering flocks.

The lapwings coasted upriver, settling on a sandbank midway between the two shores by the Kent's final curve. Looking through the binoculars, I saw that the birds all faced into the wind. The Kent must be half a mile wide here, and although the birds had no need to worry about me or the dog, as I walked onwards they inevitably flew up, breaking into smaller clusters, some heading inland towards the new seascapes of the fields, others heading out towards the shifting sands and the unknown watery ground of the bay.

I turned for home, thinking of the home-made soup waiting on the stove. Back at the weir, the heron had moved closer to the edge of the bank, its head and neck cantilevered out over the churning water. I wondered about the precision needed to stab downwards into the current to take a fish from out of that swollen flow.

Fourteen

FLOOD

December 5

We knew it was going to be bad. The ground was already sodden from over a month of rain – and every single day, more fell. I set out before breakfast, before things could get any worse. As I left the house, the cock blackbird burst out from the shelter of the clematis, then twisted and swerved down the garden calling his inimitable alarm call. So it wasn't just me that was rattled by that deeply worrying weather.

I walked to the shop for the papers and eggs, umbrella already useless, battered by the force of the wind and rain. I dumped it unceremoniously into a wheelie bin, and made my way down to the Kent at Aikrigg End. On the footpath behind the terrace of riverside houses: a man, hurrying along.

'The footbridge is closed. It's terrible down there,' he said, pointing back along the river from where he'd come.

The fenced gardens below the cottages were awash, and past the loop in the footpath was an abandoned mop on the ground – too late for that.

A couple of minutes later I reached the riverside path. It was clear that this was not going to be just another ordinary day of rain. Already the water had spilled out from its banks, drowning the entire margin of trees and the footpath on the opposite side.

Brown, murky water lapped at the edge of the footpath below me. The speed of the flow of this river was clear, and I felt, just for a moment, that even being *that* close was not a good idea. This, at 8.45am – with a whole day of unprecedented rain ahead.

I'd seen enough, turned the corner to head for home, but the footpath had been closed off with police tape on the far side of a flood – perhaps a foot or more of water lay between me and the rising ground beyond the tape. I stepped in, but soon enough the water level threatened the top of my long wellies, and anyway, the dog doesn't swim. I backtracked and noted an edge of a rising panic: would the rising river level already have cut me off from retreat? Then I remembered a cut through a gap into a small industrial estate, and ten minutes later I was home, utterly drenched.

◉ ◉ ◉

We have our own technology for measuring rainfall. The house across the road has a short flight of steps leading from the garden down to the pavement. In monsoon weather, the steps become a water feature – as if in some Italianate estate. When extreme volumes of rain drain from the fell, the run-off breaches the allotment wall, then following its own logical course, pours through the garden and cascades down the steps onto the pavement.

By lunchtime, the steady pouring of water had become a torrent, a gushing waterfall even, and the gravel garden path was being unceremoniously scoured out, carried onto the pavement, then distributed evenly along the edge of the road. I worried, naturally, that the torrent would spill over, and from there it would be only a short, impersonal route to our downward-sloping path – and to the front door. What I learned that day, though, was that our house sits exactly at the watershed; the road outside falls away in both directions. It seemed that we would be safe.

We stayed home, siren after siren blaring past on the way to some other disaster. I listened to the radio and watched news reports and videos online: stories of bridges being toppled by the force of the water, one after another after another. Road closure after road closure.

'Scroggs Bridge in Kentmere has gone.'

'There's no way in or out of Levens village.'

'People are stranded on the road at Heversham.'

'The A591 has gone.'

'Appleby Bridge has gone.'

'Eamont Bridge has gone.'

At 2.30pm Fergus came into the kitchen: 'Mum, there's a leak in the front room.' We followed. Water was dripping in a steady stream from the ceiling above the bay window. The ceiling paper bulged ominously; a significant weight of water had built up behind it. I fetched a bucket and a sharp knife, stood on a chair to pierce a hole in the paper, and the pooling water was released into the bucket in a thin stream. For the rest of the day, we checked in continuously, emptying the bucket every few hours.

At 5pm, Cal and I set off into town. Police had blocked off access to all but one of the bridges crossing the Kent. Traffic was piling into town from the north, from what was, by now, the only passable route. At the bottom of the hill, an utterly drenched policeman was ordering vehicles to turn back. He'd long since abandoned any attempt at headwear. At the back of the police station, the Kent had breached in unprecedented fashion, drowning the wide riverside path. It seemed it would annexe the police car park itself; someone's white car already lay half under water. The skate park, and whole fields opposite, were inundated. Further along, at Riverside, the river had burst again – of course it had – and we watched the spectacle of it, the shock of it. As we looked on, lives were being turned upside down.

Walking back up the hill, our road was now more river, which is something for a wide, boulevard-width road like ours.

Everywhere, gravel was being deposited, like new shingle beds on the tarmac.

There was nothing more to be done, other than stay inside, looking out at the deluge. On the radio they said: 'Stay home', 'Don't venture out', 'Don't go anywhere – the emergency services are already struggling'. We knew that alright; all day long, sirens had continually screamed up the road, heading out of town.

We put on the TV news and took in the scale of the weather's impact, of Storm Desmond, as it passed over Cumbria, drowning a whole county and more – into Lancaster where, as in Carlisle, thousands were made homeless, power stations became swimming pools, and misery spread as thickly as the rain.

At 9pm we took the dog out for the last wet walk of the day. Looking across the dark landscape, the rising hills on the eastern side of Kendal had taken on an unnatural silvery grey sheen. Our eyes adjusted, took in the information: an entire hillside on the north side of Kendal, upon which slid, in an unnatural sheen of dark-grey light, a single vast sheet of water, no – a wall of water, and it was heading straight towards the town.

December 6

You know the weather's turned when you wake and the room is light in a different kind of way. Sun, playing on pale yellow painted walls. Open the curtains to brilliance; all was glister and shine. Cars moved along the road as usual. The sense of relief that it was over – at least for us – was palpable.

We breakfasted and headed out into the morning, finding the riverside footpath open again. The river level had fallen and was down below the banks – though only just. Grimly garlanding the trees was a potent symbol of the highest point of the flood: aggregations of detritus high in the upper limbs – torn-off branches, vegetation, plastic, cans. The white car was still there in the police station car park, water dripping from the bottom of the doors. Three bright-orange, high-vis Bay Search and Rescue vehicles were lined up outside the building. The houses that backed onto the riverside path had flooded; sopping sandbags sagged uselessly in doorways and a garden wall had collapsed into rubble that spilled over the path. Someone had placed blue and white 'keep out' tape around it. Health and safety gone mad – amongst all this. At the weir, the water churned back up so that the level below was higher than that above. Then, one of those huge wire cages filled with plastic containers – the kind used to prop buildings up – came bouncing downstream.

The streets were busy, folk come to witness how the town had coped – or not, as it turned out. Wildman Street was a lake, complete with a fire engine, abandoned, up to the top of its wheels in sludgy water. We moved on towards the town centre. A police officer directed the traffic to the far side of the road, keeping it away from where floodwater remained. During the night, the water must have reached the footings of the buildings all the way across the generous thoroughfare. Everything to the right bank of the Kent – all the streets, the industrial units, the road, the cellars of all the houses – was under water. And the sense of quiet was very, very strange.

◎ ◎ ◎

In the afternoon, we drove up to Helsington, parked the car by the wee church and got out to join others who had come to look out at the land, at the Lyth Valley that had morphed from being merely flooded into a new waterland. Sunlight threw glints and shimmers onto its new sea. Out there, field-barns stood isolated in water that reached halfway up to their corrugated roofs. On one, the flood almost touched the gutters. The tops of hedgerows – those that were still visible at least, etched out some semblance of field boundaries, though of animals, there was little sign. A few sheep gathered on the top of a flood bank, and that was all. Brigsteer Wetlands, the place I'd gone with Fi to watch the bird-life out on the new water, was gone; the birds, too. Nothing moved. On the far side of the valley, a few black-headed gulls fretted at the air.

The winding curves and canalised sections of the River Gilpin were lost to the flood, mixing and flowing to places it had never been. We looked south towards the bay, though there was no bay, nor land between the bay and the valley, just one continuous plain of water. The A590, the single lifeline into and out of Furness and the more westerly areas of South Lakeland, lay somewhere underneath.

At some point in the day, I remembered with a sharp, inward wince the title of my 'Country Diary' entry in the *Guardian* published the day before the floods, about Brigsteer's recently established wetlands in the Lyth Valley: '*A Glimpse of a Watery Future*'. You couldn't make it up.

December 7

A phone call from Fi in Levens village. Stories from the flood:

The farmer from Cinderbarrow who'd gone with a village volunteer in his fibreglass boat onto the flooded Lyth Valley to rescue sheep, not knowing what on earth lay below the surface of the water, for this was utterly uncharted territory. Navigating where they could by hedge-tops and the topmost inches of fence posts, seeing beetles crowding on what little wood remained proud of the water. A mouse on a sheep's back in the boat, once they'd hauled the wet, woolly dead weight inside.

A young bullock caught by the heel in a cattle grid just below the village – no one could set it free so, damaged and distressed, someone fetched a gun. The carcass there the next day – emergency services too strained to deal with dead beasts.

Forty head of cattle swept away in the rising water; some eventually found, eighteen miles away – a few of them alive.

Horses rescued, frightened beyond control. Another mouse on a horse's back. Another horse, drowned. A barn full of young cattle up to their necks in water, and no way out.

Farms surrounded by water – nobody getting in or out. No phones. No broadband. No TV. No means of communication.

An elderly man rescued from his bungalow, perched on his bed as the water rose around him. An eighty-year-old woman driving in from Arnside to rescue her friend from the bungalow next door. And succeeding.

December 8
Near the supermarket in town, a blackbird sang, pushing out the full song more usually heard in the spring. I turned a corner, and there he was – proud in the very top of a sycamore, the only bird in the tree, like the first decoration on a Christmas tree. It was a male blackbird, giving full voice to the murky day. And it *was* a gift, I thought, this blackbird, on this day, belting out his heartening song of resurrection.

December 10
Red kites, five seconds.

December 17
Driving the backroad to Staveley. Across the fields from where the flood waters had receded, three herons followed the line of the still-swollen River Kent, one behind the other, wings lifting and falling and flexing. Descending towards the muddy riverbank, each held air in their wings, like grey, unwieldy parascenders.

December 20

Walking from Silverdale around the coast to Jenny Brown's Point, the sun began to win, breaking through dense layers of cloud. Out on the bay, groups of oystercatchers piping, at the edge of a channel; there must have been hundreds of them. They broke into small groups that lifted from the sands in the imperative of moving from one feeding ground to another. They flashed past the headland where the trees that rise in formation up the small cliffs are sculpted into waves by the wind. The oystercatchers spun past towards the northern reaches of the bay. Our teenaged people had gone ahead, nattering, as they are wont to do, disregarding anything about the landscape, or the birds. But they were out in the cold air at least, laughing as they scrambled over the cliffs and moved down into a small bay, throwing sticks for the dog into a remnant of water. In seconds she'd turned half-dog, half-mud creature.

After the walk, we called at Leighton Moss Reserve for tea and cake – of course. Then the kids had had enough, refusing to come with me to climb the observation tower. But up there, the low afternoon sunlight caught on acres of sedge, illuminating it, turning it golden. The wind made wavering pathways in it that opened and closed again in seconds. It was cold up there – biting cold – and I rummaged in my sack for a hat and gloves. The staccato whistling of teals came up from where they gathered in linear rafts out on the lagoon. I retraced my steps down to the path and sought refuge in a hide.

Out on the water, the teals whistled, and tuning in to them, I noticed their exotic colouring, the swatches of green and red on the male's head delineated by fine lines of gold, the white breast painted with radiating dots of dark grey, the sides of the body stippled in waves of black-edged feathering – all exotic *chinoiserie*. Mallards paddled across and back again.

I stopped at the small bird feeding station. Pale female

pheasants stalked the ground underneath hanging seed feeders, the males like Ming emperors. Rosy-chested chaffinches fed and zipped back up into the sheltering moss-covered trees. Blue tits and great tits fed enthusiastically, and goldfinches flaunted their gaudy apparel. Voracious feeders, the goldfinch's custom-built bill deals with each crop-full of seed in seconds, and they go straight back in for more.

A small bird flashed across the space; as I tried to seek it out amongst the trees, just a nanosecond of movement was enough. A treecreeper, spiralling the trunk in jerky movements whilst hunting out insects with that delicately curving bill. Without that pale chest, the treecreeper would easily go unnoticed, so well does his attire blend into the trunk. A robin *tick, ticked* unseen, and then from over the lagoon came the call of geese. I scanned the reed beds on the far side above where pink-footed geese flew, travelling in threes or fours, wings becoming parachutes before they landed on the restless, grey water.

In my pocket, the phone burbled. A message from the teenagers waiting in the car: *Can we go home now please?*

December 24

We were done: the food bought, the fridge bulging. In previous years we'd resorted to using nature's fridge – the shed – to store the beers. If only it were cold. Everything that could be sorted had been sorted, but then I remembered the cards I'd so far failed to deliver, and set out late in the afternoon to take the dog for an urban walk – kill two birds and all that. We wandered into town and through the market square just after dark. In the centre of the square, two slender silver birches were illuminated with Christmas lights braided through their branches.

The sound of small birds filtered down from the birches: a roost of pied wagtails. They fretted along the branches, took off, flitted up to the gutters of the buildings that lined the square, then flew in sorties back to the birches again, contact calling with each other in their sparrow-like twitterings. As the wagtails shifted restlessly, bobbing from place to place inside the trees, the festive lights lit them from underneath. Their white breasts and bellies glowed, as if they emitted radiance, like the precious silver glass bird I would be allowed to carefully unpack from its wrappings each Christmas when I was small.

December 25

Christmas morning. In the topmost branches of the sycamore down the lane, the resident jackdaw colony was silhouetted, like dark, bird-shaped weather vanes orientated towards the north.

We had the usual opening of presents before breakfast (none of us are interested in the notion of delayed gratification), and then I headed out, fortified with porridge, to walk the fell, where, it seemed, there was a complete absence of birds. The sky began to open; it had been three whole mornings without rain. Almost-blue metamorphosed out of uniform grey. But it was a short-lived moment. From the hedgerow, a single wren, in unseasonal mood, scolded me, the dog and the morning.

Washing up the breakfast pots, I looked out to our midwinter garden and the small miracle of the goldfinches. They stayed for ages, grinding up the seed, the split husks falling to the ground, with the whole performance on continuous replay. Their gaudy plumage brightened a day that by mid-morning had already turned drear.

December 26

After Christmas Day, being out in the landscape and walking from the house to the summit of Cunswick Scar was like learning to breathe again. The Scar, at least, was at the centre of a ring of cerulean blue. I reached the sprawling summit cairn and sat for a few moments looking out, eating a couple of clementines from my pocket; they loaned a citrus tang to the clear bright air. The Coniston hills were grey and monochrome, and the central mountains and Kentmere hills were dull, shadow-free. Cumulus clouds sailed at great altitude. Above the village of Staveley, Craggy Woods were rendered winter-grey in clear flat light. Ranks of cloud festered menacingly along the eastern horizon.

In the afternoon, I lit the wood burner and got settled in. There's no call for helping with the Christmas Lego these days – far from it. Later, I watched a phalanx of gulls returning from feeding in the uplands, heading back south towards the bay.

In the last half hour of light, the clouds formed into a series of successive thin bands, like a child's drawing of waves at sea. The wind pushed in from the north-west. Darkness fell like the slow turn of a dimmer switch.

December 31

As dusk began its short, transitory journey into night, I looked out from the kitchen window. There was food to prepare, but I wanted to take in the light of the final evening of the year. In the afternoon it had rained, and as I looked out it came in pulses again, clearing and returning. Heavy bands of grey showers passed over the winter-dulled slopes of Potter Fell.

It was going to be a quiet night in. Our boys were off to parties or pubs, but I don't care for the hoo-ha of New Year. For me, as a celebration, New Year has always seemed forced, and I'm not one to subscribe to the prerequisite to 'have a good time'. It's the next day that interests me, new beginnings and all that, getting out into the light, begin the year with a clear head. See what the daylight brings.

The jackdaws came flowing through the airspace above the gardens, *chack chack, chack*. They'd spent much of the afternoon flitting in and out of the bush-headed sycamore down the lane. You can stand underneath and look up through the bare branches, rain-black against the dull sky, and see the jackdaws engaged in jackdaw doings – wing rustling, vocalising quietly like blokes in the background in a pub. They preen, regard their companions, look out over the gardens, sleep.

Under the proscenium arch of the clematis, small birds flittered on and off the stage – goldfinches, blue tits, coal tits and chaffinches, though soon they would disappear to roost. A male blackbird ran onto the lawn, searching for food. He looked up, and for a split second, it seemed that our eyes met before he lifted to the top of the archway, then made a wide, swooping arc to the neighbour's weeping silver birch. From there, in those last few shorter days, it had been his practice to offer the final notes of song – my four o'clock blackbird. Somewhere in the shadows, a robin trilled an idle tune.

I wondered how the birds sensed the turning year.

◎ ◎ ◎

I drove Fergus over to Grayrigg. There was rain on the windscreen – half-hearted, the dregs of winter's worst, then just before midnight, set off to fetch him again. I stopped the car on Paddy Lane and looked up to a sky that had obligingly cleared. I climbed out, and waited for my eyes to adjust to the dark. Seams of cloud lay along the western horizon, but there was still an abundance of stars and there, the frosted transparency of the Milky Way. Soon we would be home, where I knew there was a bottle of Highland Park waiting.

Under that vast extravagance in a moonless sky, midnight arrived. Fireworks began to burst into the immeasurable darkness, blooming in slow, fading colours, red and silver and gold,

purple, green and bronze. As far south as Lancaster and Morecambe, in the small communities around the edge of Morecambe
Bay and the inland villages, over Furness in the west and all the
small places in between: stars and nebulae, born and dying in the
blink of a midwinter's eye.

POSTSCRIPT

In July 2017, it was announced that the Lake District World Heritage bid had been successful. The focus of most of the local press coverage was on the advantages to businesses across the area. No mention was made of the need for, or even the idea of, landscape restoration, or of conservation issues. This small geographical area, characterised by narrow roads and small, frequently over-crowded 'honeypot' towns such as Grasmere, Coniston and Keswick, already receives 15.8 million visitors a year; as a result of the bid, it is estimated that three per cent more visitors will come each year. This means three per cent more people on the already congested roads – attempts to travel between Kendal and Ambleside on a summer day are likely to be met with long traffic tailbacks as it is. No doubt then that three per cent additional car-parking spaces will be required. How to create these, without pouring concrete over green spaces?

In the early summer of 2017 I visited two central Lakeland valleys that are being restored on a landscape scale. In Rydal and Scandale, the farming families who manage the land are working in partnership with Natural England. Sheep have been removed from the hills, but are still maintained as viable flocks on 'inbye' land close to the farms themselves, or are sent off to lowland pastures. Both valleys have been planted up with thousands of native trees; the effect on the eye is already staggering. In a decade's time, that incipient forest will, in autumn, flicker with colour across the fellsides. With the sheep removed, some of our most rarely-found and exceptional native wild flowers – the bird's eye primrose and the late-flowering devil's bit scabious – are emerging from the soil again. Native trees are taking root on rocky outcrops and the humble bramble is seen once more. And as we know already, with trees comes massive bio-diversity.

Walking up through Rydal Park, Simon Stainer of NE pointed out the predominance of veteran trees in the landscape – oak, ash, hawthorn, beech and more. 'Every generation,' he told me, 'assumes that what they are looking at in the landscape is "normal". But without the planting of new trees, those veteran trees will continue to die away with nothing to replace them. When you see a lone tree in the hills, an old hawthorn or a Scots pine, they represent the loss of tree cover on a monumental scale.' The Rydal and Scandale re-planting projects are the largest of their kind in the Lake District.

World Heritage status continues to divide. Across the globe, communities are saying that the additional tourist numbers it creates are causing ecological disaster on sensitive eco-systems. The city of Venice is considering imposing limits on tourist numbers. Some say that the hill-farming community has achieved its goal of 'landscape preservation,' yet the bid document itself cites that much of the upland landscape is in 'poor condition.' Time will tell if there is, or is not, the will to expand the replanting of the uplands and valleys and to improve biodiversity. Set against an epidemic of species loss across the globe, were we in the Lakes to work towards this achievable goal, we might show how it is possible to buck that downward trend, to show others how the land can come alive again. After all, without wildlife, landscape is merely background.

NOTES

[1] Siegfried Sassoon, *Meredith,* pp. 163–64. Constable, London, 1948.

[2] 'The Lark Ascending', published in: Edmund Clarence Stedman, ed. *A Victorian Anthology*, 1837–1895.

[3] www.bto.org/birdtrends2010/wcrskyla.shtml

[4] David Holyoak, 'Territorial and Feeding Behaviour of the Magpie', *Bird Study*. 21:2, 117-128, DOI: 10.1080/000636574 09476407 (1974).

[5] Giraldus Cambrensis 'Topographica Hiberniae' (1187), quoted in Edward Heron-Allen, *Barnacles in Nature and in Myth*, 1928, reprinted in 2003.

[6] From 'The Leavings' in *A Fool's Errand* (2010), by kind permission of the author's Estate and The Gallery Press. www.gallerypress.com

[7] Ted Hughes, 'Curlews,' from *A Ted Hughes Bestiary*, Faber and Faber, 2014.

[8] Francesca Greenoak, *All the Birds of the Air*, Penguin, 1981.

[9] William Earnest Henley, 'The Blackbird,' in *Modern British Poetry,* Louis Untermeyer, ed. 1920.

[10] William Henry Hudson, *Adventures Among Birds*, Hutchinson and Co, 1913.

[11] Adam Foulds, *The Quickening Maze*, Vintage, 2010.

[12, 13] Reverend HA Macpherson, 'A Vertebrate Fauna of Lakeland,' published by David Douglas (1892), and re-published by Chicheley (1972).

[14] Final Report of the Conservation of The Helsfell Wolf; Kendal Museum, 2017.

[15] Liz Lochhead, *Mary Queen of Scots Got Her Head Chopped Off*, Penguin, 1989.

ACKNOWLEDGEMENTS

Thanks indeed are due to Tanya and Edmund Hoare; the Kendal Swift group; Mark Cocker; BTO ringers Hugh Jones and Glynn Anderton.

For all things curlew: Amanda Perkins of the Stiperstones and Corndon Hill Landscape Partnership Ground Nesting Birds Recovery Programme; my curlew colleagues, musician, composer and choir-leader extraordinaire, Mary Keith, wildlife photographer Ben Osborne; sculptor Bill Sample; ornithologists Tony Cross and David Tompkins.

To Susie Osborne and Helen Sample; Mary Colwell-Hector. Leo Smith of the Upper Onny Wildlife Trust; Tom Orde-Powlett of Bolton Castle; Tom Wall for his book *The Singular Stiperstones*, which greatly helped me to understand the history, social history and ecology of the area. I am most grateful to Simon Stainer of Natural England for the visit to the Rydal and Scandale valleys, for the introduction to farmer Chris Hodgson and family and for an ecologist's perspective on landscape and species regeneration.

Thanks to John Butcher of United Utilities plc: don't be embarrassed — the gate spotting website can be found at www.jdscomponents.co.uk/gates. A County Council report into the history of Helsington can be found at www.cumbriacountyhistory.org.uk/sites/default/files/Helsington%20Introduction.pdf.

To Brian Morrell and the team at Caerlaverock Wildfowl and Wetlands Trust. To Dave Borthwick. Carol Davies, Curator at Kendal Museum and Julie Darroch of Kendal College. Lucy

Mascord for explaining all things lupine at Lancashire Conservation Studios. Katherine Wilkinson, secretary of the Fell Pony Society. Dave Walker for both his time and for his excellent monograph on the golden eagles in Cumbria, *Call of the Eagle*.

To Spike Webb and Lee Schofield at RSPB Naddle Farm. Luke Steer for his paper on upland landscapes, *Treescapes: Trees, Animals, Landscape, People and 'Treetime'*. To Tim Potter, Fiona Clucas, Susan Hrynkow and Roseanne Watt. To Hylda and John Marsh for an inspiring and peaceful place to write on Mull. To the Brewery Poets for ongoing literary moral support – in particular to Po Yarwood, Clare Proctor, Caroline Gillfillan and Kerry Darbishire.

Ongoing thanks indeed to my publisher Sara Hunt, to editor Angie Harms and editorial assistant Claire Furey, and to my agent Kevin Pocklington of Jenny Brown Associates.

As ever, to my family who have shared our garden in its many transformations – from sandpits and paddling pools, to the digging of soil and making of plant borders, and who tolerated what, on my part, were some of the worst efforts at badminton known to humankind, and with whom I have shared the landscapes of south Cumbria since 1995.

Some passages were previously printed in the *Guardian* 'Country Diary'.

KAREN LLOYD is a writer of non-fiction and poetry based in Kendal, Cumbria. She is a contributor to the *Guardian Country Diary*, has written for the Family section of the *Guardian* and is a features writer for *BBC Countryfile* magazine. She contributes to a number of online blogs, including Caught by the River. She is the editor of *Curlew Calling Anthology* and works at both regional and local levels on the urgent need for curlew restoration. Karen is a member of Kendal's Brewery Poets and gained a distinction from the Creative Writing M.Litt programme at Stirling University. Her first book, *The Gathering Tide*, won a Lakeland Award and was selected in the 2016 books of the year feature in the *Observer*.